D1346798

STORIES OF TRANSFORMATIVE JUSTICE

RUTH MORRIS

Canadian Scholars' Press Inc.   Toronto   2000

Stories of Transformative Justice
Ruth Morris

First published in 2000 by
Canadian Scholars' Press Inc.
425 Adelaide Street West, Suite 200
Toronto, Ontario
M5V 3C1

CSPI acknowledges the financial support of the Government of Canada through the Book Publishing Industry Development Programme for our publishing activities.

Canadian Cataloguing in Publication Data

Morris, Ruth, 1933-
      Stories of transformative justice

ISBN 978-1-55130-174-7

1.   Criminal justice, Administration of. I. Title.

HV7419.M67 2000   364   C99-933116-7

Managing Editor: Ruth Bradley-St-Cyr
Marketing Manager: Susan Cuk
Interior design: Brad Horning
Cover design: Amy Seagram

Printed and bound in Canada

To:
My husband Ray
Whose selfless love transformed my life
That of dozens of his graduate students
And so many others

And to:
Peter, Corinne, Doug and Joy
Our four children who helped ours to be an open home
Where transformation could blossom

And to:
All those who have played
THE FORGIVENESS GAME with me,
Because forgiveness is the living water
That nurtures the tree of creativity

Acknowledgements

Every one of my books and pamphlets owes much to the patient wisdom of my husband Ray, who gives understanding, support, and technical advice on computer issues with equal grace. My relationship to Canadian Scholars' Press has encouraged my love of writing, and I owe much to every one of their staff. In particular, President Jack Wayne inspires and supports vision, and Managing Editor Ruth Bradley-St-Cyr guided this book to a much better final product. Both of them, as well as Marketing Manager Susan Cuk and Business Manager Laura McIntyre make working with Canadian Scholars Press a joy. Many good writers give up writing for lack of the kind of supports CSPI has offered me so lavishly.

Many of the stories included here have been told in our Rittenhouse workshops, and the enthusiasm of all the participants encouraged me to write them. Above all, the faithful labours and shared vision of Rittenhouse Coordinator Giselle Dias enabled those workshops to happen, and Giselle has played a special role in the continuing transformative role Rittenhouse has in my life and many others. Obviously, the book could not have been written without the inspiring people whose lives shine from its pages: Pat, Mike, Terry, David, Stacey, Joe, and all the others. The great forgivers whose lives shine throughout the book, but especially in the chapter on forgiveness, deserve acknowledgment far beyond this book, for their witness to the beauty that is in all of us.

During the final writing of the book, Rittenhouse was engaged in its biggest project ever: organizing the 9th International Conference on Penal Abolition, at which the book will be launched. Without the obsessive dedication of many people, ICOPA IX would not be taking place: most of all Gord West, Pat Sanagan, Giselle Dias again, Joan Ruzsa, and Marilyn Eisensat.

Contents

Part I
Listening: The First Step in Transformation

Part II
Transformative Processes

Part III
Key Challenges in Transformation

PART I

LISTENING:
THE FIRST STEP IN
TRANSFORMATION

Chapter 1

What is Transformative Justice?

When a storm strikes an eagle, he sets his wings in such a way that the air currents send him above the storm by their very fury.

— E. Stanley Jones

Transformative justice uses the power unleashed by the harm of a crime to let those most affected find truly creative, healing solutions. Transformative justice includes victims, offenders, their families, and their communities, and invites them to use the past to dream and create a better future. Transformative justice is an open door to the community, to the past, and to a happier future for all concerned by a problem. Transformative justice recognizes the wrongs of all victims, and recognizes also that sooner or later, we are all both victims and offenders. But it doesn't use that truth to excuse the harm to any current victims.

This may sound so obvious, you will ask, "So what's the big deal? Don't we do that already?" Not at all! Our existing legal system is a stage on which professional actors—lawyers, judges, court assistants, and police—come on, play their parts, and get pay and some kind of satisfaction from the performance, while the people most affected sit there in stunned, gagged silence. The victim, offender, and others affected are usually very unclear about what is happening, on issues that affect them powerfully. Offenders are advised never to speak for themselves, unless their lawyers decide to put them on the stand, when they are asked a series of tightly controlled questions by the legal parties, and severely restricted in telling their story as they experienced it. Victims often aren't even invited, or if they are, they are even more limited in their participation.

The feelings of both are of minimal interest in the court performance, yet those feelings will colour the lives of all the parties, and all the more so because the court process is a new violation of a painful wound. Both victim and offender are attacked by lawyers for the other side, and as for the family and community of victims and offenders: they are irrelevant!

So what does all that mean, in simple terms? We apply transformative justice in our families. When six-year-old Nancy pulls the hair of her four-year-old brother Jimmy, we don't condone the act, but parents try to get the stories from both children. They learn that Jimmy went in Nancy's room and cut the hair of her favourite doll; and before that, that the two had a major conflict over turns on the neighbour's swing-set. Life, even between two siblings in a happy family, is more complex than one offender, one victim. So the wise parent listens to both, includes both, and asks both to participate with the parents in finding solutions — solutions that are healing to all.

Our current system of justice is *retributive*. It focuses on two questions:

- Who did it?
- How can we punish them?

In our obsession with these questions, as Howard Zehr and others point out, we ignore the victims' real needs, and fail to ask the more important questions:

- Who has been hurt?
- How can we heal them?

So, many people today advocate moving from retributive to *restorative* justice. Restorative justice includes victims, and focuses on those healing questions. But even restorative justice does not go far enough. It still accepts the idea that one event now defines all that matters of right and wrong — it leaves out the past, and the social causes of all events. It's like one of those science fiction stories where time stops, and the whole world focuses on this one moment, without a past or future.

Transformative justice takes into account the past, and it recognizes distributive injustice. We live in a world where the CEO of Disney enterprises, Michael Eisner, receives over $575 million per year in compensation, while 1200 workers in a Vietnam factory making give-away Disney toys earn six to eight cents an hour. Two hundred of them fell ill from toxic solvents, poor ventilation, and exhaustion in 1997. We live in a world where 450 billionaires have as much of the world's goods as the poorest 50 percent of the entire world's population (McMurtry, p. 145). We live in a world where Native babies and Black babies die more frequently than White babies, and adults from those groups have a shorter life expectancy.

The point is not that street crime and theft (the dominant types that fill our courts and prisons) are trivial, or justifiable, but that they are part of a much broader picture. Most of those who fill our prisons have not had the minimum UN standards for their childhood met. Surely there are some broader answers, answers that can use each crime as an opportunity to transform the lives of victims, offenders, and of the whole community.

What's Wrong with What We Have?

I didn't start out talking about transformative justice. Like most others, I went to school and graduate school, and studied traditional criminology and penology. I read the usual newspapers, watched the TV "news," and assumed our system made sense, in general. But the holes in our criminal justice system are so glaring, it doesn't take long for any open-minded person to come across them, and before long, I was giving talks about what was wrong with the existing system.

My favourite line was, "There is nothing wrong with our existing justice system except that it is an expensive, unjust, immoral failure." The rest of my talk would expand on those four key points:

Expensive

The cost of maintaining a person in a North American prison is between $80 and $200 a day, not because they are luxurious, but because caging a person costs a lot in guards and security. Strangely enough, people don't like being caged, and healthy people don't co-operate wholeheartedly with the process. In contrast, most community alternatives to prisons, such as probation, bail supervision, Victim Offender Reconciliation Programs (VORP), and community service work orders, cost about five to twenty dollars a day. Even halfway houses, which are the most costly alternative because of 24-hour housing and staffing costs, are much less costly than their destructive counterpart, prisons.

Yet every one of these alternatives provide services that attempt to integrate offenders with community, treat their problems, and prepare them better in ways that will prevent re-offending. An intelligent consumer who can buy a lot of extras for less cost knows enough to take the bargain. Yet we consumers keep swallowing propaganda that leads us to buy more and more of the most costly and failed alternative: prisons. On financial grounds alone, it is worth a fresh look. A more effective use of existing alternatives for most of the 90 percent of non-violent offenders filling our prisons could easily save us about three-quarters of our entire correctional budget!

Unjust

Study after study demonstrates the highly disproportionate incarceration of indigenous people in prisons all over the world. Blacks suffer the same discrimination. A small research study I did on bail in Toronto showed that Blacks and Whites with similar bail risks and characteristics had very different outcomes: the Blacks were far more likely to be detained in custody. Our police, courts, and penal systems consistently ignore corporate crime, which causes the most social damage. But even if we accept street crime as the measure of crime, different police and court practices ensure that Black and Native youths are far more likely than Whites to fill our prisons.

Immoral

Most world nations have rejected capital punishment and torture as barbaric relics of the past. Caging people, especially when that caging is clearly aimed almost entirely at the marginalized, can hardly be considered a progressive or morally acceptable alternative. Revenge is a ravaging emotion that leaves its holder unsatisfied no matter how much pain it inflicts.

Another moral consideration is that most of those classified as offenders by our criminal justice system are youth whom we as a society have failed to protect from abusive homes, bad foster homes, or destructive and sterile institutions. A bad start does not justify them in engaging in crime. But our failure to provide them with the "UN Minimum Standards for the Rights of a Child" puts us in a strange position to wreak lifelong revenge on them by grinding them through the police-court-prison cycle for years or even decades. We should set limits on unacceptable behaviour by them. But we should not engage in an unending cycle of blame and revenge on them, for behaviour whose seeds we planted, watered, and nourished.

Failure

Recidivism rates from prisons range from about 40 percent to 85 percent, and are consistently higher than for any alternatives. Prisons fail to deter, or to protect society. My 75-year-old mother, when I first took her to visit a jail, came out exclaiming, "Ruth, you've got to get on with abolishing these places — they are nothing but schools for crime!" She is neither the first nor will she be the last to point out this obvious fact. When you take away most of a person's hope of fitting into society and gaining legitimate employment, when you make them more bitter, angry and isolated, and when you put them with other individuals whose only income-generating skills are criminal, a school for crime is what you create.

Prisons accomplish the goal of punishing, and they institutionalize people, taking away their ability to act for themselves. Claire Culhane tells the story of a newly released woman prisoner who was staying in Claire's home. Claire heard the first stirrings of her guest in the morning, and began preparing breakfast. Claire waited and waited. Some guests are slow getting moving in the morning, but the minutes dragged into two hours, and Claire became seriously worried. Finally, the door opened, and footsteps slowly descended the stairs. A shamefaced guest explained humbly, "I forgot I could open the door."

Prisons are excellent if your purpose is primitive, brutal revenge, for the dehumanizing demeaning of people is what they do best. Dennis Challeen put it well:

> We want them to have self-worth…
>   so we destroy their self-worth.
> We want them to be responsible…
>   so we take away all responsibilities.
>
> We want them to be part of our community…
>   so we isolate them from our community.

We want them to be positive and constructive...
    so we degrade them and make them useless.

We want them to be trustworthy...
    so we put them where there is no trust
We want them to be non-violent...
    so we put them where there is violence all around them.

We want them to be kind and loving people...
    so we subject them to hatred and cruelty.
We want them to quit being the tough guy...
    so we put them where the tough guy is respected.

We want them to quit hanging around losers...
    so we put all the losers in the province under one roof.
We want them to quit exploiting us...
    so we put them where they exploit each other.

We want them to take control of their lives, own their own problems,
        and quit being a parasite...
    so we make them totally dependent on us.

In fact, the Daubney Committee, a federal crime committee appointed by the Tory government in 1986 (following the Canadian Sentencing Commission in 1985, and followed by the Horner Commission in 1991, all Tory government commissions) joined a long series of Canadian commissions that, over the decades, have denounced prison as a serious solution to crime. The Daubney report says:

> "It is now generally recognized that imprisonment has not been effective in rehabilitating or reforming offenders, has not been shown to be a strong deterrent, and has achieved only temporary public protection and uneven retribution... The use of imprisonment as a main response to a wide variety of offences against the law is not a tenable approach in practical terms" (Daubney Committee, p. 75).

What's Wrong with What We Have for Victims?

It is even more important to stress that the retributive justice system approach is a dismal failure in meeting the healthy needs of victims of crime (Boers, 1992: pp. 8-12). When I began reading the literature about victims of crime and their needs, about a dozen years ago, I was astounded to discover revenge as such was not named as a primary need or drive for victims! Anger was certainly a natural reaction, but if the five core needs were met, victims' healing was assured, and revenge was not one of them. In fact, victims who get hooked on revenge remain unhealed: revenge is like a drug that is addictive but unsatisfying.

Yet our popular culture, which some have described as an addictive culture, instead of trying to support victims in meeting those five core needs, keeps trying to ram revenge down their throats. Victims who try to practice forgiveness are told by those most addicted to the revenge cult that they must not care very much about what happened, or about their loved ones who were hurt, or they would be seeking revenge, not healing!

So what are these five basic needs of victims? They are the need for answers, recognition of their wrong, safety, restitution, and to find some meaning or significance from the very event that was so painful. Let's look at these one by one.

Answers

Victims have a craving for answers, when their world has been turned upside down by a crime or injury. The first question we all ask is: "Why me?" Of course no one this side of the curtain of death can give a full answer to that spiritual riddle, but we keep needing to peck away at it, with every tragedy we face. Did I contribute in some way to the calamity? Could I do something to prevent a repetition? Am I to blame?

We need to learn what we can learn to prevent recurrences, but we also need to know we are not wholly to blame, in order to have our wrong recognized. Asking "why me?" is part of regaining a sense of sanity and control, and part of learning from pain, as well as part of asking for recognition of our wrong. We all have to go through it, but it's a lot quicker and less painful if we have supportive listeners to help us. The police and court process often blames victims, and confuses their search to answer this first great question.

Victims ask a lot of other questions that may appear trivial to outsiders. Why did you take my kid's radio and not our stereo? Why did you break a window when the basement door was unlocked? Where is my grandmother's picture now? Why did my son get in your car?

These questions are not trivial or frivolous, and when victims have no chance to ask them of the offender, who is the only one who can answer most of them, these questions linger hauntingly for years. These questions come up immediately and powerfully in victim-offender meetings arranged a decade or more after the event, because the drive for answers to them is fundamental. The fact is, a crime is an invasion of our orderly life-space, and a violation of our sense of control over it. We all maintain a delicate equilibrium in this unpredictable world, in which nature and the choices of others can disrupt our lives so easily. We try to follow common-sense rules for managing our lives. Then crime disrupts our sense of control and order, and threatens to throw us into an insane universe where anything can happen anytime, regardless of what we do! This is crazy making, and victims seek answers to reassert their sense of control over their immediate lives.

A crime that affects a loved one or even kills them leaves us out in the cold, missing this vital chapter in their lives. Painful as the answers may be, most victims want to know from the offender about their loved ones' experience, and even painful answers give the victim some peace. So answers are a fundamental need of all victims, and many questions they want to ask can only be answered by the offender or offenders.

Recognition of Their Wrong

If I had to choose just one need as the most fundamental need of victims, it would probably be this one. Victims need above all to be reassured that their community and their world recognizes how terrible their wrong was, and that they were not personally to blame for it. When this need is met, victims' path to forgiveness and healing and rebuilding is made much smoother.

Some years ago, an assailant stabbed the Pope, and the Pope impressed the world by acts of forgiveness toward this deranged man. Wonderful as this act was, and it was indeed wonderful, it was not as hard as the forgiveness expected of an emotionally battered wife toward her husband who continues to offend. The whole world recognized the wrong of the Pope; the world is still ambivalent about the right of a husband even to physically abuse, and much more ambivalent about what emotional abuse is. The Pope was secure from a recurrence of pain; the wife is sure that the abuse will continue. A fired employee, the spouse of an adulterer, a wrongfully accused person in court, all face a world that says, "You must have done something to bring it on." Their wrong is not recognized fully, and they are blamed for their own victimization, to some extent or other.

In contrast, community processes that gather together the most significant communities of victims and offenders in denouncing the wrong and supporting the victim, while seeking healing solutions for all, meet the need for recognition of wrong most fully. Victims need and deserve full recognition of their wrongs.

Police in their frustration with the difficulty of their job often blame the victim for minor lapses or qualities that may or may not have exposed them to the crime. Courts appoint a defence lawyer whose job, if they take it seriously, is to point out any ways in which the victim was to blame, and thus mitigate their client's responsibility. Our retributive justice system does not recognize — consistently or effectively or kindly — the wrongs of victims, even though it sets out to do so in a crude way. Its only measure of recognition of wrong is how many months or years the offender is locked away, an outcome influenced by many other factors such as legal precedents and technicalities, the social status and legal representation of both parties, and the nature of this particular judge and/or jury. Instead, the existing system revictimizes victims, blames them, and rubs salt in the wounds that cry out for recognition of the wrong.

Safety

What more natural need for victims than to feel safe again! Yet the more our existing system demonizes the offender, the more it separates victims from offenders and forbids normal safe exchange, the more fears are inflated. The more it angers and alienates the offender, the more the victim is right to feel the offender could turn some of that anger on the victim again. Yet every defence lawyer and prosecutor and police official will tell victims and offenders to have no direct contact with the other party. One ostensible reason is the fear of violence, and certainly contact should be supported by others, but a basic rule of our system seems to be to forbid any human instinct that wants to reach out a hand across the barrier of crime to establish communication and community. The effect of this, and of the whole court process, is to exacerbate both anger and fear, by both parties.

Thus the victim's need for safety is undermined by our processes. Nor does it help that court decisions over offender release and limits often ignore the specific fears of victims. Although victim danger is considered in most cases in release decisions, it is not the only factor, and victims often feel helpless before the seemingly crazy decisions of our legal systems, and the inability of the law to offer them basic protection and safety. Meanwhile, their fears are aggravated as the demonization of the offender and establishment of the victim as the only party threatening the offender continue to widen the breach.

In contrast, a family or community group conference gather together a circle from the whole community, including those from the offender's community, all of whom are committed to securing the safety of the victim as a primary goal. All of them also join the victim in denouncing the offender's inappropriate behaviour. What a difference!

Restitution

People often mistake what restitution means. They think of restitution as "You stole $20.62 from me, so you pay back $20.62." But in fact what was stolen was much larger than that money: it included the victim's sense of security, their belief in a world they could trust, and within reason, control. Based on this simplified notion, people say, "You can't have restitution for rape or murder." Wrong! Of course you can't restore a raped woman's faith in the world, or end a family's grief for a murdered loved one. But restitution for crimes like these is meaningful, and in fact, the more serious the crime, the greater the need for restitution.

When I was little, like most tots, I would sometimes ride my trike too fast and fall off, or otherwise scrape a knee or hand in play. I would come running to my mother, crying loudly and healthily as little children do. My mother always dropped whatever she was doing, picked me up, carried me to her rocking chair, and rocked me, cuddled me, and sang to me, till I was better. Was my knee or hand all healed? Of course not! Did the rocking do anything medical to fix it? Certainly not! But I had had restitution: the world as a safe, caring, loving place was mine again.

That is what restitution is about. Some years ago, I saw a great example of restitution at a Conference for the Wrongfully Convicted in Toronto. Eight people who had served over 150 years in prison for crimes our system now acknowledged they had not committed at all, were welcomed to the platform of that conference by Hurricane Carter, himself a major victim of wrongful conviction. As each name was announced, and their wrong briefly described, and they walked to the front to receive Hurricane's bear-hug, that audience of 300 persons rose to their feet and cheered like a home-crowd whose football team has just won the big one. It suddenly came to me that that was restitution, with roses. Did it give these victims of wrongful convictions back the decades of lives lost in living tombs called prisons? Did it make up to them for the loved ones who died while they were immured wrongfully, or the children who grew up without them? No, it does not. Restitution cannot unmake the past. But it can and does declare that a caring community is there for victims, and will do its best to recognize this wrong and prevent future ones. Restitution is about restoring our sense of a secure, warm, caring community, whether it is the arms of a mother or the warmth of a cheering audience, or a family who welcomes one with every kind of support.

But our retributive justice system remains hooked on simple restitution, on the return of the $20.62, but without any of the security or caring or recognition that are essential to real restitution. Victims want real restitution, and that is something that can only be provided by community processes that give victims and community back their true role in crime.

Significance

Significance is another favourite outcome of mine, but none needs to be singled out, for every one of these victim needs is healthy, normal, and essential for a mature community and mature spirits, to give and receive. Significance comes last in order because it is last sequentially. Eventually, there comes a time when victims have walked the path of grief as far as they can on this particular journey.

Each need has been partially but not fully met, because none of these essentially spiritual needs can ever be fully met in this world. Victims have found some answers, but not all. In the present situation and reality, they cannot obtain more of the large and small answers to the questions that torment them, but they have gone over and over it, and figured out what they can, and they are reasonably ready to sigh and move on. They have also received from this limited world as much recognition of their wrong as they can or will get. Although no one else will ever recognize as the victim does the depth of their wrong, they know that asking for more is subject to diminishing returns, and even community anger.

As for safety, victims have recovered some sense of safety. They have themselves set up systems to protect them in new ways, and the police, courts and community may have offered more. They don't feel as safe as they did before — even if the offender is dead, the victim's own sense of safety will never be the same. But they have rebuilt their own security systems, and they are prepared to move on. As for restitution, they may have recovered the $20.62, and even an apology, and some community support. Again, restitution is never complete: the wrongfully convicted don't recover so much that was lost; and a theft or assault has left a hole in some part of the victim's community. But the victim has got what they can get, and is prepared to look for something more.

At this point, victims are ready to move on to seek meaning or significance. They accept that the world will never be the same for them, but they can use their pain to try to build a world that is better for others. To use one's own pain to build a better, safer world for others is the most healing thing possible, after recognition of one's own wrong. After my own firing over issues of principle, I took mediation training, and did several organizational mediations in which I was able actually to prevent some other Director from suffering the same agony I had experienced: how ultimately satisfying! Parents of a child injured in a bike accident will fight for safer protections for cyclists. Whole movements like MADD, Mothers Against Drunk Drivers, are fuelled by this wonderful motivation (Henderson, 1996).

Yet here again, our retributive justice system focuses solely on finding and punishing the offender, and gives no scope to victims' search for significance. All the community energy and victim energy that could be turned to this beautiful quest is dissipated and misdirected in the futile drive to wrest meaning from the amount of pain we can cause the offender.

In short, as we will explain further in the concluding chapter, the existing retributive justice system we have is no more helpful to the needs of victims for healing, or communities for prevention, than it is to changing offender behaviour and integrating them into community. Whole books have been written documenting this, but the present book is dedicated to stories of a better way, so this short introduction is just to prepare you for an open look at those better ways.

Some Existing Alternatives to Prisons

One of the first questions I am asked when I speak about how futile and even destructive is our existing penal system is this, "OK, Ruth, you've convinced us prisons aren't much good. They are costly, they do more harm than good, and they don't help either victims or the community, let alone offenders. But we have to respond to crime somehow. What choices do we have that are any better?"

This question from Canadian Quakers back in 1980 prompted me to write the first pamphlet I ever wrote on criminal justice, the first of a series over the years. It was called Creative Alternatives to Prisons, and it documented eight different alternatives I knew about then, all of which were cheaper, more effective, and more helpful to all parties than prisons. That pamphlet has been reprinted and expanded five times since.

The latest version talks about 23 different existing alternatives to prisons, and I won't try to list them all here. But the 23 alternatives fall into six general categories:

Housing Alternatives

A variety of housing options for offenders provide supervision, treatment, and support in varying degrees. Many offenders get into trouble partly because of very unsuitable living environments. A supportive, safe living environment, sometimes with treatment or restrictions, can be a life-changing experience. Since a common need expressed by most victims is to have a part in making sure the offender never does this again to anyone else, such an outcome is very satisfying to victims.

Community Supervision

Probation and parole are the oldest alternatives, providing community supervision and support so the offender has someone in the community who cares about and monitors their behaviour. At its best, community supervision provides the combination of caring and control that a good parent offers; at its worst, it can be as abusive as the worst parents can. But overall, community supervision is the most tried and true alternative, and vital in preventing many young offenders from falling into the institutional-crime cycle.

Restoration Models

A variety of alternatives focus on getting offenders to pay money or do work to make up for the harm of the crime. Some, such as restitution orders, require work or money for the victim. Others like fines or community service work orders make the offender pay back the community as a whole. Restoration works best when offenders and victims and community participate in agreeing on it, for then all are committed to it, and it is realistically geared to the needs and situation of this victim and offender.

Treatment

Astonishingly enough, most court outcomes do not deal in any basic way with the very real treatment needs of most offenders. The United Nations estimates that three-quarters of the world's prisoners are untreated addicts. Mental health problems and learning disabilities also abound in prisoners. Yet the basic need for treatment is seldom addressed in courts, and only sometimes in prisons. Sending an alcoholic to a treatment program makes a lot more sense than sending them to jail.

Legal Remedies

From police discretion to discharge to parole, the legal system often recognizes that at present it does more harm than good in most lives it touches. So police, courts and prisons use legal devices to restrict their involvement. Police let most minor offenders off with a verbal warning, and although this, like all discretionary options, is very class and race biased, without it the courts and prisons would be swamped. The challenge is how to allow discretion while limiting its bias in favour of the privileged classes and races.

Co-operative Solutions

This book is about co-operative solutions, solutions that include victims, offenders, and community in responding to each crime in a way that meets their needs and empowers them. Victim offender reconciliation, court diversion programs, community group conferences, and Native sentencing circles are co-operative solutions, all of which we will be illustrating in our stories.

So there are plenty of alternatives to knee-jerk punitive penal outcomes. Every alternative meets victim needs and community needs as well as offender needs more effectively than the retribution of our tortuous legal processes. All we need is to use them more widely.

My Journey from Retributive Justice to Transformative Justice

My own journey from retributive justice has gone through many stages, and I am inviting the reader to go with me rapidly through these stages, so you can enjoy the excitement of the discoveries at the present stage of my journey. But it is hard to expect readers to skip entirely the necessary growth stages I experienced, so I will summarize a little of my journey here, to prepare you for arrival at these exciting stories of transformative justice. At the same time, we each take our own journeys, and in sharing mine, I do not mean to suggest that yours will cover the same terrain.

I have written a pamphlet on my 25-year journey in the field, called "Seven Steps from Misery Justice to Social Transformation." My seven steps are:

- Misery Justice
- Alternatives: Helping, Reforming
- Abolition
- Restorative Justice
- Transformative Justice
- Corporate Crime Consciousness
- Social Transformation

I went quite rapidly through the first stage, that of accepting a justice system that creates an equal playing field by making everyone equally miserable: victims, offenders, their families, and the wider community. In the second stage, I spent ten years devoted to building community alternatives to prisons and penal justice, and established four significant ones in Toronto. I worked hard on reforming the system in various ways during those years, and I helped a lot of prisoners and ex-prisoners, who in turn helped me in my journey.

Helping people and creating a more accepting, inclusive community are activities we can never abandon, but after ten years of arduous work butting my head up against a revenge system, I concluded that personally I was into more fundamental change, and I moved on to focus on abolition. I sought abolition not only of the archaic caging of human beings (recognizing secure care for a dangerous few will always be needed, in environments unlike prisons). After a few years working for prison abolition, I came to agree with those who said the revenge spirit at the root of current policing, courts, and prisons was the real problem. As long as the purpose of our response was revenge, we would be stuck with destructive approaches.

So I devoted a lot of effort to getting people to say "no" to what was wrong: prisons and penal approaches. While the Mennonites and others were working on the seeds of victim offender reconciliation and other ways to say "yes" to healing justice, we Quakers were focussed on saying "no" to all that was wrong in the criminal justice system.

But I recognized we needed to define as much as we could where we wanted to go, so I was very much influenced by the pioneering work of Dave Worth and Mark Yantzi, Mennonite friends in nearby Kitchener-Waterloo who created victim-offender reconciliation and talked about something they called "restorative justice." Dave said victim-offender reconciliation was not just an alternative, but the spirit behind all true alternatives. I was inclined to agree with him, but I lacked a theoretical understanding of why — until I read Howard Zehr's seminal book on restorative justice, *Changing Lenses*. *Changing Lenses* is the Bible of the restorative justice movement. Howard makes a compelling case for changing the questions we ask from "Who done it, and how can we punish them?" to "Who has been hurt, and how can we heal them?"

For awhile I went around crusading for restorative justice, and I thought my journey had ended. I knew what I did NOT want, and where I wanted to go. How much further could I go? I knew that the goal of justice should be healing of all involved, prevention of further harm, and inclusion of victims and offenders in the response to crime. All this seemed enough to me, and enough to get across to the audiences I spoke to and wrote for!

Yet after a few years, I became increasingly dissatisfied with restorative justice too. In moving on, I always tried to keep the good spirit from each previous stage of awareness; I went on helping people and working for community alternatives that included all. I went on speaking for abolition of all that was harmful in our system. And as I moved on from restorative justice, I continued to praise the restorative justice focus on healing instead of revenge, and the push for programs like victim offender reconciliation, and the recognition that victims' needs need to be respected and supported.

But I became more and more disturbed with several defects in restorative justice theory, and too much of restorative justice practice:

- The very word restorative was unhealthy for victims. A victim's first instinct is to want the world back as it was. Until a victim is ready to move on from this, to recognize they can transform the world positively from their pain, but they can't restore the world as it was, their healing is blocked. Restorative justice, although intended to speak more of a Garden of Eden kind of restoration to the universe as God envisioned it, in practice encouraged victims in imagining that you can restore a past, before some trauma changed life forever.
- Restorative theory did not take into account the enormous structural injustices at the base of our justice systems, and the extent to which they function mainly to reinforce racism and classism. Any theory or method that ignores the racism and classism that are basic to retributive justice is missing something very vital, and will serve to reinforce that racism and classism further, by not challenging it.
- Related to both of these points, the idea of restoring justice implied we had had justice, and lost it. In fact, distributive justice abounds everywhere, and most offenders are, more than the average person is, victims of distributive injustice. Do we want to restore offenders to the marginalized, enraged, disempowered condition most were in just before the offence? This makes no sense at all!

Finally, my suspicions of the flaws of restorative justice were confirmed as I saw very revenge-oriented justice officials taking over the language of restorative justice, and finding ways to use its healing approaches in punitive manners. Dave Worth expressed distress over hearing officials say, "I'm going to VORP that kid!" Any language can be co-opted, but I became convinced that the language of transformative justice is truer to our meaning, so harder to distort.

As I began to write about transformative justice and transformative models, I became entranced with family and community group conferencing, and Native sentencing and healing circles. I saw the power of transformative justice in taking crime as an opportunity, as a symptom of deeper ills, and including all directly affected by the crime in building creative solutions. Transformative justice dealt with both distributive injustice and the injustice of being victimized by a crime. It started with the current crime, supporting the victim's five needs for answers, recognition of wrong, safety, restitution, and significance. But it went beyond to the offender, and to the social roots from which the crime arose. It empowered the community, and it offered more in the way of prevention and protection than any other approach.

All this was exciting, and I would have been delighted to stop my journey there, but then I ran into Harry Glasbeek, a law professor who specializes in corporate crime. At this point in my life I had three graduate degrees in criminology, had written books and many articles, founded and headed agencies, and travelled around the world on the topic, yet I had very little awareness of corporate crime!

If this could be true of a person as steeped in the field as I, imagine the cosmic ignorance of most of the general public, who rely for their information on public media almost entirely owned and run by the largest corporations. As Harry opened my eyes to the facts on corporate crime, I had a conversion experience similar to Saul on the Road to Damascus. I was blinded by the light of truth, and yet my eyes were opened to deeper truths. And somewhat to my distress, I found my old talks did not go far enough.

Because of their ability to influence lawmaking, corporations are far more sophisticated criminals than are those who languish for years in prison. For, according to many experts on corporate crime, both in Canada and the USA, the overwhelming facts about corporate crime are these:

- many of their most harmful behaviours are not illegal
- they steal $10 for every dollar stolen by traditional criminals
- and wilfully, for profit, they take the lives of 30 people for every reported homicide!

I am still trying to take in the enormity of these facts, and the challenge of getting them across adequately in talks, without arousing in my audience either incredulity, or vengeful fury toward the corporate bosses. But this book is not about corporate crime. I merely mention it because it is vital that more of us understand its enormous part in our world, and because it sets in context the responses to street crime that we will be talking about.

While I was reeling from the shocks of corporate crime awareness, our world was being guided, increasingly, by corporate decision-making, influencing politicians of all parties, in all levels, in most countries. I became involved in the broader struggle to regain democracy and social justice for all, and so in my present stage I focus on social transformation, a transformation that includes but is not limited to our criminal justice responses.

You don't have to agree with or even follow all my steps, though, to enjoy and be inspired by the stories of transformative justice that follow. I only explain my journey because we can all learn something from each other's journeys, and because my journey sets the stage for some of the stories, and may help you in understanding them.

Conclusion: Transformation Needed Now

Transformative justice sees crime as an opportunity to build a more caring, more inclusive, more just community. Safety doesn't lie in bigger fences, harsher prisons, more police, or locking ourselves in till we ourselves are prisoners. Safety and security — real security — come from building a community where because we have cared for and included all, that community will be there for us, when trouble comes to us. For trouble comes to us all, but trouble itself is an opportunity.

My mother's favourite expression was "turning irritation into iridescence." That's the heart of what transformative justice is about. Some forms of defence use the force of the opponent in one's response. This chapter begins with the E. Stanley Jones quotation, "When a storm strikes an eagle, he sets his wings in such a way that the air currents send him above the storm by their very fury." The set of the wings is the power of transformative justice. But stories can tell it better than concepts. So let's look at how it works.

Chapter 2 shows how real empathetic listening is a key tool in transformation. Stories about everyone from bankers to robbers to social workers show how transformative caring listening can be, in and of itself. Chapters 3 and 4 wrote themselves into this book: they show how some of the prisoners I have known have transformed my life and understanding.

Then in Part II we turn to Transformative Processes, and hear stories of Circle Sentencing and Family Group Conferencing. They are beautiful stories, and they were what this whole book was supposed to be about. But there is another magic tool that demanded a chapter in itself: the power of forgiveness, and the stories of forgiveness are so powerful, they have healing and energy just in the telling and hearing of them.

Part III is on what we can do: first to transform the criminal justice system, then to transform the distributive injustice of our world. So many books are good at pointing out the problems, but weak on the solutions. This is a book of hope, and of optimism. Above all, it is a book of stories of how *every* one of us can transform impossible situations. All we have to do is choose the transformative path.

Chapter 2

The Power of Listening

Listening is a skill like any other. Some of us naturally have, or have through our family heritage, better skills to begin with. But like any other skill, we can develop the skill we have to a higher level. Life is a great training ground for growing in listening, for good listening is a powerful tool in human relationships.

Most of the stories in this section, all but the last, involve my own growing understanding of listening, so I tell them in chronological order, and the reader may be able to see my own developing understanding of listening. The third story: "Three Listeners Who Transformed My Greatest Trauma," is the only one relating to me where others did the listening to me. We can learn a lot from experiencing good and bad listening to our own struggles, and I learned a lot from that one. I hope you find these stories entertaining as well as growing.

Mike H and My Childhood Fears

Mike H was a prisoner I visited for some time in the West Detention Centre. Learning to listen to Mike's seemingly unending series of complaints about life was one of my early challenges in prison visiting. Yet behind the whining was a suffering human being, a man who struggled to express big issues in poetry, and a person who yearned along with me to help other

23

prisoners. You'll hear more about him later, but now I want to share just one story about listening and Mike. One day in 1977, Mike and I were chatting, and he made the seemingly innocent remark, "You know, Ruth, it's been years since I hurt anybody."

This is where the first listening comes in. I heard that remark, and I was utterly astonished. Mike had one of the longest records of break and entries into people's homes of anyone I had met to that date, and here he was saying he hadn't hurt anyone in years! I took a deep breath and responded.

"Mike, don't you realize that when you break into people's houses, you hurt and scare them and their *children*?" There was a pause, as Mike, in turn, recoiled in horror. Looking at his face, I could see that such a thought had never occurred to him, not once. My mind flashed back to all the hideous court scenes I had witnessed. Judges and prosecutors had told the Mikes of this world all the nasty things I had ever heard of, and lots more besides, to convey to them social disapproval. They were worthless, they were scum, they were evil, they were negligent, lazy, cruel, destructive, etc. But in all those endless words, as Mike had sat there, a helpless pawn of the lawyers and the judge, not one word had ever conveyed to Mike that he was hurting people!

"Mike," I said gently, "When I was a little girl I used to wake up in the night scared. You know why?" Of course he didn't, and he asked why. "Because, before I was even born, someone had broken into my parents' home, and I was scared he would come back and hurt me. And you know, I don't scare easily. But when you invade someone's home, you scare the parents, and you scare the kids, for years and years. You love kids, Mike. How come you never thought about what you are doing to all those kids when you break and enter?"

I could see from Mike's face that no one had ever made that connection before for him. He was very tender toward kids. He would never deliberately have hurt one. Yet none of these brilliant judges ever made him "hear" the fact that he was hurting kids all the time! There was something about the court process that turned him off: the devastating attacks on his whole being, the fact that he had no voice, and that "his lawyer" called the Crown Attorney "my friend," and went out to coffee with him later. All these made him deaf to anything that might imply he was hurting real people — even kids.

From this I learned something important: we have to feel valued in order to want to hear the other person. Besides, the victims were silenced as much as he — when had Mike ever met a victim of his? The whole process cut them off from each other, and if they heard each other in court, it was as enemies, scripted not to communicate, and not to feel for each other, or even to listen to each other.

So here was I, someone who had visited him in prison, joked with him, made calls for him, cared about him, listened to him endlessly, saying that as a child, I had been hurt by people doing the things he had been doing! And the amazing thing was, he was able to hear me. Listening did its magic, and for the first time in his life, Mike grasped that when he broke into a home, he was hurting the kids there.

The second transformative part of listening is what I learned from that exchange. I suddenly understood how vital it was that the victim get back in the scene, if we were going to communicate with "offenders." I had been a proxy victim — not a victim of Mike's, nor even a direct victim of a break and enter myself. But just by sharing my indirect experience, my fear from a break-in that had occurred before my birth, I had communicated something very important to Mike. If such an indirect sharing could do so much, how much more could a real encounter do for the Mikes of this world!

So in listening to Mike, I learned how little our retributive justice system communicated to them of the real pain and fear of victims, and I have shared that learning with the world ever since.

Listening to Policemen

One of my strange hobbies is doing call-in shows on penal abolition and other controversial topics on conservative radio shows. I find that by applying good listening, and validating people's underlying feelings and concerns, without agreeing with all their conclusions, we have a wonderful time together. These call-in shows have trained me a lot in good listening. One of my favourite stories of such an exchange came on a show in the early 1980s.

The caller began raving about bad criminals and how we should lock them up longer. He had introduced himself as a policeman, and in my work on alternatives, I was working with police, and knew their concerns. Listening to him, I felt my anger rising at his hasty judgmental comments and conclusions, but I put it aside, and listened some more. Beneath those judgements, I heard fear and some anger of his own.

My response was, "I can understand your anger. We are all concerned about those kids on the streets, and I have seen policemen risking everything to try to help and guide them." I had also seen policemen responding in much more negative ways, but this was not the moment to go into that. What I heard was his concern, and I responded to its positive element.

There was a long pause, as my caller shifted gears. Then he came back on the air in a completely different voice, and began acknowledging the truth in the concerns I was raising. From then on, we had a love duet, talking about what was wrong with the justice system, and suggesting remedies and directions. There was respect on both sides. That respect came because I had heard, beneath his hostility and hasty conclusions, a common concern for the youth that are the fodder for our justice system.

The other story of listening to a policeman was even more challenging. When I was head of the Toronto Bail Program, I created an Advisory Committee, which brought together representatives of most areas of the justice system: Crown prosecutors, police, defence lawyers, members of my Board, and a couple of other relevant agencies. At the time of this story, the Bail Program was getting well established, and it was becoming difficult to get attendance, run the meetings, and find a clear purpose, much as I believed in networking. So I was already tense when our friendly police representative, Doug, spoke up provocatively.

I should explain that this occurred in the days before community police officers, except for school presentations, were as widespread as they are now. It was Doug's peculiar fate in life to represent the Toronto police in numerous meetings with social agencies whose philosophies he generally disliked and sometimes despised. So he was often provocative, and never more so than on this occasion.

It was not the best moment for a difficult comment. I was struggling to facilitate this meeting. I had just done what I thought was a good presentation on some of the work our Bail Program was doing in supervising high need clients, waiting for trial in the community. Sgt. Doug spoke up aggressively, and challenged me with this comment. "Some day, Ruth, you're going to get somebody out in the community and they're going to commit a high profile, violent crime, and then you'll be sorry."

I drew a deep breath and prayed for patience. Miraculously, it came. I asked for guidance to hear the legitimate feeling back of that provocative remark. What I heard, the value we shared, was the concern for public safety. He thought locking people up was the way to ensure it. I believed helping them function in the community, from which they came and to which they would return, was the key. But both of us were working for public safety. I believed his enthusiasm for locking people up undermined my work for an inclusive community. He in turn was angry because my way seemed to undermine his.

Reflecting a few seconds, I was able to hear that shared positive concern, and to make this heartfelt response, "You may be right, Doug. And when that day comes, if it comes, I will be as sorry as you — not just because of the damage to this program and all the good things we are trying to do here, but because I care just as much as you do about the safety of the people in this city, and I will be hurting as you do with whoever is hurt."

No miracles this time. Doug did not become a lifelong friend and ally. But for the moment, the anger was defused, and a feeling of identity prevailed. Positive listening had turned a corner, and we were able to move forward again as a group with common goals.

Three Listeners Who Transformed My Greatest Trauma

The three stories in this section, all linked to the same experience, are stories of how being listened to helped me through the hardest trauma of my life to date. It was hardest not because of some abstract measure of pain, but because it was my loss of innocence. A friend of mine wrote me about "the loss of innocence, when we first discover that we can give of our best and finest to the world, and it does not pay us back in kind." My loss of innocence came in 1983, when after four years of founding and running the Toronto Bail Program, my Board came to differ with me on a number of issues, and pushed me closer and closer to the brink of my first firing. Here was I, an over-achiever, over-dedicated to good works and values, valedictorian of my class, a gifted musician, oozing abilities, having given my all to this program, and I was about to be fired as if I were incompetent or lazy! This came before I realized that those most vulnerable to firing are at either end of the normal curve: too far ahead of the crowd, or too far behind. Organizations like best staff who are in the comfortable middle.

At any rate, for several months I was hanging on and struggling for survival, amazed that I could be in trouble for what seemed to me like good acts: leading a successful struggle to get our marginalized clients fed when the police held them in custody through mealtimes (often up to 72 hours);

organizing the First International Conference on Prison Abolition in Toronto; and worst of all, hiring a parolee, in an agency that was constantly approaching businesses of all kinds to hire our clients, most of whom had considerable criminal records.

Of course they brought in my real weaknesses as an administrator too. Like everyone else — especially given that it was my first big job — I had some, but they had troubled no one till my Board began turning to the right in its values, while I continued on my human rights and empowerment path. I learned from that something I used to tell others suffering through similar experiences. If you are being fired over issues of principle, you need to identify and disentangle three things. First, you will never have a better chance to know your real faults. They are served up to you daily, several times a day, in all kinds of guises and sauces, nauseatingly. But to grow in grace you need to accept these, thank the giver, acknowledge your weaknesses, and then remind them that these are not the main cause of the situation.

Secondly, opponents make up the most outlandish slander. I am grateful that, for some reason, my opponents never got into my sex life with their stories. But practically every other slander imaginable, and a number quite unimaginable have been written and spoken of me in the course of my advocacy stands and my two firings because of them. You need to identify what is untrue, state quite calmly and clearly that this particular thing is false, and let it roll off. Don't get hooked on it — just living your life as the person you are is the best response in the long run.

Thirdly, you need to keep reminding everyone, including yourself, that the real causes of all this fuss are positions of principle that you have taken, and that the rest is a smokescreen to distract people from that truth. It is a lot easier to attack someone for keeping sloppy files or being late to certain kinds of meetings, than for increasing hiring of minorities, but the latter is more likely to be the cause of a firing.

But who were the three listeners who transformed this deep trauma for me? The first was my husband. The day I learned that my Board — a group I had trusted and that had worked with me so closely — had called a special meeting with me excluded ("in camera" they call it). I felt as if I had been kicked in the stomach. I, who never showed much change of colour in any situation, was so pale someone was worried I was going to have an attack. This was the first great shock of betrayal. I have since learned to loathe "in camera" sessions as the occasion of the most amazing vicious gossip and power tripping by Boards, uncorrected by even the silent presence of the primary victim. But already I sensed just how destructive it would be.

I phoned my husband to tell him, got his usual supportive response, and then I went on with the rest of my day's work, which didn't finish often till an evening meeting at night. I phoned Ray again as I was leaving for home about 9:30 p.m. He figured out when to expect me from the bus and subway, and walked two blocks to meet me. When I got home, after a walk, which included Ray's amazingly empathetic, supportive listening all the way, I found a dozen roses waiting for me, with this card:

> "I love you, woman of principle.
> Bob is proud of you, Harry is proud of you, Fred is proud of
>   you,
> And so am I!"

On the back, he had written this even more wonderful addition, which has been a theme of my life ever since:

> "When you're up to your neck in hot water,
> Be like the kettle and sing!"

Ray's listening to my pain, and his ability to applaud when the crowds were running the other way — his hearing the value of what I had given in my field — these exemplified healing listening at its best. His humorous tea kettle quip, from a World War II song, added a touch of spice that has carried us through many another crisis.

Listening does not stop events rolling on, however, and inexorably I was pressed to the precipice and finally pushed over. If the process had been agonizing, the shock and grief of separation and painful reality that followed was even worse. From being somebody, I was nobody. Many of the people I had thought of as friends abandoned me (but others were wonderful). From having a lovely central office to meet in, I tried to continue my good works in donut shop meetings and rainy bus shelters downtown — talk about feeling homeless!

My second healing listener was my mother. At this time she was in her last year of life, succumbing rapidly to the deteriorating effects of Alzheimer's disease. With her very poor recent memory recall, when we wanted a decision from her on something, we would tell her eight or ten times and take a majority vote on the responses. For awhile, I didn't want to burden her with the sorrow of my firing, nor humiliate myself further by sharing my shame with my dear mother, who thought the sun rose and set on me. But then we reflected on the Alzheimer Society advice that you should treat such victims as we do young children or coma victims — assume they understand more than you think, and give them the respect of explaining things to them.

So, valiantly, I set out one day to tell Mom that her beloved daughter had been fired over the issues of principle described above. The result was astonishing, uplifting, and inspiring. What was more, it was the same every time we told her. Each time, Mom's eyes would shine with pride, and she would say words to this effect:

> "To think, that I could have a daughter who would be fired for
> things like that! My whole life was worth living just for this.
> 'Lord, now lettest thou thy servant depart in peace.'"

Mom didn't just listen to my story and comfort me: she heard the triumph of a life loyal to the human rights principles we shared. Mom empowered me with her pride in what I had mistakenly thought was my shame!

The third gift of listening came from a group farther away. As Christmas approached, less than six months had passed since the firing, and less than three months since my friends and I had given up the hopeless struggle to overturn it. I continued to drag myself to downtown meetings, trying to breathe life into the justice coalition that had held so much promise when I held a key position, but seemed on the verge of expiring now. I felt that I had burdened my family with my open grief too much. I was trying now, especially for our children, to put on a good front for Christmas. I knew this would be the worst Christmas of my life, but I was trying to endure it with as little outward suffering as possible. Inside though, I was still bleeding daily from the rewoundings of defeat after defeat and desertion after desertion, and from the death of my belief in a fair and just world.

In this condition, I came home one afternoon in early December to find the entire dining-room table dwarfed by a giant poinsettia plant. Looking at its brilliant, living beauty in a stunned way, I reached for the card. It said, "Win or lose, you'll always be a winner with us. The John Howard Collins Bay boys." Tears came to my eyes as I thought of the lonely Christmas they would have in their prison, of the scarcity of dollars each of them had, and of the prison rules that challenged adventures like sending flowers. Yet in their poverty, they had shared love and hope with me. Out of their loneliness, they had warmed my Christmas, and Christmas took on a new colour for me. Deprived of Christmas themselves, they had given it back to me. From 175 miles away, behind prison doors, they had sensed my sadness, had valued my struggle for their rights, and having heard my state, sent me a greeting that I carry in my heart to this day.

What all three of these extraordinary listeners heard was the truth that as Henry Van Dyke has written, "Some kinds of defeat are better than victory." They reminded me that even when the world tells you you're defeated, you can take pride in living daringly, dangerously, and positively for the betterment of others. They helped validate my life path, based on the truth that the risks of loving are always better to take than the risks of shutting ourselves off from creative loving. Their kind of listening set me on and kept me on my transformative path.

Conflict Resolution with a Twist

Leaving the Bail Program led me after a year of interim university teaching to an exciting new job as Program Director at St. Stephen's Community House. My boss was a brilliant fundraiser who not only taught me much about those vital skills, but also delighted in raising money for my most creative and wild ideas! With her help, I founded both a street drop-in and a community conflict resolution program at St. Stephen's. And conflict resolution training, which I acquired from Ken Hawkins, a gifted American trainer, widened my listening skills enormously.

Conflict resolution uses the magic of mediation to show the power of good listening to one another. Here are two stories I've experienced. The first was a workplace conflict. The social service organization was a good one, and committed to mediation. One of the managers they had hired seemed to most of them to be a source of tension, conflict and problems. She had had warnings, and they were ready to fire her. But they wanted to try one last thing: mediation, with everyone participating.

We all crowded into a drab, small basement room: about fifteen staff and Board of the agency, two other skilled community mediators and myself, and Mary, the controversial manager. There were no big miracles: people were still at odds, still not trusting one another enough to work together by the end. But in the process, some real listening took place. And some things were agreed on that made the next steps gentler and kinder.

So one transformation that came out of that hot, stuffy afternoon was a moderation of the process by which one person is declared no longer welcome in a group, the blowing of a softer wind on it. But the other was a funny experience between the mediators and Mary. I often give aftercare to anyone involved in a mediation I am doing. So Mary and I exchanged phone numbers, and a week or two afterwards, we got together.

Mary told me that when she walked in that room, she took one look around. "I looked at the faces of those in my agency, and I said, 'Goodbye, old job!' But then I looked at the faces of you three on the mediation panel, and I said, 'Hello, new friends!'" Mary was right on both counts. She accepted the future, with a sense of humour, because she knew how to listen to faces.

Another story of listening and conflict resolution was the story of David. David was an ex-offender who had spent ten years in an institution for the criminally insane, and had now been out and functioning reasonably well in the community for five years. He managed by seeking friendship with some of the most caring people and agencies in Toronto. I often said I met some of the greatest people I knew through David — his taste in support was impeccable.

David did a lot of volunteer work, he took a lot of courses, he was good company and a lot of fun, and he gave generously to anyone in his path when he had any resources. But he also still carried a harvest of problems from the past: he was light-fingered with other people's money and property, figuring he had it harder than we did (which was certainly true). He had a fierce temper, which could erupt on the slightest provocation, real or imagined. And money slipped through his fingers like water, so his monthly cheque disappeared into all kinds of things immediately, leaving him bereft for the rest of the month.

In spite of all this, David was coping and progressing, and we were all enjoying him most of the time. He also had a healthy instinct to spread his needs around widely — when he had worn out one friend or agency, he would move on to another for awhile. David was progressing month by month when something untoward happened. A small religious agency where David volunteered had some American money left from a project abroad. They left it unguarded at the agency, it disappeared, and David was suddenly spending American money everywhere.

The story was circulating in David's informal community of care, and although David denied having stolen the money, everyone believed he had. But the agency that had been victimized was agonized over what to do. On the one hand they knew that with David's record, if they reported this to the law, he would go back in for a long time, and all the years of growing and breaking down the barriers would be destroyed. They didn't believe in that outcome anymore than I did.

On the other hand, they had a responsibility for this money, which had been donated by people for the project, not for David to run through. Even more important, they didn't believe in giving the message to David that this sort of theft was okay. So when I called them in 1986, offering the services of our new community conflict resolution service, they were ecstatic. This was just the kind of solution they were looking for.

The next challenge was getting David to come. Getting the second party to conflict resolution is usually the responsibility of the mediating agency, and it is the hardest part of the process. Over 90 percent of those come to conflict resolution come to a positive solution together, and over 80 percent of these resolutions are kept successfully. But most mediation services lose about half their cases from second parties who won't agree to participate in the first place. As we mentioned earlier, David was a stubborn individual with a razor's edge temper. It might seem that getting him there would be our hardest challenge.

But David had one other quality that was on our side. He was so starved for attention that I sometimes felt he would have come to his own hanging if he could be sure of a good audience. So when I explained to him that he could bring his own friends, and that between the people from Youth Challenge (as we will call the agency from here on) and the people he would invite, his whole community would be present, he was absolutely eager.

He even made a generous offer. "If they make me so mad with their accusations that I want to pop them, I'll just walk out, Ruth." When I told this to Keith, one of our expert mediators who would be on the panel, he talked David into a further step. "Tell you what, David. When you feel so mad you have to walk out, just let us know, and we'll all take a recess." It was agreed, and we had lots of recesses!

In a community conflict resolution, we seat the parties initially by sides, with an aisle between. Each group sits behind the person they are there to support. It's important to be sure that no single individual is ever alone, completely isolated. It's also important to be sure that most of those really concerned with the conflict participate in the process. Otherwise, the disputants may resolve it, and go back to their incredulous communities of support, who recharge them with their own unresolved anger and issues.

In this case, however, the situation was unique. Every one of us was there to support *both* David and the people from Youth Challenge; and every one of us believed David had stolen the money, despite his denials. David had even donated some of the American money to one of my projects before I realized what was going on! David was generous whenever he had money — his own or anyone else's.

However, we assigned people to seats on one side or the other, depending on who had invited them, and the mediation began. One couple had brought their baby, and this little tot became a symbol of the fundamental spiritual unity in the room from the beginning. Throughout the evening, he was passed from hand to hand, as people on either side dandled him on their knees.

In the first part, each party tells their story to the mediators, who try in every way to model complete, respectful listening. The mediators try to reflect back not every detail of the story, but an understanding of the fundamental feelings and values of each of the disputants. There were warm moments during each story. David was always an entertaining storyteller, and although his anger at the accusations of the Youth Challenge people was real, he also shared some of his good experiences volunteering there.

Then came the turn of Donna, the volunteer at Youth Challenge who had left the money around in a drawer, after returning from leading the trip to a Third World country. I asked her a couple of key questions.

"Donna, can you tell us what the loss of the money meant to you?"

Donna was a great participant, ready to respond and share in whatever way she was asked. She replied immediately. "I was absolutely devastated. I knew it was my fault. I should never have left it unguarded. I knew I was responsible for it, and I had to make it good. It had come from the pockets of people all over who believe in our work to help people in Africa and Latin America. I was sick at the stomach, I was so horrified."

"That must have been a dreadful experience," I responded from the heart. "What did you do when you realized the money was gone?"

"I got married right after the return, which was why I was so distracted. So I did the only thing I could do. I took the money our friends had given us for wedding gifts, and used it to pay back the lost money."

I expressed shock, as the full impact of what this theft had done to her hit all of us. I looked at David, and could see the marks of shame, as he realized that Donna's wedding gifts had melted away through his theft. Then I hit on another important question.

"Donna, can you tell us what your friendship with David meant to you before this happened?"

Again, Donna opened her heart, and let it pour out. She spoke of meeting David, of how he opened up a whole new world for her. She spoke of his sense of humour, his bright mind, his goodwill, and the good times they had together. "It hurt all of us this year that we couldn't celebrate your birthday with you, David. But we just couldn't figure out a way — not with this hanging between us."

With his loneliness and desperate need for approval, I could see how Donna's sharing reached into David's heart. He was listening to all this: her sharing of what their friendship had meant, and how painful this separation was, for them as well as for him. We were all moved.

Nevertheless, for some time after, David continued to bluster, deny, and accuse others of persecuting him. For awhile it seemed unclear whether we would get anywhere, until we took another break. During the break, one of David's supporters urged him to say whatever he needed to, to get all the truth on the table.

When they returned, David looked at Mark, the head of Youth Challenge, a deeply Christian man with a virile yet peaceful aura, who had said relatively little till now. David began by describing how he felt. "It feels like St. Michael is sitting on this shoulder (pointing to his right) saying, 'Tell the *truth*, David.' And St. Lucifer is sitting on this one (pointing to his left) saying, 'If you tell the truth, you'll go to prison.'" David paused and looked squarely at Mark, and challenged him with this: "Mark, if I tell the truth, will I go to prison?" This, despite the assurances before and all through the evening that no one wanted David to go back to prison! There was an almost audible sigh throughout the room as all of us breathed with relief. But Mark reacted immediately. Throwing his arms up toward heaven, he exclaimed, "Hallelujah, NO, David!"

Then out poured the confession from David, and from then on, we had nothing but a love-in to deal with: contrition from David, forgiveness from all, fellowship and community all around. Community and fellowship had been there all evening, but David's unacknowledged act had been in their way. Now it was out, we were indeed one loving community. The closing agreement included a retroactive birthday cake for David, at Youth Challenge, along with the payback arrangements from him, and continuing volunteer work arrangements to be resumed.

There's another piece to this true story of creative, supportive listening, and what it can do. One member of Youth Challenge offered to help David manage his money, so that he would be able to make the repayments he very much wanted to. The money was paid back years ago, and she is still helping David handle his money. David has become like an uncle to her children, and has seen them grow, as an extra member of their family. One of the truths in transformative justice is that we have to be in it for the long haul. When we are, there are long rewards.

Rejection Letter

For some years I have served on the Board of the *Journal of Prisoners on Prisons*. We reasoned that it is time we listened to those who experience personally the so-called justice system, and invite them to write scholarly critiques of the penal system itself. In most other areas, we value the expertise of those who use a product or service: why not here? The Journal accepts articles only from prisoners and ex-prisoners, but has a Board of university professors, who assist authors to document their specific points and criticisms with a broader look at the literature. In that way, prisoners learn that their problems are not unique, and therefore are not uniquely their fault, which raises their self-image.

Through the journal, they are given an opportunity to speak eloquently to a wider audience about the faults of the system they are ground through. Instead of continuing to serve solely as fodder for the system, they become experts and authorities on it, so long as they can take an academic, broad look at it, while still speaking with the authenticity of direct participant-observers.

There are so many cases of wrongful conviction, running around looking for a little support, that the issue of wrongful convictions weighs down most of us working for change in the system. Since one wrongful conviction can take several years of fulltime work for several people to overturn, and even then may not triumph, most groups feel they can't take them on. Even the few that do deal with wrongful convictions turn down a hundred cases or more for every one they agree to work on.

This story is a story of rejection, and what followed. The *Journal* took the position — correctly I fear — that we could not get into the issue of researching and documenting individual wrongful convictions. A few years ago a particularly heartrending story reached us, as a submission to the *Journal*. This American prisoner wrote a long saga of wrongful conviction and system abuse, of lack of resources and community support. Although it was a familiar story to me, it was more heartrending than most.

I remember particularly that he ended his heart-wrenching story with these words, "You are my last hope." Yet at our editorial meeting, we agreed we couldn't take his article! I volunteered to write the rejection letter, knowing that I would take time to be as supportive as possible. But I didn't look forward to throwing an article rejection into his face, on top of everything else he had suffered.

I wrote him, thanking him for all he'd shared. I acknowledged that in my sheltered, middle-class life, I had not known the kind of year-in year-out suffering that seemed the story of most of his life. I was White and he was Black; I was free, and he a prisoner; I was middle class, and he was poor. The injustices I had suffered didn't compare with his (probable) wrongful conviction.

All I could offer him, I explained, was the knowledge that his letter had opened a window to his pain, and had moved me deeply. I couldn't claim to understand fully, because I had not walked his path. But I could share a sense of his anguish, his outrage, and his protest against injustice. I then went on to explain as best I could the *Journal*'s policy on wrongful convictions, and apologize that on top of everything else, I had to say that his article just wasn't in our area of publication!

I closed rather lamely, wishing him well (in prison? — for years more? — for a wrongful conviction? — who are you kidding?) I reread it, prayed over it a bit, and sent it, figuring it was inadequate, and sounded hypocritical, but I'd done the best I knew how. I expected not to hear back at all, or possibly to get an angry response.

Imagine my astonishment when I got back, by return mail, an ecstatic letter of thanks, for my letter of rejection! What that prisoner said to me was that he understood my dilemma — he was empathizing with me. I couldn't change the colour of my skin any more than he could, or my life of privilege in most ways. I couldn't even change the *Journal*'s editorial policy. He didn't expect me to right his wrongs. What excited him was that he had felt fully heard by me, respectfully listened to, and cared about. And that was apparently more than he had expected to get, in his heart of hearts.

Robert and I corresponded for several years, and shared various adventures together. But the best moment in our relationship was this meeting of hearts, and what he taught me from it. What we most need in most dilemmas is just that: to be listened to by a loving, accepting heart. That kind of listening is at the heart of transformation.

My friend Ursula Franklin says, "Don't expect to be fully heard more than once or twice in this lifetime, Ruth. Some people never get it at all. If it happens once, be grateful. More than that is a luxury we should not expect." I think Ursula, as usual, is right. But that kind of listening is something we can give more often than that, and by doing so, transform the world. We are all hungry to be heard fully.

Bankers Can Do Creative Listening Too

Much more recently, I have been working in the community with a different kind of alienation and a different kind of challenge. In 1994 I began advocating for better access to banking services for low-income communities and individuals. In the four years since then, local bankers and representatives of our low income community have been on a journey of mutual discovery together. It took two years of meeting together to begin to understand that we could trust each other, and that the good feeling our meetings left was deeper than superficial.

It began because one of the three strongest cries of the local community I worked for, Jane-Finch, was "We want more access to banking services!" I didn't understand much about the issue at first — my husband did our family banking, and as a comfortable middle-class family, we had never had banking problems. But I was a good community developer, and that meant listening to the community's felt needs, and responding to them. Community development is about listening to the heart of one's community.

The biggest problem was that many poor people could not get bank accounts of their own, and had trouble cashing their cheques, except at extortionate Money Mart types of places. To open an account, you were required by banks to have a lot of kinds of identification, most of which poor people didn't have. As I began to visit local banks, I discovered to my surprise that some of them openly stated they didn't want our low-income community's business, and the rest felt that way but were subtler about it.

The banks felt that they made money out of large ongoing accounts that gave them lots of money to invest and few service costs. Our struggling immigrant families had small accounts and a lot of transactions, and they weren't worth it to the banks. In addition, the banks wrongly believed poor people were more likely to commit fraud, so they worried about fraud losses with our neighbourhood. In fact, the major fraud losses for banks as for all of us are to big swindlers who carry the same kind of briefcases and wear the same kinds of clothes as the bankers themselves, but I have never been able to convince the bankers completely of this fact.

Early in my work in Jane-Finch, I explored the banking issue, without making much headway. Then one day in the fall of 1993, I was in our local bank and witnessed a humiliation of a young resident who walked in proudly to open his first bank account. He encountered a clerk who seemed to be fresh from a training session on security precautions in opening low-income accounts. Among other demands was a reference from a current employer, and one from a previous bank stating six months or more of successful banking experience, hardly obtainable on your first account. My attempt at intervention on the young client's behalf failed, and I saw him leave with his head lower, his pride gone, and his optimistic enthusiasm smashed.

I wrote a letter about that experience, and shared it with Pastor Dalton Jantzi, a Mennonite pastor working in a low-income high-rise in our community. Dalton had had similar frustrations with trying to get banking services for his residents, and he urged me to share my eloquent letter with the Taskforce on Churches and Corporate Responsibility (TCCR). This group represents the churches of Canada on all kinds of social concerns about corporate behaviour, a full time job and a half. Yet they were willing to take up my letter, and were already working with the National Anti-Poverty Organization (NAPO) on the issue of low-income access to banking.

Bill Davis of TCCR knew of a conference about to happen in November 1993 called "Investors for Social Responsibility." The young man who devoted years of his life to establishing this important group was so open to our participation that the Conference invited Dalton, myself and Jeanette, three community workers from Jane-Finch now working on these issues, as well as several TCCR staff, to be their guests at the expensive conference, solely for the purpose of raising our challenging questions!

At every session, we listened courteously to presentations, and figured out which of our community experiences fitted this session. Then we raised challenging questions! It is not every group that will pay you to criticize them, and that was my first big surprise. My second was the response we got from the people at the conference. Far from hostility, they were deeply concerned, and bankers rushed up to me afterwards. Their response reminded me of the disciples at the Last Supper after Jesus said, "one of you will betray me," all asking Him, "Lord, is it I?" The bankers would give us their cards, and ask anxiously, "Was it my bank that did that?"

Of the sheaf of cards I collected, one in particular had a big impact on the next steps. Jack Klassen was a Regional Vice-President with Royal Bank, and he explained to me what I already recognized: that the banks like the rest of our culture had two conflicting values. One was competition and profit at any cost, and the other was fair play and compassion for all. Royal was very committed to the right of all Canadians to banking services, but they weren't so committed that they wanted all of our low-income community's business. Rather, they would be brokers to get all the banks to the table with us to talk about how together, they could meet our community's needs.

That offer launched one of the most amazing experiences of my life in networking and advocacy. For it came shortly before the election of the right-wing Harris government, a government that ruthlessly cut our pitiful welfare allowances by 22 percent, while giving tax breaks to the wealthy. In every way the Harris government widened the already wide gap between rich and poor, doubling food bank use, and casting more and more homeless people into the streets of Toronto.

Month after month, the Chrétien and Harris governments added to the destruction of the social safety net begun by Mulroney. In desperation, I began reading books about modern economic trends, and I learned that the Business Council on National Interests (BCNI) was a powerful lobby of Canadian CEOs of the biggest businesses. It is their agenda behind this massive attack on poor and middle class, which was destroying everything most of us had struggled to build. One homeless man froze to death directly under our Premier's office window, but the ruthless destruction went on. I also learned that the BCNI included the national heads of each of the banks I was working with. Year after year, headlines proclaimed record profits for these banks, of over a billion dollars a year.

So it was very hard to sit in the room with local bankers and bank area managers, while half the agencies in Toronto went under from funding cuts, the poor froze and went hungry, and the increasing greed agenda promoted by the corporate controlled governments exacerbated anger, bigotry and despair in the community. How do you listen respectfully to people whose organizations are stamping on your soul?

Yet somehow we managed to begin talking, and listening. I found to my surprise that the generally hated bankers never spoke in bigoted terms used all too often in the community, and expressed some real solidarity with our desire for fair play and respect for our low-income residents. One of them one day got across to me that they weren't necessarily in agreement with all the crudity being put forth by governments, despite the fact that I knew their corporate heads had laid the foundation for it. It was a hard, hard situation to keep on listening, and to respect one another, but in spite of it all, we gradually did build respect. I kept my sanity by wearing anti-poverty and social justice buttons to every meeting, and being ready always to challenge any justification of the war on the poor.

Gradually, in spite of the poisonous social atmosphere around us, we discovered respect for one another as human beings. The bankers were courteous, respectful, and genuinely concerned about the issues we raised. They were surprised at the skill levels and courtesy we community folk brought. We explored with welfare officials a lot of technological solutions like staggering cheque issuance to different times of the month and various direct deposit and easy identification schemes. I contributed little to these, but noted to my surprise that often the bankers were more flexible than the welfare officials supposed to be working for the rights of the poor they allegedly served.

The bankers insisted that major policy changes in banking policy were national, and beyond their level of influence. I argued on this, but we focussed mainly on the technical solutions, with some talk about training options, which I brought up from time to time. Finally one day after an interesting national meeting I attended, I came up with a concrete suggestion. The only real progress we had made to date in nearly two years of meetings on access was personal: we knew each other. Dalton could phone a local manager about a client he knew who couldn't get an account, and straighten it out on a one-to-one basis; the bankers could phone us about problems with community people or issues. But we knew it needed more systematic reform than after-the-fact individual interventions for the lucky few that encountered one of us.

So my proposal was this: based on my conflict resolution experience, I believed we needed to do some trainings to help both bank employees and community residents understand each other's situations and needs better.

But I also said that at this point my agency had just experienced another cut from corporate stimulated government decisions, and I could not go on even attending these meetings or putting much energy into them without some funding from the banks to our starving agency.

It took a few months of negotiating, and the communication process was funny. When the lead banker co-chairing the meeting with me began nickel and diming me on the proposal, Dalton expressed annoyance, and so did I. The bankers were surprised, and chorused, "Oh don't worry about that, that's just the way bankers work!" In a few months, all six banks agreed to fund our agency to do two kinds of trainings:

- Trainings of all bank employees in our area in understanding and dealing with cultural and class differences, and handling conflict creatively, respectfully and preventively;
- Trainings of community residents in money management and banking, so their expectations of bank employees would be as realistic as possible.

The trainings became the centre of the project, and continued in one form or other for several years. But if the trainings were the brain centre, the heart of the project was the Community Banking Group, where we continued to meet and learn to listen to one another. Our project was credited with playing a significant part in the best Valentine I ever received. On February 14, 1997, the Canadian Banking Association issued a press release modifying standards for bank account opening to realistic levels and putting many teeth in the new standards to get local banks to practice them!

The Community Banking Group went on meeting month after month. In the early days, I would say to friends with amusement, "You'll never guess what was my best meeting today — the one with our bankers!" I couldn't believe that these pillars of the financial community whose runaway capitalistic system seemed to be destroying us could have so much in common with us. And I strongly suspect that they had trouble believing the three of us who represented the community could be such good listeners, so open, so respectful, and so intelligent, while subsisting on the marginal wages and facilities of the agency world.

But over the years, more and more miracles of listening occurred in this project. One was from our friend Richard, an Area Manager with one of Canada's largest banks, and one of the most pragmatic and seemingly hard-nosed of our group. We decided to have periodic celebrations of this project, a coming together of banks and community, and these events, so different from the prevailing alienation, played a key part in the transformative process. I have learned over the years that celebrating and validating people's gifts and strengths is key to promotion of real listening.

At one of the first celebrations, we had about 90 people, 60 community residents and agency workers, and 30 from all six banks. I asked Richard to make a short speech on behalf of the banks at the occasion. I don't remember all he said, but I do know that I saw and heard a deeper person than I had seen before. The height of his remarks concerned a role-playing training we had done:

> "We were doing a role-play of a refugee coming into our bank and asking to open an account. I wanted to play myself, but Ruth insisted I play the refugee. I didn't want to do that, because I had been that banker, and I knew how I had treated people in that situation before…"

What a gigantic step forward in transformative listening Richard had taken! His humility in acknowledging to that large audience that he had not understood the refugee before opened us all up to hearing each other. In that acknowledgement, we heard a bank executive as a humble and open human being.

Another example of listening that astonished me came from Richard in his last session with us before transfer took him to a different job. We were talking about why the bank project worked in Jane-Finch but had not so far been replicated in other places. I suggested that the efforts of the banks, who tended to want fast results and de-emphasise process, were ignoring the contribution of the two-year incubating process we had been through before any of our successful project solutions sprouted.

Richard got it immediately. "But they aren't understanding that the *process* is the key!"

I gasped with astonishment and shot back, "Richard, that is such a *spiritual* statement!"

Equally quickly, he put his head in his hands, groaned, and said, "I know, I know, Ruth — it's catching!"

The spirit behind good process and good listening is catching. My other two favourite stories of bankers and listening concern my dear friend Fred, who was manager of our host bank. Shortly after he was transferred into this job and our project, when he was still trying to figure out what it was all about, our agency decided to host hearings into the impact of political cuts in social services on the people of our community. We were told to get spiritual leaders, union people, and business people on the panel hearing this day of testimony.

Following the prescription, I suggested to my staff-person organizing the day that she ask Fred to be on the panel, and to my surprise and pleasure, he accepted. Neither he nor I realized the full impact of that decision. Fred came and sat beside a woman who was head of the provincial labour council, and had been co-chair of a day that had been the largest protest demonstration in the history of Canada! I sat between them, as a kind of cushion, and tried to ensure all day long that Fred was as comfortable as possible. When people are willing to risk coming into a different world, it is our obligation to make the experience as safe and respectful as we can.

The panel sat and listened to a whole day of stories of what it is like to be poor in the Toronto of the 1990s. They heard of rising rents, of ways of going hungry without your children observing it, of the shortage of food bank resources, of the struggle for jobs, and of the shame we force on the poor, on top of their other burdens. One young woman stunned us all with the eloquence of her description of a life of sexual abuse, family abuse, mental illness, life on the streets, and learning to gain self-respect in spite of it all. She was a student at University of Toronto, single parenting two young children, organizing others to speak and act out of poverty, and carrying a student debt load approaching $70,000!

That night our staff who had organized the event each let it out in our own way. Collectively we debriefed: we expressed our grief and our anger at a society which had inflicted this burden on their own neighbours, and elected a government that continued to take from the poor to give to the rich. Each of us responded to the extreme stress of the day in our own way. Although I am famous for my high energy, I went home and took two almost consecutive naps, and still lay there exhausted. Another staff-person went on a long crying jag. Still another took it out in a vigorous evening of physical exercise of every kind.

As we talked over the experience the next morning, I suddenly thought of poor Fred, my bank manager friend. We had known the general facts beforehand, and were still emotionally overwhelmed. Fred had known almost none of this, had no one in his environment to share it with, and probably little experience in dealing with emotionally laden experiences like this. I phoned him up, got his voice message, and left a message of solidarity and support.

Fred said later that he had had a splitting headache that morning, and until I called he had not realized why. That panel experience was Step One not only in Fred's evolution into our community, but in a growing understanding of the deeper issues by our whole banking group. All this led to another miracle: an event at our Annual General Meeting led the Royal Bank to decide to second a "community banker" to work with our community in whatever capacity I thought best, for two years.

At our AGM each year we had been having community banking celebrations, inviting equal numbers of local bank employees and other bank personnel to meet elbow to elbow over community food and entertainment with our residents. A high level Royal official met Barry Rieder, a community minister with the United Church, serving one of the high-rises in our neighbourhood. When this official asked Barry where his church was, and Barry said his church was in the community itself, bells and whistles went off for that official, and he realized the bank belonged back in the community. So the idea of community bankers was born from his creative listening, and Fred Hayes became the first community banker, because of his experience with us on that panel, and other involvement in community events that summer.

Almost two years later, Fred's journey has been a wonderful one to watch. Fred and Murray (also paid by the Royal Bank, but a long-time community economic development activist) and I call ourselves the Odd Trio, or the Gang of Three. Humour and mutual respect bridge our many differences, and in spite of them, with respectful listening, we build community across the chasm that currently divides grassroots communities from large economic institutions. The path of creative listening can take us on strange — and wonderful — journeys!

Victim Offender Reconciliation: An Impossible Challenge

This story, like many of those that follow, is one I heard, rather than experienced. It was told at a conference called "Peacemaking Criminology and Restorative Justice" near Rochester, New York, in June 1997. It is a story of a crime victim who listened to his own needs, reached out, and met them creatively. The victim was a man whose love was running marathons, so he was in superb physical shape. For a living, he worked at a motel, and one night, a hold-up gang came in with guns and demanded all the money. The victim was perfectly willing to give them anything — it wasn't his money, and all he wanted was to escape unharmed from this terrifying situation.

The robbers took all the money, turned to go, and it looked as if the nightmare would end without a major disaster. But one of the two thieves turned around at the door and, apparently in cold blood, shot the victim in the chest. Doctors said he would have died except for his superb physical condition: his stomach muscles were so hardened from exercise that they turned the bullet away from his most vital parts.

Even so, the victim suffered years of pain, disability, and anguish. His running career was over, he was subject to nightmares of reliving this horror, and when he had to testify in court, he could see a horrible smirk on the face of the man who shot him. That smirk tormented him even more. He tried counselling, he got physical therapy. Nothing helped much. His life was a shadow of what it had been, and it wasn't getting any better.

So after about seven years, he decided he was going to try facing the devil, to see if he could exorcize it from his soul that way. He sought a victim-offender meeting with the man who shot him! After the usual struggles, he was luckier than most people and did find an agency that understood these things and would help him. The offender agreed immediately.

The meeting between the two was taped, and again had some remarkable surprises. Of course it covered the usual scenes: the two relived the experience, each from their own point of view. The offender expressed a great deal of contrition at the anguish his impulsive move had caused the victim. Finally, however, the offender said, "If you hadn't moved to release that alarm, I wouldn't have shot you. I was supposed to watch for problems, so when I turned around and saw you bending over to release the alarm, I *had* to shoot you. Why did you do that, if you didn't care about the money?"

It took the victim a moment to replay that bit of his memory tape. Then he remembered that he had indeed, after he thought the robbers were nearly out of the door, been bending over to put away some of the papers he had been working on before any of this happened. He was a tidy person, and needed to put away his records before he could begin calling police later and dealing with all the other critical needs from this new crisis. He explained that he had *not* been pushing any alarm — there wasn't even any alarm to push. But suddenly, after seven years, he understood for the first time that he had not been shot quite in cold blood — he had been shot because the other person was in fear of his own safety! Not that it made it excusable, but it did put a different light on that terrible action.

Now it was the victim's turn to ask a key question. "So if you didn't deliberately shoot me in cold blood, if you're really sorry about all the damage you've done in my life, why were you smirking all through that hideous trial? You seemed to be gloating at the damage you had done."

"Oh my — !" replied the offender immediately, "I wasn't grinning about or at *you*. I had a grin on my face because of the stupidity of the whole process. I had wanted to plead guilty to what we really did, but the prosecution and police wouldn't agree to that. They insisted on prosecuting me for attempted homicide, and I *didn't* do that — I never *meant* to harm you and I wasn't about to plead guilty to it. I didn't want to put you through any more than I already had, so I tried *every* way I could to cop a guilty plea, but they wouldn't let me. There we were, going through this charade which cost the taxpayer a mint and didn't do you or me any good. That's why I had a stupid smile on my face — because it was such a sick joke of a situation."

It didn't undo the years of pain, or the wrong-ness of that terrible shooting, or of the robbery in the first place. But that meeting enabled two people — each of whom had misunderstood critical moves of the other — to see behind the terrible event that separated them, a human being they could at least begin to understand. The monster disappeared, and in his place appeared a person who had done a great wrong, but who had not intended to behave as viciously as appeared. The monster had felt contrite and had tried to cut the legal process short for the victim. His grin — the grin that had haunted the victim for years — had not been a gloating grin, but one of disgust at a system that victimized everyone, and wouldn't let him spare the victim this added agonizing court trial.

The meeting didn't solve everything, but from that time on, the victim felt a new man. Old shadows faded, old nightmares went away, and he felt a sense of personal pride that he had had the courage to face his devils, and found a new power in doing so.

Stories of victim-offender reconciliation are stories of listening to one's inner voice, and then being able to listen to an offender who has wounded one so deeply. This story is remarkable for two things: the crime was extremely violent, and the victim had little encouragement and some discouragement, for seeking contact with his offender. He reached out to the offender almost as a drowning man underwater seeks the surface of the water: a powerful, instinctive drive for air. Victims need the healing release of contact with their offender, and many of them sense it. Whether they like it or not, whether the offender has many virtues or not, the healing of each is in some measure bound up in the healing of both, as these stories convey. They also show that contrary to popular criminal justice myths, the more serious the crime, the greater the need to apply healing justice methods. Deeply wounded victims need transformative healing most of all.

Chapter 3

Pat: A Story of Transformation

Anyone can play a transformative role. In this chapter I am going to share the story of how one of the most despised, lost, institutionalized prisoners I have ever met played a transformative influence in my life. In fact, Pat may well have had the most influence on my life of any prisoner I have known. It all started from the initiative of two caring and competent lawyers — yes there are such! But along the way, we will meet Terry, whose story introduced me to Pat.

Terry

Pat's involvement in my life really grew out of my friendship with another young offender named Terry. I met Terry as I met so many others during his stay in the Milton Jail. Terry at nineteen already had a seventeen-year-old wife named Jean, and a one-year-old baby girl named Angie. Terry pled with us and with the bail Judge for bail, as he felt his life and his marriage and future were slipping away from him. He sensed correctly that he was on the slippery slide toward a long cycle of incarcerations that would separate him increasingly from his family and his dreams. For all that he had an eigth grade education, Terry was eloquent, and he wrote the following letter to the Bail Court Judge:

Your Honour,

I realize your decision is arrived at by fact and suggestion by both the Crown Attorney and my lawyer, and by statements made in court by myself, but unfortunately once I'm in court I find it impossible to say anything and usually remain silent. What I have to say is very, very important to my entire future, so I felt this was the only way to express myself.

I know things do not look their best in regards to my past record. In 1973 I was charged with fraud, cheques were written to the Dominion stores for food. I was sixteen years old at the time, and very frightened of going to jail. I wrote those cheques because I was hungry, and friends with me on the street were hungry, and none of us had family to support us, and we didn't know what to do. I pleaded guilty to the charges, and was sentenced to nine months definite and six months indefinite.

In 1975 I was charged with accommodation fraud. My wife and I stayed at the Holiday Inn in Oakville for approximately two days, and I heard several guys were coming down with baseball bats looking for trouble, so I left, hoping to miss them. I was unable to make a payment on my car, and one of those fellows had co-signed so I had good reason to believe the information was true. I had not received my cheque from work yet, so was unable to check out. I left with every intention of returning to pay the $90 bill, but I was charged before I had the chance.

I appeared in the Oakville Court on the car and accommodation charges and was refused bail because I had no address and no one to go bail for me. I have now been offered temporary residence and the posting of surety bail through the untouchable kindness of the Quakers. They are being very generous in their offer, as I well realize, and they know I'm not trying to prolong justice by getting bail, nor just to be released till the trial, but for the sake of my marriage. I am married with a little girl seven months old.

When I was arrested, many things were left at loose ends between my wife and I. Because of circumstances involved, we lost everything we ever owned. She is presently staying with friends in Mississauga, but can't remain there much longer, as they are expecting relatives shortly. So my wife has to find furniture, clothes, apartment, dishes and every other necessity all by herself. She has to look after our baby, Angie, and she has to do all this on $286 a month, which welfare gives her. It is these things that will tear our marriage apart, and that I just couldn't bear. Jean and Angie are the only things in the world that have any real meaning to me. They are my life, without them I really would have no life to live.

I know my wrongs and I must pay my debts to society, and I am not challenging that, but the future of my entire life rests with your decision. I am not trying to justify what I have done, now or in the past. I am only asking that you allow me to right my wrongs the best I can, and save the only two things that have any meaning to me. It took being in custody away from my family to realize how much I love them and what a fool I've been. I can only pray that you allow me to keep what is so dear to me.

I have the low formal education of grade eight, I have a criminal record, I am nineteen years old, and approximately $10,000 in debt due to a swindler whose cons made him several dollars richer, and left my credit and financial status at a very poor level. Being in custody has allowed me to stop and realize many things. I have come to the conclusion that these four things were and are at the root of my problems. I can do nothing about my criminal record, except stay out of trouble and eventually request a pardon. My age will naturally change with time. I am making arrangements to declare personal bankruptcy so my family and I can start fresh, and do things right and cautiously this time. I intend to go to university as a mature student, working part time. Eventually I would like to become a doctor.

I now have the chance to change my life before I destroy it, and all the decisions I have made to change my life have been for two reasons: my wife Jean, and our little girl Angie. I want more than anything else in the world to get on the right track and give my family a good honest life, and I believe these decisions I have made, are a step in the right direction, but if I am not given bail, I am sure my marriage will turn to ashes, as will my dreams and my very life. I only wish I could find the words to express how I feel. I will agree to any stipulations you impose on me, and I will stick to them without fail. All I ask is that you allow me to straighten everything out with my family, get an apartment, furniture and clothes for them.

I realize that it must be difficult for you to know how I really feel, and I pray to God that you will know that what I have said here is very truthful, and that I mean every word.

Thank you, Terry

The judge at this bail hearing was at first impressed by the Quakers involved, and paid tribute to our work past and present. But the Crown attorney eventually persuaded him that Terry was a compulsive cheque writer whose offences would not be stopped by our kinds of support, so was too dangerous to be released on any bail. The court definition of dangerousness has always intrigued me: Terry's bad cheques were all small, and he had never committed other offences, yet courts daily release men who have beaten their wives and children critically, but are not conceived of as dangerous. It takes awhile to realize that our courts' definition of dangerousness is usually centred on the protection of property, and especially the property of businesses and the well off.

Moreover, the crucial evidence was that Terry had written two cheques for cars in short order, that you can only drive one car, so the second cheque and car were a compulsive desire to show off. In fact, Terry had explained to his lawyer that the first car was an ancient one bought from a used car dealer, and Terry had been as much swindled as swindler, as the car had to be junked within two weeks of purchase. Hence the second purchase and bad cheque, while reprehensible, was neither incomprehensible nor compulsive. But typical of all too many sloppy lawyers working on what they considered poor legal aid fees, the lawyer had neglected to present this vital evidence.

As soon as the Judge rendered his denial of bail, Terry and Jean both began to cry, and the Judge exited hastily. Judges usually do this when their verdict has caused pain — they don't like to see it and they don't have to. In an attempt at mercy, someone tried to allow Terry to embrace his wife briefly and hold his baby. But the handcuffs he wore made both operations very awkward. Terry was then led away, and Jean was not permitted to ride back to the jail with him. Bert, the Quaker volunteer who was to go bail in this case, dropped Jean at the jail, knowing she had arranged for someone to pick her up later.

Fortunately Bert circled the block, for as he came around again, he saw Jean walking down the road with the baby, crying and looking lost. Visiting hours were just over when they arrived, and rules are not bent for the likes of Terry and Jean.

I arranged to pick up Jean the next day to bring her to visit Terry at the jail. This seventeen-year-old teen mother had dressed up Angie in a fresh dainty pink and white outfit to see her Daddy. The three of us had a visit through the glass, and until you have experienced a visit through plate security glass, you cannot begin to grasp how alienating and cruel it is. As soon as we sat down, little Angie began playing games through the glass with her Daddy, rubbing noses across opposite sides of it, patting hands, and making faces at each other. Their struggles to transform its meaning made that hellish glass a poignant but beautiful thing.

Halfway through the visit, as arranged by Jean and me, I took Angie out and played with her in the park across the street while Terry and Jean had a comparatively private visit. As I played with this baby caught in such a stark situation, and reflected on that visit and the glass, I remembered the Biblical verse about "Now we see through a glass darkly, but then face to face" (I Corinthians 13:12). And suddenly another Bible verse I had heard often took on a deeper meaning, and I wrote it that night in a letter of hope and support to Terry:

> For I am persuaded that neither death nor life, nor angels, nor principalities, nor heights nor depths, nor power, nor things present, not things to come, nor anything else in all creation, will be able to separate us from the love of God in Christ Jesus our Lord (Romans 8:38-39).

I ended my letter with the assurance that while our love was a pale reflection of that unflagging love of God, it too was unwavering, and we would be with him and Jean through whatever legal path the courts took us, and whatever events followed.

I got back a beautiful letter in return, in which Terry wrote:

> I was becoming very cold again, as I did the last time I was in jail, but reading your letter brought warmth, kindness, and a lot of love back to my heart again... You have made me feel as if I have, after searching all my life, found out not only what

I was searching for, but I feel the "cavity" that I've had in my heart and mind since I can remember, has finally disappeared. I almost feel "light." You know, I think that was all I ever needed, because once I got your letter, it seemed as though all of a sudden my problems were solved. I felt stronger, reassured, and most of all, human.

I feel I know what I want, where I'm going, and how to get there. It all seems so clear. That verse you shared with me has also restored hope and faith to me, as I honestly felt completely shattered... Without you and the other Quakers I would have given up hope entirely, and that cavity would still be haunting my soul for years to come... Here I sit now wanting to help others and try to lighten their burdens. I feel kindness surge within, and love for my family and friends... For the first time I feel real sorrow for my deeds. There exists a drive within, that demands that I be me, the way I want to be — to right my wrongs, to be a good father, and give my family a good, clean, honest life. Many would say this is a fool's dream, and if so then I am a fool's fool, for *this will be my reality*.

I hope you can see through my outer shell, and know how I feel inside. I have never been so open with anyone before.

It was clear to all of us that Terry needed a new and better lawyer for his sentencing hearing. Marlys Edwardh has been identified by a number of sources as one of our top Canadian lawyers. When I first met her, she was Clayton Ruby's young partner, and just starting her brilliant career. Clay is probably Canada's greatest civil liberties lawyer, and shares a lot of values with us Quakers. Our working relationship has always been close, and in my early years as a volunteer I got into an informal relationship with Clay and Marlys, which no one put into words, but it worked like this: They would take on, for legal aid rates, my most forlorn protégés, and I would bail out theirs. I couldn't act as a lawyer (although I became a competent paralegal with my work in courts and prisons), and they could not legally bail out their own clients.

So I now approached Marlys to take on Terry's case. She helped us work on a contract between Terry and Jean and our family, which covered our support and their commitments in every area. We needed a joint visit to finalize it, and Marlys called the jail and arranged the visit in advance.

The entry into the jail that Marlys had organized for us was so memorable, I can still conjure it up in depth, twenty years later. Although Marlys had phoned in advance, when we arrived the guard tried to tell us we couldn't come in. Marlys exercised her persuasive powers on him: a musical voice, beautiful smile, overwhelming eloquence, and an obvious determination not to give in. He moved far enough to express precisely the prison's hierarchical view of humanity. Pointing to Marlys, he said: "*You* can come in, because you're his lawyer." Then, with a sneer of greater reluctance he pointed to me: "And *you* can come in, because you're a volunteer. But," (with disdain, and pointing to Jean) "*you* can't come in, because you're his *wife!*" The very idea, a wife having the right to see her husband! Marlys prevailed, we all three got in, and the contract was drafted, and was part of the package that overwhelmed the Milton Court that day.

Marlys prepared such a superb package for the court that this young loser not only got probation: everyone in the court was dazzled. Even the baby got in the spirit of the occasion, and when the Judge asked if Terry had family present, Angie gurgled, grinned, and waved her hand, as if on cue! People kept saying, "Who was that lawyer?" She had a full psychological report and full history on Terry. The contract Marlys had worked out with the three of us, included housing, job plans, and counselling.

From then on, Terry's and Jean's story took many sad turnings, but their sincere and desperate desire to escape the downward spiral they were in was one of many stories that drew me along in my own path of transformation. And it was Terry and Jean's court hearing that introduced me to Andy, and ultimately to Pat.

Pat: "The Hungriest Person for Help I've Ever Seen"

It was through that stunning performance that I got a call from another lawyer, Andy. After the court hearing with Terry, a number of lawyers had asked me for my number, but I was still surprised when I got a call from a lawyer called Andy, who explained he had met me in the Milton Court that day.

"I have a client I'd like you to meet. His name is Pat, and he's being held on a robbery charge. He's got one of the longest records I've seen. It's mostly petty stuff — theft and a few small drug charges, getting into fights and that kind of thing. But it goes on for pages. He's been in institutions pretty continuously from the time he was fourteen till now — he's 26, except for one four-month period when his brother Alec helped him stay out.

"Pat doesn't have any work record or skills. He is the scapegoat in a large multi-problem family. At the present time he is co-charged with Alec in a robbery. Several of their other brothers have been in prison too. Their Dad is a chronic alcoholic. Pat may have a bit of a drinking problem himself." (That turned out to be the understatement of the century!) "He's also functionally illiterate, but he's been getting help from a literacy volunteer in the jail. Oh, — and I almost forgot, he's attempted suicide about seven times."

When he paused for breath I tried not to gasp. Up till now most of my prisoner protégés had been smooth middle-class con men types. I had not taken on any lower-class "rounders" like Pat, much more typical of the men the system processes in and out regularly. No member of my family had ever had a drink of alcohol, and my life had been pretty sheltered. I'd never even seen a person under the influence of alcohol or drugs, except once or twice at a distance, on the street. I gulped, and tried to respond.

"So," I managed to get out, "just what did you think I could do for him?"

There was no hesitation on Andy's part. "He's the hungriest person for help I've ever seen," he responded with utter sincerity. That did it. How could I refuse a plea like that? I agreed to see Pat, and we would take it from there. Although I am supposed to be the person of faith, I have often been carried to heights of faith-filled risk-taking by the faith of others, and this was a case in point. My first visit to Pat took place in the presence of the whole Quaker jail program group in the Milton jail. He didn't speak up, and he seemed quite strange to me, what little I could figure out of him. When I reported this to Andy, Andy just said, "Pat was embarrassed to talk with you in front of the whole group. He needs a one to one visit to open up." So off I trotted, somewhat reluctantly given the 35-mile drive, for a one-to-one visit with a man who sounded like a walking time-bomb, and whose first impression on me was that he was pretty odd.

There was no magic at that first meeting, but I did begin to pick up on the hunger Andy had talked about. Pat told me about his tragic family background, about his yearning to be part of the real world, about his lack of knowing what it was like to experience community holidays outside of institutional bars. He mentioned Betty, his literacy volunteer, who was helping him learn to read for the first time. Most of all, he talked about his brother Alec, and asked me to go see Alec, who wanted to talk with me also.

Alec was in the West Detention Centre. He was a lot more presentable than Pat, but also faced heavy charges. Alec had a young wife who was threatening to leave him because of the sentence he was serving and the charge he faced with Pat. If Linda left him, she would take custody of their four-year-old son Matt, whom Alec adored. Here was a young man facing problems that would have overwhelmed us:

- The two years less a day sentence he was about to start serving;
- An outstanding charge on robbery that would probably net him years more in prison;
- The probable break-up of his marriage and loss of his only child.

Alec was a likeable young man. For all the problems he faced, he kept coming back to Pat. He told how no one in the family but himself really believed in Pat. Linda had been very kind, and allowed Alec to take Pat in their home once for four months, and that showed Pat could do it, because he had stayed out of institutions for the longest ever. But with Alec facing years inside, who was there to help Pat now?

Alec had heard of my visits to Pat, and he was terribly grateful. He kept trying to sell me more on Pat, as if his own life depended on my investment in his brother's life. "With me in here, Pat has nobody," Alec said repeatedly. Still, I listened to his challenges, and wondered what he most needed. At the end of the interview, I asked him: "So is there anything I can do for you, Alec?"

Without hesitation, he looked at me with his whole soul in his eyes and said, "Just help my brother, please. He has no one else." As I heard that plea and saw his eyes, focussed solely on his brother's need, another image flashed before me. Some years before, two children went boating with a family friend in the Niagara River. The boat owner was unfamiliar with the river and its dangerous current. He passed the sign warning not to go nearer the Falls without noticing it, then began to hear the thundering waters, and tried to turn it round. The motor failed as they struggled against the mighty Niagara. Desperately remembering his promise to take care of his friend's children, he had the two children put on the only life jackets in the boat.

As they swept nearer and nearer the Falls, the boat was overturned, and the teenage girl, her eight-year-old brother and the boat owner were swept into the fierce waters. The owner was swept over the brink to his death, but both children experienced miracles. The little boy became the only person ever to go over the brink with no powerful protection and live — he was found by the amazed crew of the Maid of the Mist boat which takes tourists near the foot of the Falls to get a spectacular view. They certainly got a spectacular view that day as they spotted a little yellow blob, which turned out to be a living child, bobbing about in the churning waters! His very lightness probably swept him over the murderous rocks. He blacked out during his incredible experience, but was otherwise uninjured.

However, his teenage sister had her own miracle. She was within feet of the Falls, screaming and struggling, when an off-duty policeman saw her and tried to save her. Yelling at her to try for the edge, he tried to wade out a very few feet to save her. The current was too strong, and he might have died too, but another tourist grabbed a tree, stepped into the water, and held out a hand to the policeman. That human chain was able to pull the girl in.

A wonderful story, but what does it have to do with playing the transformation game? The next line is the fit. When they hauled that girl in, closer to the brink of death than anyone had ever come without going over, she was screaming not, "Save me, save me!" but "Save my brother!" Alec reminded me so much of her, with his pleas to save his brother, despite his own perilous situation.

So I heeded Alec's plea and continued to visit Pat. But I still knew I was over my head with Pat, and had a tiger by the tail, without even knowing the nature of tigers. As a result, I responded in a somewhat lukewarm way when Andy, the lawyer, said he wanted to try for bail for Pat, and would like me to testify. I was into risking, and I wanted to help, so I agreed, but I wondered what I would say, and more importantly, if they gave Pat bail, what I would do! Andy's dogged persistence impressed me the more because I had seen so many lawyers who lacked any of his caring, second mile approach. I once witnessed a Chicago lawyer who gave a case summary spiel to the judge, then looked down at his papers and said, "Oh, sorry — wrong case!" He tried another one on, while his bewildered and disheartened client of the day just sat there, knowing how little his life mattered to his lawyer.

The bail hearing was held in a funny little country courthouse that took me a while to find. My mother was living with me now, and I brought her along. She had never heard me testify in court before, and found the whole experience fascinating. The courthouse itself resembled — and may have been — an old church building mildly remodelled. It made me think that when we lose the substance of sound religious faith, we need more courthouses.

I had enough experience in courts by now that faces and experiences were beginning to repeat. Both the Crown attorney and the chief police witness had testified against other protégés of mine, and I had prayed for them, and for the grace to cross the invisible but powerful barriers that separated those of us on opposite "sides" of this thing we called a justice system. This particularly Crown attorney was easier than many to pray for and communicate with, and my prayers enabled me to dialogue with him about other cases we both knew in the court intervals. I knew he would not be unfair in his presentation here.

Andy did a good job of presenting our case, and I spoke as well as I could, but the Crown prosecutor held forth eloquently on the rich topic of Pat's record, and his poor chances not to re-offend. The judge concurred with the Crown, and I have to admit I was more relieved than disappointed. Not so Andy, who said right away, "We're going to appeal this, Ruth. With all we had going, we should have won." He plunked down his own money for the transcript for the appeal, and I admired his faith without sharing all his enthusiasm for our project.

Alec had had to be present for the hearing too, although meaningful bail was impossible for him since he was serving time for the other offence already. But the two of them were chained together, so when I went to speak to Pat, to extend my sympathy to him, I met Alec too. I had never encountered a situation quite like this — it was not part of my suburban upbringing — so I muttered something to Pat about "I'm sorry, it's too bad, but I guess you've faced these kinds of denials before." I realized much later how little I understood the meaning of denial to Pat, but while I was there, Alec spoke to me warmly, from the heart, "Thank you for all you are doing for my brother, Ruth."

Andy was as good as his word. In a few weeks I got a call from him that the Supreme Court Bail Review was booked for the next Monday, and could I come testify? He was hoping that Betty, Pat's literacy teacher, would be there too. By this time, with the enthusiasm of Alec and Andy for Pat, and with my own regular visits beginning to bridge the lifetime of different experiences that separated Pat and me, I was becoming keen myself.

I was feeling somewhat more optimistic than before. I had continued to visit Pat and Alec and Alec's wife and had begun to feel almost part of the extended family, understanding a little of their traumas and challenges, and identifying with them. We had firmed up arrangements for Pat to stay at St. Leonard's House, after an initial period with us, which made me feel more hopeful. Andy continued to express faith in Pat's progress — he said Pat kept telling him how much the support of Betty and me was doing for him. Another life-skills teacher was also a positive element. Rereading the previous transcript made Andy feel he should have won it and that we had every chance on this appeal.

All this made me feel much more cheerful about coming, although by now I hated bail hearings in general. My only other appearance at a Supreme Court review had been before a judge so harsh that when he denied bail in our exemplary case, all the other lawyers present had found excuses to withdraw and defer their cases that day. They hoped that any future judge would give them and their clients more of a chance. This had amused the judge, who wanted to get on to another trial he was doing, anyway.

Another thing about bail proceedings and court proceedings in general was the amount of time spent — or wasted — depending on how you looked at it. Delays are what courts do best. One of their biggest punishments for friends and family of accused — and victims — is the time taken in waiting, deferral, waiting, deferral, waiting, deferral... If you lost, it was depressing of course, and if you won, there were more time delays in waiting to get papers, waiting to be admitted, driving to another office, waiting some more, driving to the jail, and waiting for the JP, and for your friend, and to sign. That was for those of us fortunate enough to have cars. The obstacles were heavier still for those without.

So I looked forward to this day with distinctly mixed feelings. I sat in court and watched the judge for the day — Judge Griffiths, adjudicate one bail case, to see which way the land lay. I was mildly disheartened when bail was denied, but not wholly discouraged. The judge had at least listened well, acted courteously, and given sensible reasons for his decision. I was still more amazed when Andy asked for and got permission to move our case up next, because he had two witnesses waiting. That the court would actually consider our time was a novel and heady thought for me!

The Judge was feeling fairly negative to begin with. Both Judge Griffiths and the Crown shot down Andy's argument about Pat's Failure to Appear record being only one time. Andy said then that he had two witnesses, which puzzled me again, because he had phoned me a day or two before, to say that unfortunately Betty's job wouldn't give her the time off for this, so she wouldn't be there. The Supreme Court was a larger and more formal setting than others, with people waiting for a number of hearings. As a result, I couldn't guess who the other players were.

Andy called me to the stand and there was the usual slight awkwardness as I asked to affirm, not swear. But I was getting experienced at this, and a combination of prayer and experience set me at my ease. Andy began by stating all my professional qualifications from my résumé, and all I had to answer was "Yes," as he read off each one. Next he asked me about my volunteer work and about the work of our Quaker committee with a variety of prisoners. He was laying a firm groundwork, doing his best to impress the court that I was professionally and personally in a position to know what I was doing. Then Andy surprised me by asking a general question, "Tell me about your relationship with Mr. S. and what you would like to do with him."

A witness was only allowed to answer the questions asked, and a lawyer who asked narrow questions or the wrong questions could handicap ones usefulness greatly, so this was a wonderful opening I had not expected. I talked not only about Pat's apparent readiness and motivation, but also about the variety of resources I had been looking into for him: a couple of possible jobs, the St. Leonard's House to stay, and various young and older Quakers to add to his depth of friends.

I knew by now the habits of Crown attorneys in situations like this, so the Crown's questions did not surprise me. His questions were reasonable: did I know the length of Pat's record? Yes, indeed! Did my information about it come from Pat, or from his lawyer? From his lawyer. Courts believe, for some unfathomable reason, the word of lawyers of all stripes and persuasions, and doubt that of accused persons equally consistently, so my answer was important.

The Crown then asked if I had ever taken on anyone with a record as long as Pat's. This was a tough challenge. One or two prisoners I had met could match Pat, but no one we had taken in personally was in his league. Yet I had become friends with a number of chronic offenders, and was able to talk about my experience with them, partly though not completely answering his legitimate challenge.

As the Crown was running out of traditional Crown questions for someone like me, I waited eagerly for questions from the judge. The judge's questions would be the first clear indication of his attitude. Roughly two-thirds of judges appreciated the intervention of community volunteers like myself, and my credentials — academic and otherwise — always impressed such judges. The rest tended to be more cynical and regarded volunteers as a bit soiled by the company they were keeping, or too naive to listen to. It was important to see if this judge were going to take me seriously. So I was very disappointed when he had no questions at all, and I returned to my seat slightly discouraged. Still I felt I had done all I could, and was eager to hear who Andy's other witness was.

To my surprise, they called Betty to the stand! As I learned later, she had just not been able to stand going to work that morning, leaving Pat abandoned by her, so she took a day of unpaid leave to come and testify for him. This was the first clue about the kind of person that she was. Betty was more inexperienced than I in anything to do with courts, but she radiated a Christian grace and faith along with an infectious belief in Pat and an excitement about his opening the world of literacy. I was proud to be on the same side with such a human being. She spoke of seeing Pat on the verge of a major learning breakthrough, a key event in his life. She added how important it was to his self-image to build on this eagerness by gaining release for him at this critical time.

The Crown threw a tricky question at her, asking if she would continue to work with Pat in the jail if he were not released. Of course she had to say yes, but Andy rescued her by asking her to describe the conditions for learning in the Milton Jail. She replied with zest, "In one word, deplorable!" She went on to describe how there was one room for all legal visits and schooling visits and she had had to move three times last visit and ended up working in a hallway with all kinds of interruptions and distractions.

Betty told me afterwards that she had arrived while I was testifying, and picking up my previous experience, felt she would be making a fool of herself trying to testify. Then she replied to her own self-criticism: "No, I'm here to speak for Pat, and if I make a fool of myself, it doesn't matter." In that spirit, of course she did wonderfully, because it is when we forget our own egos that we come through best to great challenges.

When Betty sat down, another big surprise happened. Before the Crown even got up, the judge turned to him and said that in all the circumstances, this was such an unusual opportunity for rehabilitation for this man, he was inclined to give these people a chance to try to help Pat, and to order his release. When the judge said that, I knew what our Quaker founder George Fox meant when he said, "I felt a great opening." Betty, who is very religious, felt it too, and we were sitting there side by side, never having spoken to each other yet, but feeling the tremendous power of God in that courtroom, and both nearly in tears from the beauty of the Spirit.

The Crown attorney was quite taken aback, and understandably so: he had an almost perfect client for a detention order, and he was about to be snatched away from him! The Crown began a half-hearted speech he had prepared about what a menace Pat was, but halfway through the judge cut in with these words, "I know all that, and it is all very well. But I have seen men like this young man before, and I have seen how few opportunities come their way. We have heard two families in this community, families with resources and integrity, come forward prepared to give their all to help him become a part of our community. Opportunities like that don't come twice in the life of a man like this, and I'm not going to be the one to stand in the way."

I have told that story many times, and written it a few, and I can never repeat those words without tears coming to my eyes. People talk about great moments in courtrooms when some clever attorney outsmarts another, or some surprise witness brings a new bit of evidence. They may be great in one way but, in my lifetime, that was surely one of the greatest spiritual moments I will ever experience in any courtroom.

The judge returned a little to this world, concluding his words to the Crown with, "What I am interested in hearing from you are the conditions of release you would propose." At that moment, the whole room seemed full of light, and even the Crown got in the mood of the occasion. When Andy learned from me that we were prepared to go $2000 property bail without further discussion, the Crown said that was too much — $1000 was plenty!

We continued in this incredible spirit, all working together for everyone's good, for the public surely can only benefit if the Pats of this world finally find a place where they can be a giving, valued part of our communities. Everyone there was concerned for Pat too, and aware of his tragic self-destructiveness.

I had signed enough bails by that time that I had some idea of the process, but the Supreme Court one was a little more complicated. One of us had to wait for the papers, and take them out to Milton, to extract Pat from the jail there. Betty had to get back to the remainder of her day's work, and I was thrilled to have the chance to bring liberation to Pat, to surprise him with this incredible news. So Andy told me what to do, and while the papers were being prepared, Betty and I had the chance to visit for the first time, to talk about plans together, before she went on her way.

It was certainly one of the most wonderful beginnings to a profound partnership that one could have. We were both on a spiritual high from the judge's powerful venture in faith for Pat, and for us. I let Betty buy the tea, as I could see she was so full of thankfulness to God for what was happening that she would burst with it if she didn't have some outlet. We shared our dreams for Pat in the weeks to come, and ideas to work together in helping Pat build a life outside of institutions.

By the time I got the papers it was afternoon, although the hearings had begun at 10 a.m. Going home on the bus and subway with those bail papers, I was still so radiant, and singing to myself that people were looking at me to see what was going on with this lady. Every once in awhile I would pull that bail paper out of my purse, and look at it and think: there lies a man's freedom, and his chance to try again, with God's help.

The drive to Milton took another hour and a half. Lawyers have a choice on whether they bring their clients to bail hearings, and lots of them don't. I often feel it is an uncaring thing to leave the client out of a scene that is all about his or her rights and life. But Pat's lack of life-skills stood out a mile. It was the same quality that had alienated me at first, and made me feel he was odd. I knew Andy had been correct, not uncaring, in deciding that Pat's presence in court would work against our goal. So Pat had been waiting all day for the outcome. When no word came by lunch-time, he was sure that, as nearly always in life, he had lost again.

So when he got called to come down for a visit with me, Pat thought I had come to tell him he didn't get bail. Then he walked in and saw me sitting there with a Justice of the Peace, and he knew the wonderful truth. Tough, streetwise Pat burst into tears. He knew that I would not be there with a JP unless bail had been granted. Pat put his head in his hands a moment, crying with the inexperience of a man who doesn't allow tears, and then he hugged me, with tears still running down his face. The JP showed an astonishing amount of tact by leaving the room for a few moments so Pat could recover, and I found myself with a tough streetwise 26-year-old chronic offender leaning his face on my shoulder and sobbing his heart out. I recalled my callous words a few weeks ago about how used he must be to rejections, and I learned for all time that no human being is ever so accustomed to rejection that it doesn't hurt right down to the depths of their soul. How blind we are to think that rejection and neglect ever stop hurting their targets.

When the JP came back we got the paperwork done fairly quickly, and then the jail had to process his release. Before very long we were on our way. I had a free Pat in my car for the first time in my life, and Pat had succeeded in getting bail for probably the first time in his career. Alec was being held at Maplehurst, a provincial prison also in Milton and near the jail, so we agreed we would stop by and see him, if the prison let us, which they did, somewhat to my surprise. (Many prisons refuse visits by those with criminal records to those inside.)

I still remember that scene vividly, after all these years. The joy those two brothers shared made both their faces glow: Pat's with the wonder of new hope, a first experience in having a chance to make it with people, outside of his loyal brother, who believed in him; Alec with unselfish pride that his brother was going to have a chance, at last. A number of times Pat would start talking about his hopes, his plans, his ideas, and then break off, apologize to Alec, as he saw that every word was reminding Alec of the things he could not do, facing a substantial prison term already. Each time Alec would say hastily and sincerely, "No, no, Pat — that's great! You do it for both of us! And don't let the Morrises down. Make us all proud of you."

So it was a bittersweet experience, but because of the vicarious pleasure Alec had in Pat's liberation, the sweet outweighed the bitter. We drove back from Milton quite high, back to what was one of my children's favourite holidays of the year: Halloween. We always made individual costumes based on each one's idea of what she or he wanted to be that year. Our older children went trick or treating independently, but little Joy at seven needed someone to accompany her. Instead of having a parent go, we let Pat go out with her, and I don't know who was more excited: Pat experiencing his first Halloween in many years, possibly the first not blurred by his alcoholic father's problems and other family issues; or Joy, proud as always of her new costume, and sharing her love as she always did with her new friend straight from prison.

But the transition was rugged for all of us from the beginning. Pat was very reluctant to go into St. Leonard's. He begged to stay with our family, away from the influence of other ex-offenders and their temptations. We insisted, but he screwed up badly that first night, bringing drugs and police down on the halfway house in an escapade for which my friend the Director forgave both Pat and me with wonderful graciousness. But it closed that door for Pat, and left us with him staying with us, and no other options. I knew this would be no rose garden, and that even with Pat's desperate desire to make it and our eagerness to help, he might still not make it. But I felt in the depths of my heart how wonderful and right it was to be trying together this venture in healing humanity.

Pat's teaching reached me through the night at St. Leonard's House too. One of the other men in the house, Dennis, looked twice as street-y as Pat, a real rough and ready type. But Dennis, who had also spent his life in institutions and was barely literate himself, had risked everything in dogging Pat's steps that night and saving him from various even worse catastrophes. Dennis had several long talks with Pat, trying to persuade him he didn't have to drink and screw up to be accepted by the other men in the house. There were good angels in strange shapes everywhere, and Dennis and I always cherished each other in the years to come from the shared experience of Pat's first night out.

Pat's relationship to money was otherworldly. When he came out, he had three cents to his name, and almost his first act was to put his three cents into Joy's UNICEF collection box. On the other hand, there was something about Pat that attracted the visionary gesture in others. A member of our Quaker prayer group, who had been praying for Pat for weeks, pressed a twenty-dollar bill in my hand for him, saying, "This is not charity, or a loan. This is an *investment* in a new life." We were all investing, in a big way.

That was the beginning of one of the most memorable six months of my life. I am credited with a number of "achievements" — starting things, getting awards, writing books, speaking at major events. But I have more than a dim suspicion that when I cross over into the next life, those six months with Pat will stand me in better stead than any of the recognized achievements. They began with a roaring start, a harbinger of things to come. After the first few days, we would be facing a weekend, and weekends are times of special peril for those who have few skills in finding constructive use of leisure time. It would be Pat's first weekend out in many years, and he needed a lot of support. On the other hand, my Dad in Buffalo had cancer, and I had promised to visit him that weekend.

I could think of only one excellent resource: Betty. It had been a wonderful experience at court to meet someone in a relationship that began clearly on the spiritual plane. Having shared that radiant mystical joyous courtroom experience, Betty and I began our relationship sharing not only spiritual ideas but also a common awareness of the light of God all around us as we spoke and felt the beauty of this day. We had agreed to take Pat in, but she was eager to help in any way, and had urged me to call her as needed. And now, already, we did need her. So I picked up the phone and asked: could she and Mel take Pat for that first weekend?

She had to consult with Mel, but when she did, the answer came back affirmatively. So I dropped Pat off on my way to Buffalo, and wondered as I spent that weekend with my parents, how Pat and Betty and Mel were doing. Lucky I didn't have an inkling! For when I dropped by on my way back home to pick up Pat, what a story I heard from Betty of that memorable weekend. Pat had been difficult in a variety of ways on Saturday, drinking more and more. None of us had any guidelines or clues on his drinking problem, and this was the first indication that it was going to be a whopper. In fact, even prisoners with virtually no drinking problem often overindulge when first released, in trying to blot out the harsh memories of incarceration, and the sense of helplessness and worthlessness as they confront a world for which they are utterly unprepared. Pat's preparation was less than anyone's was and his drinking problem pre-existed, so he seized every opportunity to drink. This was our first discovery that with Pat, opportunities to drink and get drugs existed as universally as the air we breathe reaches us.

So Saturday night Pat went out to have a serious binge, and proceeded to do just that. Somehow, with his strange ability to find a home when it seemed most unlikely, despite an equal ability to get hopelessly lost at other times, Pat made his way back to Betty and Mel's, stone drunk, late Saturday night. Not only that, but this was also our first introduction to a sequence we were to see often. Pat felt terribly guilty when he drank too much, so to blot out the pain, he would take drugs. Again, Pat had an unbelievable ability to attract free drugs on the streets, wherever he was. Drugs came to him like a magnet, without money, and without effort. If only the good things of life came to Pat with a fraction of that ease!

Pat's guilt over mucking up his first weekend with his wonderful, generous hosts was so overwhelming that he decided to end it all, to show how sorry he was, so he tried to kill himself by overdosing on drugs. But by the time he got to Betty's home, he was feeling sorry about that too, and realized this was not exactly the way to make amends. So he told Betty what he had done. Betty and Mel spent hours trying to get a doctor to their home to deal with Pat's overdose. By the time a doctor actually came, Pat refused his services, and soon dozed off to sleep. It turned out that, although Betty and Mel were thoroughly frightened by now, Pat was so accustomed to drugs that the dose he had taken was by no means fatal, but the drugs did put him to sleep.

Not for long, however. When Betty and Mel had finally fallen into an exhausted sleep, Pat woke up, more depressed than ever. Those who have never faced serious depressions have no idea how overwhelming they are. Pat's depressions were frequent, came most often and most severely at night, and usually overwhelmed his very limited sense of trust in himself and in life. A psychiatrist friend of mine said once, "Pat, you need sometime to see one of those depressions through to the bottom, and see, without alcohol, drugs or anything else, what is on the other side of them." Good advice, but hard to follow.

On this occasion, there were just two sleeping exhausted and inexperienced hosts, and a desperately depressed Pat, guiltier than ever for having screwed up their weekend, adding drugs to the guilt he already had about alcohol. He decided on an action he had taken a number of times before. Finding a kitchen knife, he sliced his wrists, and began bleeding to death. He bled all over the bed, all over the carpets. As the blood of his life continued to trickle out, some dim sense of what he was throwing away came to him. Was he going to throw away the first real opportunity life had given him, the first weekend that he had it?

Full of apologies, he went to wake up Betty, with words of abject guilt. He had screwed up worse than ever, but he had decided to live. Would she help bind up his wrists so he could? Betty, wakened out of the first heavy sleep of exhaustion, rose to the occasion with a Christian grace I still marvel at. As she contemplated the wreckage of her bloodied bedclothes, rugs, and home, and saw a drunk, drugged, horribly bleeding Pat as her only compensation, and heard his miserable apologies, she began binding his wounds physically, and emotionally bound them much more with these amazing words, "No, Pat, you are NOT a failure! This is a victory, because you have chosen to live." I am still awe-struck, and know that only from the Divine could such strength and integrity and love emanate.

When Pat had had an episode like this, he was exhausted, and slept deeply. And when he awoke again, he was in a funk. Repentance overwhelmed him, to the point where he could barely speak. So they spent the next day till I came, trying to bring him out of his total funk of despair, combined with a hangover, post-drug reaction, and recovery from his wrist wounds. As I heard the story, I felt my own guilt for having foisted this experience on my new friends, even less experienced than I in the wonders of a world inhabited by Pats.

Bewildered myself at what to do with a deeply depressed, morose Pat, I had trouble getting any words out of him as we headed back to Milton to see Alec again in the hope that Alec could talk some sense into Pat. What a situation — to depend on one weak, imprisoned brother as the best support for the other! Most of my conversational efforts in the car got nowhere, because as I gradually learned, when Pat was depressed, the struggle to do anything, even say a word, was enormous. Depression drains energy from us more than any hard exercise, and Pat's depressions were like solid blocks of ice: thick, cold, and brutally immovable.

Finally though, Pat himself came out of it enough to begin shaking his head. "Those people, those people," he muttered. Then he brought the wonder of it out, "Those people, Ruth — after the weekend I gave them, they asked me back, and they meant it!" Pat had never encountered Christian grace so wide and so deep, nor for that matter, had I. Tough as the months ahead were for all of us, the grace of a Betty who could say "It's a victory, Pat — you've decided to live!" and who could invite him back after that weekend, set Pat on a new road, a road into community.

Alec tried his best to put Pat back on track too. Alec was obviously distressed by what had happened, but with a surprising amount of wisdom recognized that the only way was to go forward, trying to learn from the missteps of that first weekend. So we returned home, and tried to make a new beginning in our own home. One pledge I had made to my husband was that we would not take into our home someone actively inebriated, nor allow either alcohol or other drugs to be kept in the home. This created some interesting scenes. There was no liquor store or tavern within half a mile of our home. Pat's worst depressions came at night, and overwhelmed by depression, craving alcohol or drugs to numb it, he would sneak out of the house, and we would usually not know he was gone till morning.

The pattern continued: he would drink till drunk, then take drugs to dull the awareness of his failure and the continued depression, sometimes in a mild suicide effort. More despondent than ever, he would often slice his wrists in a heavier attempt to end it all, or he would strike out at someone in a tavern or similar spot and get into a brawl. Either way, he would usually end the episode in a psychiatric ward of the nearest hospital with such a facility. I learned so much from Pat, and here came an astonishing lesson. Hospital after hospital would wait till morning had left Pat in a sodden depression, no longer trying to pull the bandages off his wrists and finish the job, just lying there passively, hungover, more depressed than ever, but quiet. Not caring what lay behind the quiet, they welcomed it as a sign he was no longer a danger to himself or others, released whatever restraints they had that were physically preventing suicide, asked him a couple of routine questions, and turned him out!

Once one hospital made a referral to public health, who called us in a very helpful spirit. They tried to help us find more resources in the local community for any and all of Pat's problems, and their spirit gave me a lifelong respect for public health as the frontline troops in community integration. But it would take more than a few good efforts like this to overcome the lifetime of problems layered in Pat.

We kept Pat a few weeks, tried to find what he most wanted, and tried to get him into programs that would meet those needs. For the first time in my life, I began to experience the kind of rejection Pat and his peers had known all their lives. When I knocked on doors for myself, I usually got in: I was bright, middle class, well-mannered, had contacts and resources in the community, and had a track record and presentation of someone who accomplished what I set out to do. I took for granted this response, never having thought about it. Now when I knocked on doors for Pat, I got a different response. People were still usually somewhat polite to me, but when it came to accepting Pat, the doors began closing, and some of them slammed in my face as well as his.

Once during one of the bail appeal periods, I was talking to Andy, Pat's lawyer about Andy's excellent record in returning my calls promptly. I jokingly mentioned my husband's comment, "Don't ever expect someone to return a call unless they are trying to sell you something."

Andy had laughed and said a little sadly, "That's the trouble, Ruth; the people you and I are trying to help, nobody is buying."

The most typical response came from a woman who listened to me over the phone, and then said, "You sound like a nice, capable person who wants to help people. If you want to help people, I can put you in touch with lots of people who want and need and will use help. This guy sounds like a real loser. You're wasting your time with him, and I'm not going to waste my time on him. But if you want to help someone worth helping, just let me know." I bitterly resented such speeches: on Pat's behalf, and on behalf of all the lost legions he represented. Who were these people to determine the saved and the damned, and offer no crust of bread, no sip of water to the Pats of this world?

One of the things Pat and I shared was an ability and commitment to say thank you to those who deserved it. Pat asked my help early on to write a thank-you letter to Andy, his remarkable lawyer, who richly deserved it. But deserving it or not, few lawyers — particularly few of those who devote their life to going to bat for the most marginalized — get such letters. And I drafted a two-page thank-you letter to the judge who had made this remarkable decision. I began the letter to the judge on November 3, just four days after his momentous decision:

> Ever since you ordered the release of Pat — on Monday, I have been wanting to write to thank you for giving him this chance to make a fresh start, and us the chance to do what we can to help him carry it out. But I've been kept busy making sure things started off on the right track.
>
> I'm sure it must be awe-inspiring to sit on the bench and have such important decisions to make which affect lives so deeply, based on a few sheets of paper and the way in which lawyers and occasionally witnesses express themselves at one short hearing. We in the community have a different set of data and impressions to work with, but it is always hard for any of us to know for sure how wise our judgements have been. I think it must be especially hard for judges, because you seldom learn how a particular decision does turn out, so one reason I wanted to write you was to let you know that if motivation means anything, you certainly made the right decision for Pat.

Then I went on to tell him about Andy's statement on Pat's deep hunger for help, and Pat's starting gratitude to everyone concerned and eagerness to make it. I continued:

> There certainly is no guarantee that Pat will make it. You and I both know that with his history, many factors are working heavily against him, but if he doesn't, it won't be for lack of a sincere effort on his part as well as Betty Hillmer's and ours.
>
> The way in which you listened, and the concern you expressed not to miss this opportunity at rehabilitation for Pat, are things all of us appreciated so much. I have found in Betty Hillmer

far more of a resource than I had counted on. Pat is the first prisoner she has become involved in and excited about working to help, and there is something very special about one's first venture. I think you sensed the combination of wonderful warmth and wisdom in her from her brief testimony. She and I are finding it a joy to work together in plans to help Pat.

The community of support I spoke of is also materializing, including many unexpected bonuses. Just this morning I learned Pat has a nearly complete hearing loss on one side from a fight, some months ago, which has never been checked out. I was able to get the Canadian Hearing Society, which happens to be next door to my work, to arrange for a complete check-up, which they offered to do for him without charge.

Pat has expressed very beautifully to us in his own simple words his sense of a newly opening world, and of the discovery that there are a lot of people who care to be concerned about people like him. Pat's struggle yesterday to write (despite his literacy problems) a letter of thanks to his lawyer demonstrates a quality of thoughtfulness in him, which bodes well. He also mentioned this morning, on his own initiative, that he would like to make restitution to the man who lost $125 to the three of them, as soon as he is earning any money.

Then I described the moment in the Milton Jail when Pat discovered he had succeeded in getting bail this time, and let the judge who took that risk hear the joy and hope it brought to that battered soul. I concluded my letter to the judge:

When Andrew first spoke with me about the possibility of help for Pat, I remember saying, "I don't know whether I can help Pat — but I'll talk with him and see what I think." And I remember too that as I thought about Pat's long record and difficult past, I thought to myself, "I know I as one human being can't 'help Pat' by myself. But God can help Pat when Pat is ready for help, and God can use anybody." I believe God is using all of us, and that you too played a very wonderful part in that Divine reaching out. The risk we are all taking includes a very real risk of failure. But more and more I believe we are here to grow in spirit and in loving one another, and I would rather risk failure with love than the failure of withdrawing into a cocoon of safety and non-involvement. Henry Van Dyke says, "Some kinds of failure are better than success," and that's the way I feel about the disappointments we have encountered in this work.

Thanks for your part in making our venture of faith possible.

The venture of faith continued, with daily surprises in both directions. Pat was so needy that I could not leave him to his own devices for long, so I began taking him to work at my job at Friends House, and he found it an accepting atmosphere. It was like having a child attached while I was trying to do my job, however, and I struggled with it. One day as we were riding the subway to work Pat came out spontaneously with his own religious revelation.

"You know Ruth," he began, "I've never been religious, or thought much about it. I always thought religion was for good middle-class people who lived in nice houses and had nice jobs and went to churches on Sunday, opened their Bibles, read them, and went home. But when I see you and Betty and your prayer group and her church, and the way all of you care about someone like me, and what their religion means to them — then I know that that kind of religion is *about* and *for* someone like me. And I want that kind of religion."

In amidst all his problems, Pat kept coming up with amazing gems like that. One day he said, "Sometime I'm going to get all my problems under control, and when I do, then I can help people who are institutionalized like I've been." We agreed that no one else could help someone as well as someone who had been there. Then Pat paid me a wonderful compliment, saying that I seemed to understand what it was like even though I had not been there myself. During this period we managed to get out on bail an immigration detainee who had been incarcerated just over a year. We had a celebration dinner, and then Ray set off to take him to his family — observing that other people got high on drugs, I got high on bail!

I had always been good at math but I began to say that the most challenging mathematical formula I had ever had to solve was how much money to give Pat when he had to report to the police or do some other errand at the opposite end of Toronto. Give him too little and with his unerring ability to get lost, I would get a call from some impossible part of

Toronto with a lost Pat to go get, since he couldn't find his way without getting into more trouble. Give him too much, and it translated into money for alcohol, which led to another binge of alcohol and drugs!

By late November we had hit a new low in our resources and resilience, and Pat's depressions were out of control. We learned that he had had dreadful experiences in mental hospitals in the East and was terrified of them. I was no enthusiast for mental hospitals or institutions of any kind, but Pat's problems were beyond any of us. We didn't want to see him lose this precious bail opportunity, so I began trying to talk him into signing himself into a local mental hospital for a limited period.

He was very resistant, but finally, reluctantly agreed. Then I learned something brand new and shocking: you can be considered inadequate to be admitted to a mental hospital! This seemed to me an ultimate degradation, but Pat was rejected initially as insufficiently motivated. Apparently he had been in our mental hospitals too and had a bad record of signing out too soon. I reflected on Jesus' words, "Come unto me, all ye that labour and are heavy laden." He said nothing about prognosis or motivation or intelligence or any of the other things Pat was always getting rejected for!

Most social institutions, I learned by now, picked and chose the ones they wanted, the cream of their crop, and the Pats of this world fell through the crevices between, always failing to make the cream standard. Jails and prisons got the residue, and were therefore our social destination for Pat. But mental hospitals were a little more open, and after some difficulty, we persuaded them to take Pat, and him to sign in. Given their mutual suspicion of one another, we were rightly dubious how long this one would last.

About this time I heard a Christmas story of a prisoner named Peg-leg (for obvious reasons) who miraculously got a Christmas pass from jail. He actually didn't have much family himself, so he collected names and numbers of families from all his jail friends, and spent a happy Christmas sending news and love and other messages from those inside to those outside. Yet Peg-leg was one of the condemned, one of those we considered and labelled all bad.

As Christmas approached I would sometimes argue with Pat in his deep depressions. Often these days I felt myself surrounded by a vivid sense of God's presence, and I asked Pat if he couldn't feel it too. He assured me he could not, but it led to a deep discussion of how God was present in the venture we were working on together.

While Pat was in the mental hospital, I was struggling to get him into the alcohol treatment unit. It is enough of a job to get an alcoholic to admit their problem, without having to fight a system denying them treatment, when they finally tentatively and often reluctantly reach out for a helping hand. We were in that situation, with the hospital not co-operating, so I phoned Vivian, the Quaker psychiatrist who was offering powerful and wonderful free support to Pat and us in this whole experience. I concluded without any difficulty that the hospital would listen with more attention to a psychiatrist than to a mere social worker and friend of the client, so I approached Viv with the problem.

The alcohol program was due to start the next Monday, so if the hospital didn't move quickly, Pat would end up spending his 30 days in a general ward twiddling his thumbs, taking tranquillizers, and losing even more of his fragile self-image and hope. Vivian phoned me back within twenty minutes, completely steamed up. She had first phoned Pat's ward, and spoken with the nurse, who denied that he was there. "That's the story of his life," she exclaimed, "You've had him a day and a half, and you don't even know you've got him!"

Actually being ignored is just the first half of the story of lives like Pat's. Vivian next encountered the other half. She phoned the alcohol unit and was told, yes they knew Pat, and they had had him before. He had not done well on their program, and they doubted they would try him again. Vivian told them that was ALSO the story of Pat's life: being rejected again and again in various settings, often on the basis of past performance, but sometimes just because of his general background and "unimportance."

This exchange reminded me of a place I heard of, a fine home for disturbed children, which takes those who have blown most other opportunities. The first thing they do is burn the child's file from most other agencies! Of course I know, and they know, the drawbacks of such an approach. But the compensatory beauty of it is that it symbolizes the willingness to give that human being a fresh chance to break away from old destructive cycles. That was precisely what we were trying to do with Pat. I kept telling doctors and other authorities that I knew they were right logically on his prognosis. I didn't usually have to spell out the but to follow, because they could see it in the gleam in my eye. Often they came round when they caught our enthusiasm and our faith that, in his own mixed-up way, Pat was more motivated now than he had ever been.

Betty more than backed my two-woman movement for Pat. She visited Pat on the alcoholic unit (yes, they did give in and take him!) and preached our gospel to three different people there. She would open by asking them innocently, "Do you believe people can change?"

"Of course!" they would answer enthusiastically. Why else would they be in work like this? But then Betty would follow with her stumper.

"Do you believe Pat S. can change?" Confronted with the inconsistency, and catching also the fire in her eye and the love in her heart, they came on board with us. I phoned his doctor's secretary and recruited her to our Pat club. Viv said the key thing was for Pat himself to convince them he was truly motivated this time. So I got Pat on the phone in the afternoon. Until then, he had been in a deep depression, but when he learned he was to be given a chance at the alcohol program, he perked up and began talking about his determination to make it. His stubbornness, so often turned to dysfunctional decisions, was pointed in the right direction.

Of course stubborn was a word that applied well to all three of us. Pat could hardly have found two more stubborn individuals to help him than Betty and me. I had warned him that if he once asked for help from me and I agreed, he wouldn't be able to shake me off easily. Betty said she had never in her life had such a clear sense of being used by God. Many people were praying for Pat, and the coincidences and small miracles that kept happening seemed direct outcomes of all this spiritual energy directed toward one seemingly lost and hitherto neglected human being. Betty observed one day, "I feel I have made a commitment to teach this man to read, and now I have to get things in a place where I can keep this commitment!"

As Christmas approached that year, I reflected on all I was learning from Pat and my other prisoner friends. I wrote a poem about risking:

> What a risk God takes in breathing
> Into tiny infant frame
> All the blessings of creation
> Loving each new life the same.
>
> He must know each child will fail him,
> Bicker with his fellow man,
> Losing touch with his creator,
> Putting self before God's plan.
>
> But God risks the pain of loving,
> Putting trust in mortal man;
> Though he knows the risk he's taking,
> As we fail him once again.

Yet how often when we're looking
At a risk in giving aid
To a child of God in trouble,
We require prompt thanks, full paid.

Can't we learn from God the Father,
Giving love is full of pain,
But the joy is in the giving,
And we suffer not in vain.

Join our Father in the venture
Into slum and jail and pain,
Learn the risks with him of loving,
Lose with him — and *living* gain.

I reflected on all our new experiences in our Christmas letter that year, and added that

redemptive love is a challenge God calls us to today, not a worn-out Biblical once and for all idea... Sometimes people think we are sacrificing in these adventures, but we have gained so much from these prisoner friends of ours, we feel deep joy through all the tribulations, and a humble gratitude toward our friends who share so much of themselves with us, too. Giving of oneself is such a wonderful release from the bonds of our own selfishness and fears.

While in England we came across a Quaker poster by Harold Loukes that says so well what we have learned:

An act of love that fails
is just as much a part of the divine process
as an act of love that succeeds,

for love is measured by its own fullness,
not by its reception.
— Harold Loukes

In that spirit, we don't believe any love shared is ever truly lost.

If a sense of great joy hasn't come through by now, it should
have! It doesn't take Christmas to indicate to us how much we
have to be thankful for this year, and how grateful we are to
God for his love and direction. More than ever, we believe we
are here for growing in spirit — and what a glorious experience
it is when we let down our guards and let ourselves grow with
God, in love toward all his children.

Inch by inch we were moving toward Pat's first Christmas outside of
institutions. We had celebrated Halloween with him the day he got out, but
a big goal we all looked forward to was the first Christmas. Over the years
since, I have learned that Christmas is more a time of sorrow, depression,
loneliness and grief for most of the marginalized, than of family and joy and
celebration. It is ironic that Jesus came to bring comfort to the very ones
who feel their isolation and rejection most at the time the overly comfortable
celebrate His birthday.

But at this time Christmas was still a time of great joy for us, and we
wanted so much to share that joy with Pat, and celebrate his first Christmas
in the wide world with him. That hope got us through some rough patches.
For various reasons it was decided Pat would spend Christmas itself with
Betty and her family, but I remember singing "O Holy Night" as a solo at a
Christmas Eve service that year, and feeling it as I had never felt it before.
It was indeed a Holy Night, the wonder of the birth of hope in the world
echoing in my heart with the wonder of this struggle for a miracle that we
were living. Above all, the reality that we had made it, and that Pat was
going to see Christmas in a real home, not an institution.

By Christmas we were aware that Pat's alcohol problem was profound.
He tried antabuse, a drug or injection that created a powerful allergic
reaction so that any alcohol consumed would make the person very sick
indeed. The problem was that the pills could be tongued and disposed of,
and Pat's ambivalence led to good and bad patches. Still, we were muddling
along.

In January Pat decided he wanted to enter a life-skills course at the
community college where Betty taught. It would cost $40, and Betty and I
talked about how to raise that money. I don't remember which of us came
up with the idea, but we decided to use it as an opportunity to show Pat
how many people believed in and supported his struggle. We bought a
simple card, and solicited donations of $1 and signatures — it was easy!

We got 40 people between us in a few days, signing on their faith that Pat deserved a chance to build a life in our community.

That is the mystery about all this. Probably a lot of those people, if you ask the question another way, might come through with punitive or negative comments about releasing a Pat into their community. But put a couple of faith-filled folk behind him, and ask for a simple vote of confidence in a struggling human being as we described him, and no one ever said "No." So inch by inch we continued to move forward, yet Pat's ghosts kept haunting him, and his depressions and periodic binges would recur.

On one hilarious occasion I had secured him an interview with the Addiction Research Foundation, which took weeks of waiting. Pat had gone on one of his alcohol-drugs-suicide episodes just before, and he came back in a total funk, barely able to function. But I wasn't going to blow this long awaited appointment over an issue that was so close to the core of all his problems. So I brought him down to the interview, and came in with him.

Pat in a funk could hardly speak. You were lucky if on provocation you got a few nods and head-shakes. So the social worker interviewing him needed me to assist in communication. She was a capable young woman and tried her best, but what Pat couldn't seem to grasp was that she was blind, so his nods and head-shakes were utterly useless! I spent the whole hour trying to establish communication between a non-verbal depressed Pat and a willing but visually blind social worker.

Finally the time came for the trial on the charges with which Pat and Alec were co-charged. By the time they came to trial, the incident they were charged with was fifteen months old. Jury trials have long waiting times for those who request them, and this was comparatively quick. But naturally, after fifteen months memories were very faded, and any effects of swift and sure justice were much reduced, even had the course of justice been an effective one.

As I watched the trial, I got a strange picture. The charge concerned four drunken men, all of whom had been in trouble before. The driver turned state's evidence against Pat and Alec, so wasn't charged. All four agreed that the victim had been relieved of $120, which was his, in order to continue a drinking binge, and that he had not been happy about sharing it. The issue that took it to court was whether threats or violence were used. Pat and Alec were charged with robbery instead of theft: this may sound a silly distinction for such a huge expense and fuss, but in the eyes of our legal system robbery carries a seven year maximum, and theft two years.

Yet because of a dispute over the nature of a $120 offence, Pat alone spent four months of dead time before we bailed him out, at a cost of $7000 to the taxpayer. Without the combined miracle of Betty, Andy, myself, and that amazing judge, he would have spent another eleven months, costing another $20,000! Another mindblower was that the complainant told me out in the hall, during one of the many breaks where lawyers were arguing over what the jury could and could not hear, that the Crown paid a taxi fare of $69 each day, to bring him to testify. As this was the second day, his taxi fares had gone beyond the disputed sum already. As with many complainants, all he had wanted from start to finish was to get his $120 back, and that was the one thing he was least likely to get out of this messy process.

On the second day of the trial, Alec's wife phoned me, and I brought her to the trial, along with one of Pat and Alec's sisters. Some of the scenes that day were funny, with the jury sitting in its little room waiting to hear what they would be allowed to hear, while lawyers researched arguments in the law library on the same topic. Meanwhile Alec's wife and I talked with the complainant, out in the hall, and she straightened him out on facts. For example, the driver, who had turned police evidence so was not charged, was the one who had thought up the idea of taking the money in the first place! This is often the case in our legal system: the one most guilty agrees to testify, so is never charged.

The trial itself was eight days long. I got to see Pat being cross-examined on the second day, and it was painful. Pat was someone who couldn't think analytically if his life depended on it. Ask him why he kept slashing his wrists, and he stared blankly at you: it was the kind of question the Pats of this world didn't approach, preferring to take life as it unfolded. So when asked on the stand why he would expect someone he barely knew to buy him free beer, he looked bad. Hence the Crown asked a lot of questions which I, having a good impression of the four occupants of that car by now, could have volunteered a number of good answers to. But Pat would hang his head, answering nothing, and giving an impression of guilt, stupidity, or both.

On one occasion I inadvertently helped him out. The Crown asked, "Is it your usual kind of behaviour, that you ask someone you've known only four hours to buy you a case of beer that he won't be sharing in?" Pat was standing there with that vacant hangdog air. I knew so well that it was *exactly* typical of his usual behaviour, I couldn't help nodding to myself.

We were continually amazed that perfect strangers gave Pat free liquor and drugs, wherever he went. Pat apparently saw me nodding, as he suddenly came to himself and said, "Yes, that's exactly the kind of thing I do. I walk into a beer parlour, sit down at a table, and ask them to buy me a drink, and they usually do." But that was the only question he was able to respond to in that way.

One irony of the jury process is that the cat is more often than not out of the bag before the jury is sent out of the room. For instance, the Crown can bring in the person's whole criminal record if he takes the stand, but only in certain phrasings and ways. At one point the Crown said, "Isn't it true that you are likely to have used violence because you have used violence repeatedly in crimes in the past?" Actually, these "violent crimes" were barroom brawls with all parties drunk and no money involved, but the convictions didn't show the distinction between those and robbery very clearly.

The defence attorney objected to the question, and the jury was sent out. Whatever the ultimate decision of the court, the jury had heard a very damaging question, and being told to forget it by the judge only set it more firmly in their minds, without any corrective information being added in. But the constant parade in and out of the jury trains them to march better than kindergarten parades train five year olds.

On the last day of the trial, I was also attending the trial of another prisoner, who was being tried in the next courtroom for rape. I talked with complainants, witnesses, relatives, lawyers, and when I could, with my friends the accused. I even talked with the marshals whose job it is to enforce order, bring glasses of water, and carry out protocol. It was a strange experience to be talking one moment with the rape complainant, and five minutes later on the same hallway bench, with the parents of the accused. It was mentally and spiritually tiring, bridging the gaps so widened by our justice system.

One thing Pat had going for him was that he himself believed most sincerely that he had talked the complainant into giving over the money, so it was theft not robbery. But his own sense of innocence didn't come through as well as it should have on the stand, because of his background. A bigger plus was that the complainant had the same background, and was if possible an even worse witness. It was clear something had happened to the poor fellow, but quite unclear what. If I hadn't known Pat so well, and begun to learn how his world thought and spoke, I would have been convinced they were both lying most of the time.

The jury came in with the heaviest verdicts permitted by the evidence: theft against Alec, robbery against Pat. It was a heavy decision, and I felt for Pat, who had emphasized again and again that he had never before fought a charge, because he believed in pleading guilty to what he had done. It was strong evidence, he felt, that this once when he had pled innocent, it must be for good cause. But unfortunately the jury didn't buy it, and Pat faced more years inside.

A disheartening thing was that the courts paid little attention to our miracle: those many months outside of community living, so hard-won, so painstakingly gained day by day. No one in the courts felt it was remarkable to note this dramatic change in the sequence of Pat's life, and our testimony for him at sentencing weighed little compared to the long record of offences. This judge was less open to the possibility of change than the other one had been. So Pat began serving time again.

Because of his long record, inside as well as out, he ended up in a maximum security institution, on 23½ hour a day lockup. I got occasional letters from him, describing how he was returning to a vegetable-like state. "I am sleeping more and more, because there is nothing else to do. I get depressed more too, and feel like I am going back…" He was slipping into that shadow life prisons and other institutions make of human beings. The human garbage disposal system had him in its grip again.

I wrote Pat letters, with thoughts such as these:

> My prayer for you this Christmas is that you find something you are able to believe in and work for with your whole heart. You have the potential to do wonderful things, and as we have tried to tell you many times, you have a lot of strength. But it has been so wounded by the experiences of your childhood and past. Sometimes I long to go back into your childhood with you, Pat, and protect and comfort you from the many hurts that set you on the downward path you were on so long. Did you ever think about the fact that you were born just as lovely a child as all the great people you can think of, and God loves you just as much as them, right now? There is nothing but the hurts of childhood and of institutions and the world since then, stopping you from being the person God and you want you to be. If Betty and we can do anything for you, it is in seeing and loving the real you inside, and showing you yourself, with all the potential you have.

In a letter that same December inside, Alec wrote, "I'd first of all like to tell you that for the time I've known you, life for me has been more easy to understand. My hardships fewer, and this long time away from home easier to bear. I hope to show my thanks for your time and thoughtfulness by making a good life for myself, and helping others in the way you helped me. It feels so good to know there is always someone there you can talk to."

In the course of Alec's own incarceration, he had a very bad experience in a generally fairly good treatment oriented institution (the only one of its kind in Ontario). Alec ended up breaking up a solitary cell, when he had been betrayed by the guards, after voluntarily signing himself in to keep cool, and then being abandoned there over a long weekend despite numerous requests by him for relief. He was threatened with transfer to a maximum security institution like Pat's. I talked with a friendly superintendent at the jail Alec was transferred to in the meantime, and he amazed me by saying in response to my story that he would have broken up the cell too in those circumstances. He even volunteered that if I could get Alec a job offer, he would get him transferred to a Community Residential Centre — a minimum security institution almost like a halfway house.

Although I knew nothing about CRCs, and had few job resources, I looked into it, called people up, and among all our resources, we miraculously got the job offer. Alec ended up in the community, in a CRC it was true, but he phoned me ecstatically, and I will always remember his words: "I went outside and was sweeping leaves, Ruth, and neighbours were passing by and they smiled and spoke to me, just like I was a regular person!" Being given a chance to rediscover his real personhood was all Alec needed. He continued to make progress, and never looked back. When he got full parole, he established a good life in the community, and never offended again.

Pat's was a tougher situation. He regressed inside the institutions, got in repeated trouble, and expressed anger toward me for "mothering" him. It was in some ways as if he had progressed from early childhood to adolescent rebellion against constructive parenting input. I was most shocked when on one visit he said he had no drinking problem; now that he was getting treatment for his emotional problems, he would drink normally when he got out! We had some strong exchanges on that, and some breaks in correspondence, as I tried to explain to him that treatment doesn't change who we are, just how we cope with who we are. But we kept muddling on, and Pat also wrote lovely letters to Joy, our youngest, who was a fount of love for high need people.

Pat finally got out, and kept minimal contact with us. This was a pattern with many high need folks we worked with: we didn't write them off, but if they weren't making it, they didn't want to face us. Yet I heard from or of him from time to time, and he seemed to be improving some, gradually. Then in 1982, three years later, I heard from a woman he had married out west, who said Pat was in some trouble again, had attempted suicide several times, but had got religion deeply, and was a good step-dad to her two children.

That was the last letter I had about Pat, until a year or two later, a sister of Pat's phoned to tell me he had died of a drug overdose — whether intentional or accidental, no one knew. So what is transformative about Pat's story? Transformation isn't always a simple happy ending, but it is about transforming lives, and Pat's story transformed more lives than almost any I know of. I have told it again and again, and for all his objectionable ways and failures, I have never told it to the most conservative group without their being with him all the way. Pat shared his soul's struggle with us, and through him we have been able to share it with so many people who never had a window into the human drama of the Pats of this world.

Pat and Alec, but Pat most of all, transformed my life, and my ability to reach into and empathize with others. From a sheltered, well-intentioned middle-class person, I became someone who understood much more about the world all around me, the shadow world that so few of us middle-class dwellers understand. Pat transformed me. Or God did, through Pat's openness and desperate call for help.

Did we transform Pat? Only God knows, but I think we did. Through these adventures, Pat discovered he could make it in the world, that he could do things that had been impossible, and that he could be loved and accepted not just by us, but by the communities we introduced him to. Pat became literate, and his horizons expanded. The clouds that hung so heavily over him didn't go away, and eventually they caused his early death. But through those months and years, Pat got to share some of God's sunlight with the more fortunate. That's transformation enough for me.

Chapter 4

Anyone Can Make a Difference: Widening Circles of Prison Work

Pat was my first opening, and the deepest. But Mike was another Pat who also had a deep impact on our family, and whose contact with us was transformative for many. Pat was one of several that drew me in deeper, and expanded the kinds of people I was able to work with enormously. I began keeping a diary at this time, because I realized — and many people told me — that my life was a soap opera of potential stories, novels, and true adventures. It was unfolding faster than I could keep track of, so I began writing every four weeks or so a short summary of highlights of the period, and it reads like a rich smorgasbord of prisoner lives.

My own life was a welter of prisoners and ex-prisoners. In a report I wrote on my service work with prisoners from 1977 to 1978 I listed relationships with 24 different prisoners. In jail there are few gifts you have to give, and the gift of a friend outside is special. Those I was close to would pass my name — with my permission — on to other prisoners, and the circle kept widening, like circles in a pond after a pebble is thrown in. My ventures of faith with the first Mike I bailed out and with Pat and his brother led to a transformation in my life, and a whole new world opening up, for me and for many of those I visited or corresponded with.

Rally was our first prisoner friend, who had helped interpret for us when our nervous group of eight volunteers in the Quaker Jail Program first entered the Don Jail. He interpreted not from one formal language to another, but between the worlds most prisoners had known and the insulated world we middle-class volunteers came from. An American Black, Rally had been involved with the criminal justice system since he was eight, but had also been a professional football player. Glenn was a man charged with fraud whose family became among our strongest supporters and vice versa. Steve was a policeman's son, with a penchant for break and entry, who enlivened our lives in so many ways.

Bryan was struggling with drugs, and we took him in at the request of a caring Judge and another prison volunteer. He taught us some of the forms of Far Eastern meditation that he was learning to escape the prison of addictions. Gordon was a sixteen-year-old who was charged with armed robbery. His hard manner contrasted with his naivety — he did not even know what "appeal" meant — legally or socially, and he had little idea what was happening to him in the legal process.

Most of our prisoners lacked supportive homes, and many had grown up in a series of abusive foster homes and institutions. We also took in a refugee family who were in a stateless condition, having fled one country to arrive in Chile just before the coup there forced them to flee again. They were literally people without a country. The father was not charged with any crime other than being unwanted by Canada as well, yet he had spent six months in jail before an aggressive law firm managed to get a bond for him, and we bonded him and took him and his wife and two children in. Their lack of English and our lack of Spanish made for an interesting living arrangement, but Lorne, the very caring student lawyer on the case, came out once a month or so and translated for us and caught us up on communication! Lorne was another student with Clay and Marlys, and it was no surprise to me that he later became one of the best and most selfless refugee lawyers in Toronto.

I wrote an article at this time describing a fairly typical day in my life. On a quiet day at home with nothing major happening, these events came to me:

- The wife of a prisoner-friend called about transportation to Maplehurst Correctional Centre for a visit. She shared her enthusiasm about a nursery school she had found for their child.
- I wrote a letter to a prisoner friend we had almost lost touch with. He was back in jail, lonelier than ever. I tried to use our mutual mistakes to build a deeper relationship.

- I took a call from a doctor, who was asking about Addiction Research Foundation's involvement with an ex-prisoner we were working with.
- I received a call from a friend we met through a prisoner, asking information about Toronto area prisons, as another friend of hers had just been sentenced to three years.
- I spoke to a lawyer for a seventeen-year-old boy we met through our Don Jail program, about possible help for the boy.
- I wrote a long letter to American Quakers about a prisoner in the USA whose conviction might be overturned and who wanted to come to Canada. They had asked our help for him if he did come.
- I confirmed arrangements for an evening meeting of a new support group for agencies and people trying to do supportive work with prisoners and ex-prisoners.

I concluded the article with these thoughts:

As a family we involve ourselves deeply with about seven prisoners at a time, inside or outside prison, and these relationships have been lasting. They are moving for us as well as for them. Going bail for people, and visiting those in prison, and giving families rides or other help are more than isolated acts of charity. They allow our middle-class horizons to be broadened by the world they live in. We are grateful for the love and gifts they give us, transforming us into better people through that of God in these new friends.

We admit our faults to them, just as we see them with their faults exposed, and we learn to love one another, warts and all. We rejoice with those who rejoice, weep with those who weep, and laugh at our own follies along with theirs. It is one of the most glorious adventures we have found in life: the risk of loving. One of our prisoner friends muttered to me over the phone the other night, "The trouble with you people is you don't ever know when to give up on a guy."

For I am persuaded that neither death nor life
Nor angels, nor principalities
Nor things present, nor things to come,

Nor powers, nor height, nor depth,
Nor anything else in all creation
Will be able to separate us from the love of God
In Christ Jesus our Lord.

                                                    Romans 8:38-39

It is interesting to see that at this time, nearly twenty years before I took up the cause of transformative justice or thought of this book, I referred to the prisoners' transforming effect on us.

All this had a profound impact not only on us, but also on our family. Joy, our youngest, was particularly close to the ex-prisoners, and they took to her with a warmth and comfort that was often greater than my relationship with them. Many of them were starved for relationships, but terrified of adult relationships, which had mostly been abusive and rejecting. Although I was learning, I still bore all the trappings, vocabulary and degrees of a highly educated, very privileged upper-middle-class person. Joy on the other hand, was a young child, loving, innocent, and very simply open.

They latched onto her sweet openness in the same way many of them adored pets: a dog or cat does not judge a human being's value, and reject them — we do. Joy was safe in the same way, with the added benefit of being human, so able to satisfy their starved sense of never having been part of a family, and their stunted yearnings for real fatherhood. All this had a profound impact on her. Joy would sometimes accompany me to court, or to a jail visit (though she was not allowed to visit in the way I was). Joy remembers best a prisoner named Mike, who was a lot like Pat, and whom we met shortly after Pat.

Mike: Dreaming of Freedom

Unlike Pat, Mike had some education and was thoroughly literate. But like him, Mike was heavily institutionalized, very needy, and talked a better ballgame inside than he could deliver when he was released. The pattern of institutionalized people is that they have a struggle to last more than 48 hours on the street: the transition is overwhelmingly traumatic for them, and yet they are also miserable and often suicidal inside, because institutions — especially prisons — fail to satisfy so many basic human needs.

Almost exactly a year after I first met Pat, I began visiting Mike. Mike was a whiner. He had so many gripes it took most of my visits just to hear them listed. I met him first in the Milton Jail, where he complained bitterly about the absence of supports for friendless men released from jails and prisons. He had found an obscure law, unrepealed he claimed, which required that every released prisoner be given a horse and saddle to his home destination, and he said he was going to claim it! He told again and again how on his last release, at a place many miles from any supports, he was released with just 25 cents in his pocket, and of course he got in trouble immediately again. He was the only prisoner that the guards actually thanked me for visiting, because it got him off the range for awhile.

Mike was a writer of poetry. It didn't scan, but it was a cry from his heart, and showed an ability in him, despite the male working class culture of inhibition, to examine and share his feelings. One of his poems was like a short autobiography of his childhood:

> When I was a kid, many times I wanted to die.
> I would hide in places, so no one could see me cry.
> Had no one to hold me in their arms,
> Until the pain went away, by warmth of their charms.
>
> Why my old man drank so much, I never did know,
> I was too small, and he didn't let his inner self show.
> So even way back then, it was all plain to see,
> My Dad, well he never did really love me.
>
> Then at twelve, in the cold, cold dawn,
> I left home and a most stormy life was drawn.
> Until today, I have never looked back,
> Have been mostly in prison, on the wrong track...

Some of Mike's poetry dealt with the peculiar torture of prisons:

> There are guards and officials who find pleasure
> To see your mind and manhood wilt with pressure.
> But if your mind and beliefs remain strong,
> You will surely overcome all inflicted wrong.

The trouble with controlling institutions, as I was learning, was that in their efforts to take away the power to do wrong from inmates, they gave too much power to do wrong to those with absolute control of them. Far from transforming men like Mike and Pat, they turned weak guards, vulnerable to power addiction, into sadistic brutes. They also conditioned institutionalized inmates into playing a series of unhealthy games, in the course of which they lost much of their ability to make constructive choices in our world.

Mike's letters were articulate. Our relationship began in 1978, and I tried to build into planning with Mike all I had begun to learn from working with Pat. By July I had offered to help Mike if he were granted bail. He wrote me gratefully, "With the much needed assistance you're prepared to give me, I honestly believe I will make it. Let's face it, the rest of my life is at stake. If I don't make it this time, I never will. It's unfortunate I didn't have the opportunity you're offering now, years ago, but its not too late."

Once Mike knew he had a good listening-ear and a real friend, he had room for concerns for others. He was interested in my life and doings, and he brought me regularly the troubles of others. Through Mike more than anyone else, I added to my list of prisoners. He felt he was choosing ones who would really use the friendship and resources I brought most appropriately, and obviously enjoyed the satisfaction of feeling he was helping others through this linking service.

I gave Mike a list of halfway houses, with ratings by myself and others. I added, "Any of them could work out at various points. The main thing is, you need somebody around to help fill in the cracks and gaps in what halfway houses can do. I am prepared to go to court and be that person, if you are absolutely serious about making the effort, but it is a very great effort." I asked a friendly chaplain to discuss a possible contract with Mike, saying what each of us would contribute to helping him make this transition. Having learned a few pitfalls by now, I wrote Mike, "You have to be more committed to making it than you are to relieving depressions through drink or other alternatives when you find things tough outside…"

Mike wrote me equally frankly. "To be perfectly honest, I have never lived in a family setting where there was love, honesty and communication. This has affected and bothered me a great deal through my life, but I don't talk too much about it. You know I have been 'in' a long time and I want out. This time I want it to work, Ruth, and I am scared to many degrees. It's the adjusting that has me upset.

"You mentioned the possibilities of my living with you and your family until I am somewhat adjusted, and then perhaps going to a halfway house.

Going directly to the latter has me a bit shaky. I do wish it didn't, but it does. Ruth, only if your whole family are agreeable, and that you don't feel I will be too much of a strain for all of you, I would really appreciate it if I could stay with you temporarily."

Shades of Pat — unfamiliar with a real home, but terrified of a halfway house or other solution! Mike went on to affirm wholeheartedly that he would honour whatever stipulations we felt necessary.

We did sign a contract with Mike on August 4, 1978, which included his residing with us, and refraining from smoking, drinking or drugs while there. Open honest communication by all parties was agreed to, and continued contact at least weekly whenever Mike moved out. He agreed to pay something toward room and board as soon as he had an income, and to do a share of household chores. Nothing very revolutionary, but we had discovered that institutions destroyed people's sense of normal interaction so thoroughly that it was important to spell it all out.

To make matters worse, in that same month of August 1978 a new crisis arose. Someone in authority got the bright idea of transferring Mike to a very heavy unit with a lot of the most dangerous inmates and no protection. Mike was in protective custody for warning guards of an escape plot that included the planned killing of a guard. Mike naturally refused to leave protective custody, and he was then put on limited diet and denied the few privileges he had. Moreover he was threatened that he would be dragged to the new unit in a few days if he didn't co-operate. His desperate messages to me drew my intervention, and I was able to reach the Ombudsman and two chaplains, who managed to stop this insane process.

Another prisoner, Bob, whom I had met in Milton and became quite close to, arrived at the Toronto West Detention Centre. In the course of visiting him I learned for the first time that he was charged with rape, not once, but several times! Had I known that initially, I doubt if I would have become quite so friendly with him. My own views, formed by the outside world as well as the views of other prisoners, were that squealers and rapists were in a bit of another category — yet now I found myself visiting with and close to one squealer and one accused rapist! It didn't make me feel better about those offences, but it moved me a step nearer to understanding that every life has its own story to tell, and that God somehow truly manages to love us all, without loving all the conduct of any one of us.

Meanwhile Mike's letters began to speak yearningly of being part of the family, of being tempted to call me Mom. Mike was already attached deeply to Joy and he wrote, "Please say Hi to my little angel, and tell her I send my love with a hug and kiss. I would like to send her a little letter, and I was going to, but how do you write to a child? I'd enjoy taking her someplace when I get out, perhaps to the zoo. Oh, if Joy draws any pictures or writes me, you must remember that delaying the mail is a federal offence!" Mike, who lived in constant tension, went on to say he felt too content to write more. The prospect of a home was filling empty crannies of his soul he hadn't known could be filled.

We continued to dialogue about his life in our family, and he wrote, "No matter how calloused one's inner self may be, everyone deep down needs and wants love. I really don't know all the values of love, though I never wanted nor want to go back in time, to be nurtured with that basic warmth and caring you talk about. What I didn't get as a child, I needed then — not now.... After so many years pass, something dies inside of you. Unfortunately, I love in degrees. I love a woman one way, people such as you in another; but I stop it before it gets too close, or when it becomes a threat to me. Children and animals I love the most, and I put up no walls."

Mike went on in the same letter to dream about what he would do first when he got out. It was something I encouraged him to do, because I had learned that the shock could lead to disaster if you hadn't explored and tasted concrete steps beforehand. Mike wrote, "My first plans when I get out should be to hit the welfare, then to the pawn shop to see if I can get a few dollars together, so I can get my hair cut and styled. If there's a park near your place, maybe one of the kids will take a walk with me for the first couple of days, or maybe if the kids want, we could go to the zoo. I want to do these things the first two or three days I'm out, along with going to the rehab centre you were telling me about. And I want to make a few phone calls to see if I can set up interviews for a job..."

Mike spent most of his time in segregation, because of his role in saving the lives of a couple of guards from two violent inmates who had planned to kill them in an escape attempt. This story was confirmed later by institutional officials. So ironically, although Mike had done the officials a favour, he had to be put in protective custody in isolation, for his own safety. This added to his sense of isolation and loneliness.

One day Father Massey Lombardi, a caring Catholic chaplain we both knew, came to visit Mike in segregation. Mike took one look at him and said, "You need a rest more than you need to listen to me." Mike urged him to lie down and take a siesta, and two hours later Massey arose from a rare rest, uninterrupted by the demands of the needy world! Mike knew how to care for caregivers, sharing the gift of his isolation with Father Lombardi, and amusing all who heard it by transforming the loneliness of Mike's isolation into a haven of rest for an exhausted priest.

In August, Mike had another 90-day bail review, and despite my testimony, the judge confirmed the detention order. Mike decided to switch to a woman lawyer, Nola Garten, who took the case with all the energy some lawyers reserved for top paying clients. Like most prisoners, Mike was on legal aid.

Mike's Supreme Court Bail Review was set for September 18. He asked not to be present for it, preferring to reduce the stress in that way. On the day of the hearing, Mike wrote one of his strongest poems, which he dedicated to our family, and called SOLITUDE:

> From where I sit, I see the wall,
> So strong and cold, but why so tall?
> Every day I see the dying souls of men
> Tomorrow will bring the same again.
>
> No one laughs, and no one smiles,
> I wish someone would sit and talk awhile.
>
> So if I were you and you were me,
> Then you could feel, and you could see,
> To be with you is all I care,
> But I am here, and you are there.

Meanwhile Joy sent Mike a picture of herself, which he loved, and he dedicated another poem he wrote especially to her. Mike wrote me humbly:

> It's hard for me to understand how you've been so patient with me lately. Have you considered at all wishing you hadn't made such commitments to me? ... In all fairness, I'm not sure we should go through the bail hearing as planned — the commitments. The closer and better my chances of getting out, the more uptight I get. I guess I'm trying to tell you I'm

very much afraid — afraid of you, your family, living in your family environment, the commitments, and getting close. I've never committed myself to anyone or anything, and as far as getting close to people, I'm always controlled and never let it go too far — just a hi-bye sort of thing...

You know how I feel? Like someone not knowing how to swim, being thrown in water over my head with a couple hundred people standing around, but they can't help me. It's swim or drown. Ruth, exposing my emotionality makes me feel very vulnerable and insecure. Once exposed I haven't any defences, and all my life I lived in a cold environment with high walls within myself to survive.

Mike expressed so well the terror he and Pat and others had of freedom. They were truly damned if they did and damned if they didn't. Institutional life was so suffocating they were suicidal and utterly depressed inside, but the risk of living and loving outside was so unfamiliar they were petrified of it, and sure they would fail and let us down. Both of them expressed clearly what others tried to tell us less articulately: that being exposed to family love for the first time was a strange mix of heaven and hell. The warmth of the love, the rays of its sunlight were the most beautiful thing they had ever seen. But their own glasshouses of protection from all the pain of their lives prevented their FEELING that love penetrate into themselves. So they could see all that beauty, but they could not experience it reaching into and warming their own hearts.

Nevertheless, we went ahead preparing for a November Bail Appeal, and Nola prepared an excellent affidavit which Mike signed in November. It detailed his recent history — he had been held in custody on comparatively minor charges of breaking and entering since February 2nd, which was longer than many sentences for his charges. Delays had not been his choice. He had been promised a trial date for early October, but now it was not due till January 1979, and even that date was not firm. His co-accused, who was out of custody, had demanded a trial by jury, which was what caused the length of delay in trial, and kept Mike inside so many months. Father Lombardi's willingness to help and our contract were all in the strong affidavit.

With Nola's skilled support, and the logical argument that Mike had served more time by now than he likely would have been sentenced, Mike was released on bail to us, to live in our home. Unfortunately, after a heart-warming first day and a half, his anxiety to get things done overcame him.

Father Lombardi had promised he would help Mike get proper glasses again — Mike could not read properly without glasses and he had not had prescription ones inside. Mike was determined to go out the second evening to see Father Lombardi downtown, to get $50 to get the glasses. I pled with him, I offered to lend him the money myself — I knew that for him to leave our house and venture out into the wilds of Toronto this early was probably fatal to his hopes. But he insisted he could do it, and he insisted he *must* do it. He left, and we got a call 24 hours later that he was in custody for some minor offence.

The next event was even more dramatic. Three police cars came screaming up to our driveway, together. In all our eventful life, this had never happened before, and we surmised it had something to do with Mike. We watched the corps of police come down our driveway with interest. Their main question to us was where Mike was, but all we knew was that he was in custody. They explained that he had been in custody but with his gift of the gab, he had somehow persuaded someone with a minor charge and no record to exchange names and papers, and Mike had walked out, freed on recognizance in the name of this malleable young man! Escaping custody in this way was rather spectacular, and embarrassing to the courts; hence the exciting numbers of police cars and police who visited us.

We didn't hear from Mike for several days, and since we had signed a large bail for him, I felt obliged to go to court and pull the bail. It was an obligation of sureties to do so if they had lost control of the situation, as I clearly had. I remained haunted by the agonizing session I had had pleading with Mike not to go out, and finally seeing him leave to his destruction.

Mike was rearrested in a few days, and we heard he was back in jail. I waited to hear from him, and finally wrote him. We sent him a homemade Christmas card from one of Joy's classmates, which said, "To a nice person," and I told Mike that if he could just understand he was a nice person, most of his problems would be solved. I wrote him my evaluation of what had happened in his brief time out:

> In some ways it isn't much easier for me to write you than for you to write me. I had a hunch when you escaped custody that you were running away from facing us as much as anything else. I think it is hard for you, or for most people, to realize that some kinds of love and caring don't depend on good

behaviour and putting your best foot forward, but go on loving the Christ spirit in you, no matter what. I don't say I wasn't very disappointed, more for what you did to yourself and others than to us. There were some times I was angry, and some things I was angry about, but it doesn't change the fact that we care about you and want to help you build on what we've all learned for a still better try next time you get out.

The things I find harder to understand than to forgive are why you didn't call us at all after that last call. The only time I really got mad at you was when I had to spend a whole afternoon doing what I utterly loathed doing, fighting the bureaucracy and getting shot down by them all for my bad judgement, because I had to pull the huge Peel bail, with you loose on an escape custody. A simple call from you would have been so helpful, Mike; it would have meant a lot just to know you were alive, and what you were thinking about. But as I said, the most important thing is what we can learn together from this.

Some of the things learned are that you have a lot of strengths — you related well to every member of our family, and you had everyone who met you rooting for you to make it. You planned things well up to a point, till you started pressing yourself and the world to get it all done too fast. You showed a capacity to give as well as receive in relationships, and that is so important.

I wanted to share with you a thought about daring to love. You have shown you can do it now, Mike, and the most important thing now is to bear the pain of going on loving through difficulties and disappointments, whether the disappointment is in yourself or in others. Don't lose the courage to keep on loving and being assured of our love. Love is always worth whatever pain goes with it, because love is of God, and in fact whenever we love we are part of God, directly sharing His spirit.

One of the problems that stopped us this time is that there is a tremendous inner tension in you, Mike. Most of us have some inner tension, but yours is bigger than most. And because it would be nice to get rid of it, one way to deal with it is to think: "If only I could get out of segregation, it would go away and I'd feel ok"; or, "If only that judge or guard treated me more like they should, I would feel ok"; or "If only I could get to the doctor, I'd feel ok"; or "If only I could get welfare started I'd be ok." The last one was, "If only I could get glasses and some decent clothes, I'd feel ok." All those things needed doing, but the feeling of not being ok is inside you, and rushing and pushing harder to tend to those things only makes you destroy the things you have. Somehow you have to accept the fact that YOU ARE OKAY, inside you, and then you"ll be able to bear all those other frustrations for short periods.

I went on to recommend the book *I'm OK, You're OK*. I complimented him again on the things he had done well, and closed with these words: "More than ever, I know you can make your way out of this, but it is up to you to think deeply about what stopped you this time so you can avoid that particular hazard next time. Nothing is ever lost, nothing is every impossible, as long as we keep love in our hearts and keep trying. God bless you, and we'll be thinking of you on Christmas."

Mike and I continued to exchange letters, trying to make sense out of the sad outcome of our dreams in his short release period. Mike wrote us that he had felt happiness even while spending Christmas Day in that bleak jail. I wrote him, "The one thing I am surest of is that God IS pure love. It is because you felt that love in our family and in our relations with you that you felt happiness on Christmas Day, even in the jail — because you had partaken of God's love in giving as well as receiving it. So God is not far away from you. God is very much with you, right there, right now... One of the saints said, 'Remember that God was seeking you long before you began to seek Him.'"

Mike wrote us back, explaining why he had not contacted us after his escape from custody:

First off, though you felt I was putting your home in jeopardy, I didn't feel that way. At the time all I could think of was staying one step ahead of the police. I only had about twenty-some days to my Brampton trial date, when I escaped, and I knew I'd have to surrender myself that day. There was no way I was going to run out on you Ruth... If I would have contacted you or Nola before January 3 you would have asked me to give myself up and I knew I would have had to. The other reason and most important one was I was too ashamed to contact you. I could have been in Buffalo two hours after I took off, if I were going to skip my bail. The above certainly doesn't justify my not calling you, and no matter how heavy my heart is now for not doing so, I can't express more, as I don't know what else I can say as to how I feel.

Our older daughter and I were reading Tolstoy short stories together, and Corinne and I both loved "Father Sergius." The ending had lines to this effect, "I realized then that she was what I was meant to be, but had not achieved. Whereas I had done things believing them to be for God, I really did them for man, while she did them for God, believing she did them for man..." Through all these events, our children as well as Ray and I were being transformed. In September I found myself visiting and bailing out a transsexual. I had barely known that such people existed a couple of years before, and my feelings on homosexuality were very mixed. But when I met this tormented child of God, my horizons expanded, and I chuckled at what would happen if she/he visited our Friends Meeting as promised.

I was still haunted by that poignant moment when I had pleaded with Mike not to go out, and he had insisted. We had prepared everything so carefully, even providing Viv as a volunteer psychiatrist and counsellor, and our home as a safe place to be. We understood that he had a pattern of re-offending within 48 hours, and we were determined to see him through that invisible barrier. We had done everything we could think of. What did it take to bring transformation into these troubled lives? I was about to find an answer: a resource that came too late to help our Pat and Mike, but which was born out of their suffering, all our failures, and our mutual love. That resources has offered transformation to many Pats and Mikes, and as with the originals, some have been able to grasp the lifeline, and for others it has slipped through their fingers. But all have found a place that is there for them, which accepts and welcomes them for who they are.

Father Lombardi had been the object of Mike's trip. That failed trip brought Father Lombardi and me closer together. Massey Lombardi and I had already become friends through the prison work, and shared a sense of caring for the most forgotten, the Pats and Mikes. We talked about the failure of our whole plan for Mike, and the fact that even if there were enough homes as committed as ours for the Pats and Mikes of this world, the transition from institutional life to the warm sun of a caring home was too abrupt for them.

So although we still felt caring homes like ours were a vital part of the solution, we realized some other environments were needed. Massey and I set out to found a halfway house that would be small, caring, non-institutional, and designed for those who had spent their lives between prisons and mental hospitals, who could not show motivation in the usual ways, but who were as ready as they would ever be. I wanted to call it the "Can't Fail Halfway House," reasoning that these men would fail if given the chance! But we ended up calling it "My Brothers' Place," and it remains one of the most wonderful outcomes of that period in our lives. Mike and Pat were the inspiration for the many years I dedicated to creating and maintaining that unique caring resource, an eight bed home for men who had no community support and few chances in life. Above all, Mike's ornery determination to make that foolish trip for glasses to Father Lombardi's home brought disaster to Mike, but was the critical seed that grew into a home which has helped scores of Pats and Mikes.

At the time we began My Brothers Place, we had to knock on 200 doors of nearest neighbours and tell them we were bringing to their neighbourhood the very people most group home foes imagine every group home will bring: chronic, active adult offenders! It was one of the most fearsome tasks life has offered me, and the experience inspired Joy in 1987 to write a song, to a familiar folk tune:

1. She's worked in many places,
   And lived in many towns,
   She's studied here and studied there
   And passed most social bounds!

   All waifs and strays, they love her;
   They follow her like hounds,
   That's why on this cold morning,
   Upon your door she pounds!

CHORUS:
   Oh neighbour please don't protest,
   I'm setting up next door
   a halfway house for rounders,
   hardened criminals and more!

2. They're no real threat or danger;
   We've had them live with us.
   They're not much worse than lots of folks
   You see get on the bus.

   Just 'cause they're poor and m'norities,
   It's them the p'lice mistrust —
   And then you think they're Sons of Sam,
   And make a great big fuss!

CHORUS

(TUNE: Grandpa's Whiskers)

In early January 1979, Mike came up for trial on the original charges on which he had been waiting for trial all this time. I was still very frustrated by our inability collectively to break through the chains of Mike's institutionalization, and felt that if I testified, any Crown would ask me about what happened, and my testimony would do Mike more harm than good. But Nola called me and said that she wanted me to be there just for moral support for Mike, because it would mean a lot to him to have me present. Always delighted when a lawyer thought of their client's feelings, I agreed immediately, and she agreed she wouldn't ask me to testify. But instead she asked me for an affidavit about my willingness to give Mike further support, which I was happy to provide.

So I went to court in January, expecting to hear Mike get penitentiary time (more than two years) for his charges, not because they were heavy charges, but because with his record and his recent bail failure, he was a sitting duck for the legal system to knock down. That was when the second answer to my wonder about transformation came.

Nola was asking for a sentence of eighteen months, the Crown for at least three to seven years. I admired Nola in every way, but I didn't think she had much to work with here. I was wrong. She had pulled out all the stops: a good lawyer visits and communicates with their client, knows the law and processes, and does all their homework thoroughly. Nola was more than a good lawyer; she was a brilliant one. She had obtained letter after letter documenting the other side of Mike: she even got a letter from the Assistant Warden of the jail, expressing thanks to Mike for what he had done in saving the lives of their guards, and support for him on this occasion!

Equally impressively, she had committed it all to memory, and presented Mike's history and background and the facts of the case without needing to look at her papers — which was both professionally brilliant and much more effective. It also testified to the fact that she had cared enough about this chronic "loser" to do a lot of work. The volume of work was clearer still as she began to present the court with letter after letter, documenting a side to Mike's life which courts seldom hear about in lives like his. The Judge seemed particularly impressed by Vivian's letter, from a professional psychiatrist who had worked with Mike, saying that she felt he would not benefit from further institutionalization, but needed to build on the community roots he was establishing through our circle.

When Nola and the Crown had finished, the Judge began. He summed up very well the gist of all the Crown had presented, and then went on to Nola's case. He said that despite the reasonableness of the Crown's recommendation, and Nola's own recommendation of eighteen months, he wanted to look at this whole situation with fresh eyes:

> I don't want to see the law get in the way of doing what is needed — of doing what is right and best. We often exaggerate the difference between the interest of the public and the interest of the accused. They are not that far apart. The public are individuals LIKE the accused. He is part of society...
>
> I remember one person I took in my home when I was a defence attorney. He got high on drugs and pulled a gun on my niece — I'm thankful it was my niece and not my daughter, who is high-strung. But my niece is cool, and invited him to have tea with her while they discussed what was to be done. He was sitting there drinking tea with her and still holding the gun when male relatives came home and disarmed him. He had to serve a few more years, but eventually he was rehabilitated. I don't know how far we have to go in trusting these people to rehabilitate them, but I'd suggest that's about as far as I'm willing to go...

He went on to state some more conventional feelings about alcoholism being no excuse for bad behaviour. "We can't build fences around all our cliffs because someone might jump off them. A person has to be responsible for his behaviour." He also talked about breaking and entering being a serious offence with which he had no sympathy. He discounted a number of points that Nola had made, and talked at length about the guilty plea by Mike. "A person shouldn't be credited for a guilty plea because he saved the community the cost of a trial, because everyone is entitled to the full protection of the law. But a guilty plea WHEN YOU ARE GUILTY indicates a right state of mind." Having seen how often defence lawyers join with police to get their clients to plead guilty, in order to strike a deal and save everyone trouble, even when the client maintains his innocence, I have come to appreciate Judge Lovekin's sensitivity more with every passing year.

He continued by quoting twice Vivian's statement that continued incarceration would not help rehabilitate Michael. "That is a concrete medical opinion. That is evidence." He was also impressed by Mike's having saved a guard's life. "That is not talk about intentions — that is a concrete act, and I am impressed by it." He referred to each of the professionals Nola had brought letters of support from, and then concluded:

> The public interest must be protected. But *what is the public interest*? It is that he be saved for himself and for society as a whole. He is part of society. I don't even have to believe he has a 50/50 chance. I would take the risk if he has a one in ten chance. You have to be a realist and go out and look for the one sheep that has strayed.
>
> I am willing *on the particular facts of this case* to take a gamble, but I can only justify that gamble on conditions that will enable society to be protected. "Vengeance is mine," said the Lord. Vengeance is not my job, I am not God. But I do have to protect society. I think this man is at a critical turning point in his life. I cannot bring myself to deny him that last chance.

He went on to ask the Crown Attorney to propose what to do in the circumstances. The Crown had got the message and said he assumed he meant probation terms? The Judge said he was open to any wisdom from anyone. So they adjourned, and worked co-operatively on an outcome that would respond to those eloquent words, some of the wisest thoughts I have ever heard in a courtroom. At the end of the hearing first the Judge and then the Crown commended Nola as a credit to her profession, a well deserved but rare kind of accolade.

As with the miraculous hearing for Pat, the Light shone in that courtroom. I was amazed, and I was dazzled, and I have never forgotten the miracle of those moments. Telling two such courtroom stories in a short space may give the impression that courtrooms are places of light, wisdom, and mystical experience. In fact those are the only two such experiences I have had in courtrooms in a life filled with courts. But each took a dedicated defence lawyer, a visionary judge, a desperately yearning offender, and community people who cared. Out of those, God wove a miracle.

Mike's miracle didn't have the direct result that Pat's had had. Mike was still responsible for the minor charges he had acquired during his brief period on bail in December, including his escape from court. So he went back to serve time, but without any new time on the charge which had originally held him so long. Mike served time at a prison some distance from Toronto, and we were reduced to letters only. He thanked me for my habit of seeing the good in him, and went on grumbling about the daily frustrations of life inside.

I wrote Judge Allan Lovekin a letter of thanks for the vision he had shown, which said in part:

> I was especially moved by the personal experience you described of having taken a prisoner in and having had such a frightening experience for your niece. What impressed me most in the whole tenor of your comments was that you recognized one has to go on from risk to risk, in being creative in this world.
>
> I often think that the real message of the crucifixion for me is that God didn't quit loving the world after that betrayal of His love, and I believe He is constantly calling us to that kind of redemptive loving and living in our world. As you correctly pointed out, the only real hope for society's safety from people like Mike is in that kind of effort with him. It is often overlooked that the risks of giving up are incalculable for society, as well as for the offender...

Mike continued to write a mixture of needy personal concerns and of quite mature words about the challenges we all share. When I wrote him that I had been laid up in bed for a month with a bad back, he was deeply concerned, and responded: "You expressed your experience with helplessness and uselessness, and how it eats away at your soul. I suppose that's why I'm so unsure of myself, and have fears that rip my gut apart, knowing a lot of damage is done, and I might not make it... People don't seem to realize the severe damage loneliness does over a long period of time. How the H —— do you cope with loneliness locked up in a cell 24 hours a day? If I were physically beaten I could handle it. That can be treated — but how do you treat loneliness? How do you cope with it? Then you've got the guy next door (like now) who flips out and smashes up and slashes up. How do you cope with insanity without going insane yourself?

"Ruth, I can't thank you enough for all the help and support you give me, along with the encouragement..." A letter like that went a long way to make up for all the frustrations and barriers. Yet after all we had shared, Mike gradually slipped away, dropped contact, and I don't know to this day how far our transformative sharing impacted on his directions. So many ex-prisoners fade into the unknown, but the light we have shared in some way illumines our lives and shines a few rays in the dark corners of this world.

Widening Circles of Prison Work

Not being able very often to see dramatic success in the community with the prisoners most lost was hard. But transformation showed in some of the poems and letters that these prisoners sent me:

> I've only begun in my new way, and have a long way to go to get the continued peace I desire, but now I know where to look. And I learn more each day that my search is rewarded not by itself, but by keeping my heart and will open to faith. It's hard for me to give up myself all the time, and there are parts of my old self I'd like to keep even though I know they're wrong. But time is on my side, and so is God...

Another prisoner shared his experience of prison with me in poetry:

> Tears come and tears go
> And dry on pale greyed face,
> That grows each month, years older,
> In this, the hating place.

But the same prisoner also expressed the hope beyond prison:

These walls and bars around me
Have no way to compare
With my own self-made prison
I built about my soul.

The bars were of uncaring,
The walls of hurt and greed,
My jailer my indifference,
To other people's need.

No more am I in bondage,
And my soul has been relieved,
For in giving up my soul to God,
My freedom I've received.

Three more short stories conclude this chapter on prisoner experiences as mutually transforming. Marco was a man who had been in and out of jails and prisons for at least ten years. Then he met Donna Carroll, a life-skills volunteer and friend of Betty (of Pat fame). She found out from him that addictive gambling was his problem. He had actually studied for the priesthood, but when his gambling addiction took over, just like any other gambler he stole in all kinds of ways to support his habit. So Donna went out in the community and found Gamblers Anonymous, and got a representative to come in and talk with Marco. Both men were excited about working together. Marco said in ten years of prisons and courts this was the first time anyone had bothered to find out what was behind all this bad behaviour!

Robin Kobryn, one of our Quaker volunteers picked up the ball. He wrote the court a wonderful letter explaining who we were, how we knew Marco, and what we had learned. He urged the court to give Marco the chance to work with Gamblers Anonymous. The lawyer handling the case said Robin's letter transformed the whole hearing. The Judge said he had been going to give Marco three years with a recommendation for no parole, because of the repetitive nature of his record. But Robin's letter cast real light and hope on the situation. The sentence was for fifteen months with a recommendation Marco be sent to a nearby institution where he could work with the Gamblers Anonymous volunteer, and a further recommendation for parole, provided the connection to GA continued. Robin was twenty at the time, and showed that age is no impediment to playing a key role in transforming justice.

Secondly, I had an experience in the fall of 1977 that was like a living parable. I had begun to visit a prisoner in Toronto West Detention Centre who was an electrician with a drinking problem. He was supposed to stay with us for a few days when he got out, but was having difficulties getting to us. He phoned desperately in the afternoon, down to his last ten cents, wanting directions to our place. Then he phoned from near an intersection three miles from us, so I told him to go to the corner and stay put there, in front of the big Zeller's department store, and I would pick him up there.

I drove there immediately and found to my horror that the Zeller's had closed about four months before, and a Canadian Tire had taken its place. There were three big plazas on that corner, and looking for Jim was like looking for the proverbial needle in a haystack. I drove around all of them, in the rain and cold and growing dark, worried where he was and how we could possibly find each other. Finally I said a little prayer that God would guide us to each other, or look after him in some other way. I felt guided to drive back to the Canadian Tire store, have one last look, and then proceed home. I had already left a phone message at home with my older children with directions for Jim in case he phoned again.

When I got to the Canadian Tire store, and Jim still wasn't there, I noticed a car making stalled engine sounds. The same car had been there, making these sounds when I first arrived. It occurred to me that if this trip were to make any sense, and God had any purpose in it, I should help someone I could reach. I got out of my car, went over to the two men, and asked if I could phone someone for them, or help in any way. They asked me to check for them at a nearby gas station. As I was walking back to my car, a car pulled up, and Jim got out. He and his friend had been looking around for me too. The truth that hit me overwhelmingly was this: we would both have left without seeing the other if I had not stopped to help the occupants of the stalled car!

It brought home to me again in a new, powerful way the truth expressed in a Tolstoy story which concludes, "The most important person in the world is the one you are with now, the most important time is now, and the most important thing is to do whatever you can to help them now." The other transforming aspect to this experience was that the small miracle I had experienced made me fresh and strong for the challenges that faced us with Jim.

Finally, here is a story of transformation among the most despised of the despised. In most jails there is a section reserved for the mentally ill prisoners, the lowest of the low, the "nut-bars" as they were jeeringly called at the time of this story. Why we house mentally ill people in jails is a point which has eluded me all my life, but my efforts on that one have so far not borne fruit. So at least at this time the Quakers were given the opportunity to run a volunteer program in the section of the Don Jail where these lonely desperate souls were deposited, with even less privileges and volunteer resources than other prisoners.

This was the second week of the new program, and we decided to do creative listening, in which various questions are asked, and a small object is passed around while each person answers the question or passes the object on without comment. No negative comments are to be made — it is an opportunity to be listened to with full attention, respect and love.

Early in the session, our friends shared openly their grief and humiliation at being labelled "nut-bars" and "crazies" — branded even among the branded. Their honesty and openness made one wonder at times about our definition of sanity. If this kind of truthfulness and sensitivity is crazy, what are we? We were deeply moved when they spoke of how much our sessions meant to them, and then offered to share half of their time with us with others on the unit, who had no visitors at all. The reality of the parable of the widow's mite came home to me.

But the gift that moved me even more came in response to a question my partner Jake asked: "Sometimes we think only of the wrongs we have done, and the things we have failed to do. Let's share something we've done that has helped somebody." One by one, people who in the eyes of the world had had few opportunities to give, shared their personal offerings of love. For each, a spark of pride and self-worth kindled a little as he shared.

Last in the circle was Paul, who was most clearly handicapped. The group had already been very supportive of him. When his turn came, he almost blushed, and said, "Aw, I've never been able to help anybody." The whole group joined in gently encouraging him. After a heart-warming series of positive thoughts and nurturing ideas, he finally added, "Well, sometimes I do try to help drunks."

There were exclamations of approval all round. Then someone asked, "And how do you help drunks, Paul?"

"Well," he said with embarrassment, "I give 'em a QUARRR-ter — when I have one." An imaginative soul said, "That's nice, because they can buy food with it."

But this thought was too much for the sense of humour of even this generous group. Laughter flowed, shared by Paul, for no one was crazy enough to imagine that a practising alcoholic would spend cold cash on food. But a further burst of imagination struck one member. Realizing Paul needed help to find meaning in his contribution, this brother in pain spoke up: "That *is* helping them though, because with your money they can buy real booze instead of drinking Aqua Velva, which rots their guts."

There were murmurs of approval, along with some amusement still, and the conversation moved on. But Paul had been nurtured by acceptance. His love offering had been received for the spirit behind it, not for its practicality. Which of our love offerings doesn't need that spirit? Love comes in many shapes and depths: I caught a profound glimpse of it in the jail that night. That kind of love is the basis of transformation.

You Can Do It Too

One common reaction to stories of my adventures with Pat and Mike is to assume I am different from ordinary people. One of the ways we dispose of people who go far in the risks of loving is to saint them, and thus miss the ways in which we too can gain the fun of their lives and growing. You don't have to take in a Pat or Mike to learn from their lives, and expand your horizons in whatever ways your life permits, even if it is only in being more understanding and respectful of the Pats and Mikes of this world.

Every life has its own challenges, and no one can deal with all of them at once. While I was working with Pat and Mike, I missed a lot of chances to involve myself in the lives of indigenous friends along with Joleigh, Nancy, Gini and other Quakers working on those issues. When my mother developed Alzheimer's and we took care of her for years, we found we could no longer care for needy prisoners, as long as she was with us. Every life has its limits, and its priorities. These stories are not a guilt trip because you don't do precisely what Ray and I did, but an invitation to expand your understanding and empathy so that your community includes, in whatever ways you can show it, Pat, Mike, Paul, and all marginalized people.

I dislike being sainted almost as much as I disliked being pilloried by people threatened by our reaching beyond the usual social boundaries. For one thing, I am not a saint and when people expect me to be so, I inevitably fall off the pedestal they have put me on, and then they are angry with me for disappointing them. For another, in sainting me, they fail to accept me for the full human being I am, a person with many flaws and many failings, but one who happens to have accepted some transforming challenges. Those transforming challenges have made me a more exciting and fulfilled person in many ways, but I didn't start out different. I made some simple choices open to every one of us. The choices we make transform us or stunt us.

People sometimes say, "I could never do the things you do, Ruth." My response is, "Yes, you could. But your life may have different challenges. I did not start out taking a thief, a con artist and a murderer into my house at once. I started out by saying Yes one day to an invitation to visit the Don Jail. Two weeks later, I said Yes to the call in my heart to bail a wrongfully charged person out. Then I got involved in advocating for him in the courts. And so, on and on it went. One step leads to another, and God doesn't usually throw us in water over our heads; God leads us step by step, as we are willing."

That is the process of transformation. But on a simpler scale, the stories of Paul and the others reminds us of the fact that most people are in prison for non-violent offences, and that those who are mentally challenged and emotionally challenged and deprived of most life opportunities are far more likely to wind up there. Every life has its own story, and Pat's saga shows it so well. Pat was in many ways a repulsive person on the surface, and a person who blew every one of the few opportunities Betty and I struggled to get him. Yet beneath that he was so clearly a desperately needy person, aching to give and receive love, deeply grateful for those who could see through his facade. Pat was like the Beast in Beauty and the Beast, and all the Pats of this world need is for a Beauty to love them, to enable both of them to be transformed.

There is a beautiful story in Kazantakis' life of St. Francis, of the great time when God called St. Francis to kiss the leper. In this version of the tale, after St. Francis not only kisses the leper but also carries him for miles, the leper suddenly becomes Jesus Christ. Francis' struggling disciple Brother Leo thinks this means Jesus made a special trip for their enlightenment on this occasion. But Francis, transfigured, says, "No, that's not it at all. Don't you see, Brother Leo, it means — it means that every time we kiss one of our lepers, they become Jesus Christ." And every time, in any measure any of us resolves in any way to embrace one of our lepers, both they and we touch the transforming power that can make us all Christs.

I had an uncle who used to say that we missed the point of Jesus' life by emphasizing his divinity instead of recognizing his humanity. If Jesus was divine entirely, then his life need not challenge us: it is beyond us. If Francis is a saint, he is out of our league. If Ruth Morris is saintly, she is just an oddity who may irritate me or give me an emotional high of admiration, but her life is irrelevant to mine. I don't have to think how I could apply the witness of these people to my life. But we are meant to think exactly that: How can we apply the witness of Jesus, Francis, Mother Theresa, Gandhi, or Coretta King to my life? Each of us has our own life limits, and we are not all meant to witness in the same way, but we are all meant to witness! Sainting *other* people gets *us* off the hook, and we miss the true inspiration of their lives.

Once more, heady stuff. But if you think we are talking extremes that only a few can access, read on. The next chapters, about the power of transformative justice, show that given the right opportunity, most people can touch the magic of transforming love. Then Chapter 6, all about forgiveness, carries us to the heaven on earth of stories where people reach for forgiveness, often without any structure or others to help them, and find the healing and transformation in that amazing act of will.

Transformation is not about an emotion: it is about a commitment to a process of good will, and anyone can do it. You can choose it each day in the way you respond to every person and situation that annoys or hurts you. As I said in the chorus to a song I wrote in New Zealand, borrowing Bob Dylan's tune and theme of "Blowin' in the Wind":

The power to transform is blowing in the wind,
The power to transform is in us all.

PART II

TRANSFORMATIVE PROCESSES

Chapter 5

Circle Sentencing and Family Group Conferencing: Communities Take Charge

This chapter tells stories of how justice already is often applied in transformative ways, where cultural traditions, newer legal options, or creative people enable it to happen. Let me say to begin with that any method can be done well or badly, although some are inherently more prone to destructiveness and others naturally give scope to positive interpretations. But just as a Beethoven symphony can be played out of tune or rhythm, or in a lacklustre way, transformative justice processes can be abused by authoritarian people, or others who miss their spirit. This is particularly true when we are surrounded by a culture accustomed to a "justice system" based on patriarchy, revenge, and hierarchy. It's hard to leave all that baggage behind by changing the form.

So we begin here by going back to indigenous cultures, which recognized the importance of a healing process that would strengthen the whole community, heal the victim, and find a way to reintegrate offenders. All transformative processes are to some extent rooted in those healthy indigenous cultures that recognized the importance of empowering a healing community, dedicated to including all its members. In a dim way, we are beginning to recognize it too.

Most of our modern police forces acknowledge they could not do their jobs without community support, and the many variations of "community policing" attempt in some way or other to bring the community back into the picture. Yet the rest of our justice system, including the rest of policing, systematically exclude the community from the whole process of justice, and the community's vital role in making it happen.

Circle Sentencing: Aboriginal Justice Shows the Way

It has taken me years to sort out the differences between Native healing circles and Native sentencing circles, but it is really quite simple. The Native healing circle is the original, purer form of Native justice, as it was practised before Western "justice systems" intruded. Native sentencing circles are modern adaptations in which our judges participate, and where ultimate power still resides with our courts. Although sentencing circles usually work remarkably well, they are to some extent a hybrid, and can be adversely affected by the power and agenda of our revenge oriented system. Even so, they are usually an improvement over our courts, for wherever the community is allowed to have a voice, and wherever victims and offenders are heard instead of being forced through a legal script, transformation is possible.

When I tell the many stories where transformative justice has created magic moments for victims and offenders and community, I often say, "It sounds like a fairy story, it is so beautiful. It doesn't always work out this way, even with transformative methods. But more often than I would have believed possible, it does. And in 25 years of work with our court system, I have never seen this kind of magical transformation happen. Our system is designed so that transformation is virtually impossible."

So let's look at the indigenous systems that use the power of a healing, caring community to enable that magic to happen. Our first story comes from Africa, and shows how the two justice approaches would handle the same situation, side by side.

A Tale of Two Justices

This story (Leach 1992) happened in West Africa in the early 1990s. A lively party was going on, with food, dancing, and drinks. Gilbert felt Boukary was paying Gilbert's girlfriend too much attention, and that Boukary had also done that in the past. He decided to confront Boukary, and with both under the influence of alcohol, their argument got out of hand. Before anyone could stop it, Boukary had been stabbed!

Had Western justice been followed, the anger of Boukary's family would have led them to charge Gilbert through the police and courts. Gilbert would be arrested and put in a tiny stifling jail with inadequate water for drinking or washing. A week later he would be transferred to a large prison where he would be slowly starved along with 700 other prisoners. Under these privations he would fall ill and become increasingly bitter and listless. Because the prison is far from home, he would have no visits, and he would gradually be forgotten in his home village.

After a year or so, he would get a trial, if he were lucky. While inside he would learn new ways of stealing and getting into trouble. Cut off from village life, he would be frightened of returning. He would be especially scared of Boukary's family, so he would decide to stay in the city. He would commit increasingly serious crimes over a period of time, and spend longer and longer in prison. His life would be greatly shortened, and his contact with his own community lost.

On the other hand, what actually happened through traditional village justice began similarly, but took a very different course. Boukary's family was still angry, and wanted something done. Boukary was off work during a time when the family needed work done in the fields. So Boukary's family talked to the village elders, who called a meeting.

One elder reminded the others that Gilbert had been unsettled since the death of his mother. A frail woman reminded them that this was Gilbert's first crime, and he had always been gentle. After long discussion, it was decided Gilbert must make amends to Boukary's family. He would work half-time in their fields, to make up for what Boukary could not do.

Gilbert was grateful that he was not expelled from the village, which might have been an outcome for such a serious crime. He worked alongside Boukary's family during the long hot summer, and this common experience in hard work built increasing mutual respect. Gilbert found in Boukary's mother some of what he had missed in his own. Both families were touched when others from the village helped from time to time. Gilbert became engaged to a girl from the village, and when they got married, Gilbert moved into a new house which many villagers, including Boukary and his family, built for them.

One of the interesting aspects of this true story of Gilbert and Boukary is how work together in the fields gradually drew the two sides together. One of the things about crime is that it is a unique, exceptional event in the life of both parties, especially of victims. The categories "victim" and "offender" are important, but they are never the only roles the two have played in life. A part of any good healing process is to help each see the other as a whole human being, someone whose senses operate like theirs, who enjoys good food like they do, suffers when someone they love is hurt, and bleeds like anyone else, to paraphrase Shakespeare's Shylock.

When any solution brings the two together in a setting such as working in the fields together, it enables this grasp of the wholeness of the other party to take place. The myth of the monster and the victim melts before the knowledge that at bottom we all share fundamental human qualities, joys, and dilemmas. Extended contact over a long period of time is not always a good or appropriate outcome, but a key part of the success of all transformative outcomes is enabling victim and offender through some kind of deeper knowledge of one another, to see each other as part of their communities, and as part of the whole community.

Our next story is one where a judge enabled a Native community to bring back old forms with new inspiration.

The Frank Brown Story

Frank Brown belonged to the Heiltsuk nation on Vancouver Island, a fishing village of 1200 indigenous people (Northey, 1991). Like so many who went on to live troubled lives, Frank grew up with an alcoholic father, but Frank's father died when Frank was eight. By the time Frank was fourteen, he had been living on the streets of Vancouver, was charged with the robbery and beating of a bootlegger, and seemed certain to find himself in a youth detention centre.

But at this point, a transformative option was chosen, first by a judge, then by Frank's community. Judge Cunliffe Barnett made British Columbia history by accepting for the first time that the Native community would deal with Frank in their traditional way. The Native village had seen many of its teenagers lost to suicide and alcoholism. They saw this as an opportunity to try to save one of their own from the dead-end, deathly road of institutionalization.

Frank's Elders met, and asked him to spend eight months alone on a deserted island, an hour from the village. Perhaps the double gift of grace — first by a white Judge, then by his own leaders — gave Frank the grace to find peace and spiritual renewal in that lonely preserve of nature. Whatever the cause, Frank's transformation changed not only him, but also many others. He became a leader in cultural renewal for his people, and in organizing the first ocean-going canoe voyage by West Coast Indians in the twentieth century! He also produced and helped write an hour long video on his own life. Frank established a rediscovery camp for youth to experience Native culture and wilderness on an island near the one which had been his home for eight long months.

In November 1990 Frank celebrated a "washing-off feast," the first to be held in decades. In fact until 1951 it had been declared illegal. Judge Barnett was presented with a ceremonial paddle in honour of his courageous risk-taking twelve years before. By taking that creative risk, a risk which still held Frank responsible and challenged him, the community — both the Judge and the Native community — offered Frank an opportunity at personal transformation, and his story certainly shows how fully he opened his life to it. In all true transformation, the glow is passed along to others, as Frank's was.

"Making Angels out of Assholes"

It is hard for anyone to understand a different culture, and all the more so when that culture has continued to exist, in spite of many efforts to exterminate it, within our dominating western culture, for 500 years. So I have struggled to understand Native healing circles and circle sentencing. I include the comments of Trish Monture-Okanee and Sakej Henderson, although they are not stories in the strict sense, because they illuminate the indigenous perspective on our justice system and theirs.

In March 1995 I went to a remarkable conference in Saskatoon on "restorative justice." The conference was full of leaders in the new models. Trish Monture-Okanee in her opening speech said, "There is no word for justice in our Native languages. The nearest word is harmony. Harmony means to be nice, kind and responsible in aboriginal thinking, and if there is one thing this system isn't, it's 'nice, kind, or responsible.'"

Trish also challenged the whole concept of "alternatives" in a way that has stuck with me ever since. "Alternative to what?" she asked, and went on to answer her own question, "To courts and jails. The big stick is still there. I am tired of being an alternative and marginalized and other. Aboriginal justice systems are our way, and they are the real thing. The Creator put Aboriginal people in this land. The Creator in Her Wisdom put us down here. 'Alternatives' conceptualizes me as inferior... I had trouble with law school because law is the study of the oppression of my people. You tell us to change, but your people have not made commitments to stop colonizing. The Canadian justice system is a system that entrenches total colonization of relationships. Every oppression that Aboriginal people have survived was delivered by the legal system. The study of the law is the study of oppression."

Sakej Youngblood Henderson, who followed her in speaking, was just as eloquent. He began by pointing out that the two icons of Eurocentric thinking, Socrates and Jesus, who taught Europeans most of what they claim to believe, were both executed by the finest justice systems of their day: "Your system calls itself order, and tries to pass off sovereignty from above as order. It tries to eradicate indigenous thought, because it cannot deal with its own contradictions. For five centuries Eurocentric theory has used violence and terrorism as the foundation of social order, and called it justice."

Sakej Henderson moved me deeply, this brilliant eloquent and empathetic man, when he said that every member of his family and his wife's family had been to jail. He said this related to the Native people's need to indulge in white men's vices to prove their equality:

> Native justice, in contrast with Eurocentric justice, is preventive, and relates to how we raise children. Justice comes from the heart. White governments did all they could to destroy Native child-rearing practices.
>
> Sovereignty in our language means trying to act like a big God — it is false. Sovereignty from above is telling everyone how to act, and if they don't we'll put you in jail, because we don't know how to deal with disorder. But a state doesn't breathe. It is an artefact of language, and not as fragile or precious as people. We must heal ourselves from 500 years of oppression. We need to return to our old Healing Systems.
>
> At a meeting of Justice Ministers in Canada last year they agreed the Canadian criminal justice system has failed and continues to fail. The aboriginal people call the Justice Ministers, "Keepers of all the bad experiences." My Grandfather used to say, "You really think you can make angels out of assholes with a piece of paper?" Now I understand that it is the human soul that has to do the work. You cannot be just in one part of your life, and unjust in the rest.

Those presentations had a powerful impact on me. Since then increasingly I reject the use of "alternatives" to describe healthy community ways of responding to crime. Instead I say, "Community is the way. Courts and prisons are the failed alternatives." Even we Whites can grow enough to learn from Native wisdom!

A Judge Supports Circle Sentencing

Judge Barry Stuart is someone who has never let the power of his office go to his head. In that same spirit, he has used the opportunity of being a judge to support circle sentencing wherever possible. Circle sentencing is a method going back to indigenous days. The exact format varies, but basically it includes the offender, the victim, and the whole community. Usually the elders play a special role as well, but the sacred feather is passed around; whoever holds the feather has everyone's respectful attention, and may speak only truth. Although not immune to power abuse, circle sentencing is far more inclusive of community and respectful of the voices of victim and offender than our courts.

My friend Teresa Hanlon who did her thesis on Native justice, explained to me that in the original Native healing circles, the complete process included four times of going around the circle:

> First, people introduced themselves, stating how they related to this situation and simply, why they were here.
>
> Secondly, each person spoke to the victim, offering their support and their recognition of the wrong done to that victim.
>
> Third, each person spoke to the offender, expressing their disapproval of the offence along with their concern for the offender as a valued member of the community
>
> Fourth, each person gave his or her recommendations for solutions, which the Elder facilitating the circle pulled together in a final consensus.

I can imagine no more perfect process for meeting the needs of victim, offender, and community. Introductions begin to build community. The primary need to recognize the victim's wrong and assure them of community support for their safety is the top priority after introductions. Then the dual needs to repudiate the offender's behaviour but include the offender himself in the community are addressed, separating the sin from the sinner. Finally the whole group works together for a common consensus on a transformative outcome. Unfortunately, the process is usually abridged and altered in Native sentencing circles. Nevertheless, it still retains much of its power, as this story told by Judge Barry Stuart illustrates.

Because our courts will not and in some ways cannot under current law relinquish their power completely, Judge Stuart has to mingle his presence with the Native circle, and in general, some interesting hybrids have arisen. But most judges who care enough to use it give the circle as much respect and authority as possible, and Barry Stuart is no exception.

The best circle sentencing is truly transformative justice: it does not stop with the offence, and isolate it from history and the community; it looks at the whole picture. So it takes awhile! Judge Stuart begins this story by noting that some of his fellow judges made fun of the amount of time he took over a single case. When you hear a few facts and a guilty plea and rattle off "Six years" to this one, and "Eighteen months!" to that one, you can get through a lot of "cases" in an afternoon. But when you invite the community to participate in a healing, transforming process, that is another matter.

Judge Stuart includes the community in consultation, and one day they asked him to take to a circle a case of a fourteen-year-old Native girl who was charged with underage drinking. He groaned inwardly if not outwardly, and thought what his fellow judges would say to his spending half a day on such a trivial charge! He tried explaining this to the Native people who had brought the request, but they were adamant. They felt this incident would help the community get to the bottom of some of its key issues.

He reluctantly agreed, and as it turned out, they didn't spend half a day on the case: they spent the whole day on it! That simple charge and the circle of truth probing it brought out issues of a lack of recreation for youth, of adult abuse of alcohol, of family disruption, of problems with education and its opportunities, of severe unemployment and its impact, and many more. By late afternoon they had looked at community issues never before shared so openly, all together. They looked around the circle with an air of well-merited satisfaction, and were drawing toward a close.

Then someone said, "But what about the teenage girl?"

One of the wise elders replied thoughtfully, "I think we've dealt with that."

Neither Judge Stuart nor I are suggesting that exposing and healing the social roots is the whole story in dealing with most crime. But those roots are so significant and so seldom explored in our system that I find this story very healing. It restores the balance. Sometimes we can transform a whole community by tracing the ripples in its pond from the fall of a tiny pebble.

Judge Stuart is remarkable, but not unique. Several Canadian judges have pioneered in bringing back to all of us the valuable heritage of Native justice. It amused me that when a Canadian court allowed a Native offender to experience a sentencing circle, while his White Canadian co-accused had to go through our Western courts, the lawyer for the White Canadian protested that this was not fair to his client! So obvious is it that Native justice is a superior option for offenders, but it is equally superior for victims and community.

Since writing most of this chapter, I was co-speaker at a Winnipeg Conference with Judge Bria Huculak. The judge is a dynamic petite woman who appears in spirit, sense of humour and character much like my dynamic youngest daughter, but who has to be older given that she, like Judge Stuart, has been pioneering in promoting Native sentencing circles for more than a decade. People like Bria and Barry, humble and empowering to us all, defy the universal impact of the corruption of power, and give one hope that we can transform our destructive justice systems with the beauty of healing justice models.

There is a Native legend that just before Columbus' voyage a Native spiritual leader prophesied thus:

> Something harmful is coming to our shores soon. It will cause much destruction for about 500 years, but as long as we keep faith with our spiritual traditions, it will be just a glitch. At the end of 500 years, Native culture and spirituality will revive, and prevail.

It seems to me — as I look at the collapse of our greed-based economy, our realization that the rape of the environment and the widening gap between rich and poor cannot continue — that the prophecy is being fulfilled. For Native spirituality is flowering among us, its ceremonies often opening our own conferences, its truths beginning to be understood by us as well as them. A major area where the glitch is passing is in our old shallow revenge based justice systems. Native healing circles, which touch the dynamic power of the whole caring community, and bring deeper life to victims and offenders, are a part of all our future.

The next section shows how they have lit a spark that has transformed the whole youth justice system of New Zealand, with legislation that includes all young offenders, and impacted profoundly on policing systems in Australia. Truly we are seeing the dawn of an era where as the prophet Amos says; "Justice can roll down like waters, and righteousness like a mighty stream."

New Zealand and Australia Try Family Group Conferencing

I had the privilege of visiting New Zealand in 1994 and 1997. While there, and in a much briefer foray into Australia, I learned about Family Group Conferencing, sometimes called Community Group Conferencing. I was astonished to discover that my proposal to legislate a parallel system of "transformative justice courts," and offer prolonged support and a healing process to victims, offenders, and their families, was remarkably similar to the system for all young offenders in New Zealand!

In fact, when I came to New Zealand in 1997 I had the privilege of visiting Judge Mick Brown in his home. Judge Brown is a Maori Judge, who had been practising his version of Maori Family Conferencing for ten years, when in 1989, a dramatic change occurred. The all too usual response of our "criminal justice systems" to an individual who takes creative risks to improve the system is that he or she is attacked and thrown out. Instead, Judge Brown found his system legislated as the approved method for all juveniles in New Zealand, and he himself was appointed to oversee the process!

Thus began an amazing saga in New Zealand history, which has been going on for ten years, a quiet positive miracle in a world inflamed with regressive moves. Family Group Conferences spread quickly to Australia, and Sergeant Terry O'Connell of Australia has travelled around the world spreading the word, along with others from Australia and New Zealand.

We will begin this section with four stories from New Zealand, showing the power of family group conferencing. The first story was of an initiative taken by Samoan families without waiting for a conference, but the fact that family group conferences had been the legislated response to all juvenile offences for four years when it happened set the stage for this remarkable event.

Death and Forgiveness: A Samoan Story

I heard one story again and again, from Marie Sullivan and others, during my 1994 trip to New Zealand. From the South Island to the North Island, in large cities and small towns, wherever I went, people would ask me with shining eyes, "Have you heard about the story of the two little five-year-olds?" Like all great stories, it includes both tragedy and triumph.

Two five-year-old boys, whose parents usually picked them up from kindergarten, were leaving school. The parents were slightly delayed that day, the boys tried to cross the road by themselves, and — tragedy struck. A speeding car struck both children, and sped off without stopping. The parents arrived, already troubled by being a little late for the pickup. Imagine their devastation when they found a crowd around the two little broken bodies, long past human aid.

The driver of the speeding car was another young person, and after he recovered from his initial panic, he turned himself in. Both the family of the offender and the families of the victim were from the Samoan community, which had a long tradition of healing justice. Before the authorities could get into the act, the families of the victims and the family of the offender approached one another. They decided to follow Samoan tradition, and with the support of the Samoan community, they were ceremonially united. Victims and offender actually met with open arms.

The thought of meeting with open arms the person who has killed our child immediately causes us Westerners to draw back. "I could never do that!" we exclaim. "How could they? Didn't they love their children?" But the ceremonies go far beyond the final step of open arms. They include recognition of guilt, taking responsibility, the whole community sharing the grief and wrong, and only finally, reconciliation. Strange that we whose culture is allegedly steeped in Christianity, and whose founder said, "Love your enemies, do good to those that hurt you and despitefully use you," find this idea so much harder to take in than people from what we have called primitive cultures!

But the world is hungry for reconciliation, and this event captured the heart of all New Zealand. It happened shortly before Christmas, and everywhere I went on my speaking tour, people spoke of it as bringing the true spirit of Christmas back to them. It is one of many stories, most of which will be told in the chapter on forgiveness, where people reach out instinctively for mutual healing from great pain, even when the legal structures discourage them. We include it here because it happened in a country where the legal structures encourage reconciliation and healing, and those legal structures set the stage for a whole country to celebrate together, a Christmas miracle of forgiveness.

"You Don't Ever Have to be Afraid of Me Again"

Marie Sullivan of New Zealand told me another story about family group conferences. Marie was near a building where a family group conference was taking place. She saw people emerging, and was surprised to note that a fairly unemotional staff-person was trying to hide his tears. So Marie asked him what had happened, and he told this story.

John was a fifteen-year-old who had assaulted, terrified, and humiliated Pete, a smaller boy of about the same age. For resolution, it went to an FGC (family group conference), and relatives and friends of both were encouraged to participate. Most offenders are overwhelmed and frightened by the experience of a community united in condemning their behaviour, and very penitent about what they did. But John tried to cover up his fear and nervousness with a cocky, irresponsible attitude that was rubbing everyone the wrong way.

After this unpromising beginning, the time came for Pete's mother to speak about how the assault had affected her son, herself, and her family. She said words to this effect; "Pete's Dad died just nine months ago. It has been ghastly for him, for me, for all of us. Pete was keeping it inside till recently, when he began to talk about it: his grief, his anger, his sense of being lost and alone. His grades had gone from good to failing, and about a month ago, after he began to face it in a better way, they got back to average. Now he is so frightened and hurt and upset I know he is back down where he was. It's just not fair that so much should happen to my boy, in such a short time."

Pete's mother broke down at this point and began sobbing. The whole room fell silent, united in support of her grief and that of her family. Then a wonderful thing happened. The grandmother of John, who had played a large role in his childhood, got up and came across the circle. Putting her arms around Pete's mother, she said, "I understand what you mean. My son, John's father, died seven years ago, and if he were still alive, I don't think we'd be here today." She too broke down and the two women clung together, finding community in tears, and in common grief for the loved ones they had lost.

His grandmother's act penetrated all John's cockiness. Seeing his grandmother crying, re-wounded by his act and attitude, he melted, and from that moment the Conference became a love-in. Everyone joined in working for support for Pete and his family, preventive measures for John, and a glimpse at the factors that had led to the incident from the whole community's perspective. It was a highly successful Conference, as most are, and when it was over and people were leaving, John thought he could do something without anyone noticing. He approached Pete tentatively, and stuck out his hand fearfully, afraid that it would be rejected. He said in a hesitant but deeply sincere voice, "I just want you to know that you don't ever have to be afraid of me again. I would never, never want to hurt you after this."

The hand was not taken. Pete, who had also been deeply moved by the Conference, instead flung his arms around John in a man to man hug, and said, "I know, I know!" At this point, the others noticed what had happened, and the joyful tears of the adults joined with the reconciliation of the boys. It was the aftermath of those tears that Marie had seen, as the still overwhelmed group was leaving that transforming meeting.

This is one of those stories that sounds too good to be true, but it is true, and so are many, many more. Can you imagine that kind of reconciliation and beauty coming out of our court process?

Drunken Driving Causing Death

No, it doesn't always work out that beautifully. So let's hear a story where people are not all reconciled, but where something good comes out of it anyway. This story is told by Jim Consedine and Helen Bowen in their book *Restorative Justice: Contemporary Themes and Practice*. It is a careful account of a family group conference that was voluntarily initiated in New Zealand in an adult case in December of 1997. Family Group Conferencing is mandated for juveniles in New Zealand, but not for adults. However, this story shows that when so many people know of it, as they do in New Zealand because of the youth legislation, it will often be sought to bring more healing and resolution to victims and more preventive impact on offenders.

Derek pled guilty to several driving offences, especially driving while drunk, which caused the death of Michael in January 1997. A community leader in their city was aware that tension was growing from the unresolved anger of the victim's family, so she suggested a Conference. The idea was accepted. Michael's grandparents, Derek, his partner and his mother, and the facilitator were all present. Conferences in New Zealand usually open with a Maori prayer. In the introductions that followed, Michael's grandparents described the unimaginable pain of being told by phone that their grandson had been killed, and having to inform other relatives. His grandfather said he hoped nothing like it would ever happen to anyone again.

In fact throughout this conference, as in many, a theme of it was that all the victims, including the partner of the offender who had herself been badly injured, wanted above all to prevent Derek's ever doing this again. The hope of this significant outcome is a main motivator in these conferences: that my pain may at least prevent someone else's agony. This selfless goal inspires many victims to keep going through the long, dark tunnel of grief and rebuilding.

The offender's mother also described receiving a phone call in which she was told of the accident, that her son was the driver, and that Michael, whose mother she knew slightly, was dead. One of the strongest ways to get through to offenders is when they see their own dearest family members suffering from their acts, as well as the pain of the victims. Derek saw vividly the pain of both his mother and his partner. Derek's partner cried throughout her introduction, saying she should have been driving, but she was too drunk. She talked about her own injuries, having to have her leg reconstructed, skin grafts, metal plates in her face, and a glass tube as an artificial tear duct. But above all, she told the victim's grandparents again and again how sorry she was for what had happened to them.

Michael's grandfather expressed anger that the car lacked a fitness warrant and the offender's license had been suspended since 1994. He went on to describe in depth the grief of his daughter (Michael's mother) and of Michael's little sister, who had combed his hair in his coffin. He said his children were too grieved to attend this meeting. Michael's sister had written a letter wishing she could have died instead of Michael.

The offender, Derek, said repeatedly how sorry he was. Michael's grandfather passed three pictures around: one of Michael alive beside his motorcycle, one of him in his coffin, and a third at the graveside, showing the grief of Michael's parents. The offender held the pictures in his hand, after looking at them, through most of the session.

The grandmother of the victim went on to point out that the offender had a free trip to the hospital, while some of their burial expenses were not covered, and how unjust this was. The grandfather spoke of the horror he had been through in helping to dig his grandson's grave. He talked about his sleepless nights, thinking about Michael.

Toward the end, the offender's partner described the day of the accident from their point of view. During the Conference, the offender acknowledged he now knew he was an alcoholic, that he was actively committed to AA, and declared repeatedly that he would never, never do anything like this again. He often appeared transfixed, staring at one person after another as they spoke. The impact on him was visible and powerful.

As the meeting drew toward a close, with the victim's family accepting the strong commitments made by the offender, the grandfather said it was easy to be full of vengeance, but now he felt better. "What we want is that you should never do it again. The fact that you sit there today showing genuine remorse will be of benefit to you and your family, and to mine." The grandmother added, "You are alive, you have the chance to make the most of your life. Do the best you can. Please make your life worthwhile."

The meeting ended on that note. Not exactly a love-in! But for those concerned about accountability, how could there be more accountability than that session? The grandmother's last wish is a common one too: that the offender who has taken our loved one's life makes up in his own life for the loss.

The whole story of Derek and Michael says to me that Conferencing can be very worthwhile as a step along the road to forgiveness and healing. It isn't the final step in most cases, but unlike our court processes, it is not a step backward, but a move toward peace and healing.

"I Wish I Could Turn Back the Hand of Time"

Our last story from New Zealand was given to me by Judge McElrea, a powerful fan of Conferencing in New Zealand. Judge McElrea himself was the judge involved in this case. He gave me a copy of the actual report on this story, on condition that all identifying details be changed in any publication; but except for names, dates, and places, everything is just as it happened here. A local minister agreed to facilitate the process, and had some background in observing them, but never facilitating them, before.

The fact is that when you are working with healthy processes, they are not as hard to facilitate as people think. A leader in a Mediation Service in Winnipeg told recently of how she had taken pride in getting a rather difficult victim and offender case to agree to meet with her and another facilitator, some years ago. The only problem was the victim and offender thought it was Tuesday night, and she and the other facilitator thought it was Wednesday. She got a call during the day Wednesday from the victim saying that she and the offender had met on the steps of the agency the previous evening. Finding the door locked and no one there, they had talked it all over, worked it out, and come up with some recommendations as their solution, and she hoped that was ok! So much for the essential role of us professionals. But back to Judge McElrea's story.

Norman was a rather typical young boy headed for trouble. He broke into a local takeaway bar and stole money from it. While waiting for trial on this charge, he followed a woman carrying a bag up a hill toward her home, shoved her violently, grabbed her bag and ran away. Judge McElrea asked for a Family Group Conference, and the facilitator worked hard on this.

The owners of the bar, Mr. and Mrs. Chong, came from an Oriental background where it was the custom to be represented by intermediaries, so even after several visits from the facilitator, they chose to ask a neighbour to represent them at the hearing, but Mrs. Chong attended as well. Mrs. Phelps, the woman who had been attacked and had her bag snatched, also chose to send a representative, but she wrote a letter herself to Norman:

> I am writing this because I can't be at the Conference, and I want you to go straight and keep out of trouble from now on. Here's what I think Norman.
>
> FIRST, your greatest need is to learn how to say NO.
>
> Say "NO" to your friend who tells you or asks you to snatch someone else's property. Just say, "NO — not my style, brother!"
>
> Say "NO" to your hands when they want to grab someone else's belongings.
>
> Say "NO" to your feet when they want to run to mischief.
>
> In some countries theft is punished by cutting off the offending limb. In New Zealand, we put people in prison. That means the whole person is put in prison, not just the hands or the feet. Perhaps that is a bit unfair.
>
> You have a good brain and a good heart and a lot of other good things. Why should they all be put in prison because your hands snatched and your feet ran? Don't let your hands misbehave; don't let your feet misbehave. If you can control your hands and your feet and learn to say "NO!" you need never go to prison again, and more than that, you will be a man whom everyone can admire.

Everyone in this room admires how you look; and the way you stand. From now on, we want to admire the way you control your hands and feet, and the way you learn to say "No" to mischief.

"No thanks, brother! Not my style nowadays!" Say that to your friends, to your hands, and to your feet, when mischief threatens you.

Your friend, Mrs. Phelps

This remarkable letter shows what creative messages can come across when victims are allowed to express themselves directly. Who has more motivation to try to get the point across than a direct victim does?

But before the letter was shared, the Conference opened in the usual New Zealand way: people introduced themselves, and a prayer was said. Then the facilitator explained the reasons for the Family Group Conference. The aims were to deal with past hurts, seek any possible conciliation and reparation, and to make the offender accountable for his actions. The charges were read and Norman acknowledged he had done them.

An intermediary then explained the feelings of the Chongs, whose bar had been robbed. They lived in Norman's neighbourhood, and they wanted his attitudes to change. They weren't in favour of prison particularly, but they wanted to be sure Norman would not seek revenge for their pressing charges. They wanted to be sure he had changed, and then they might be willing to meet him again.

Mrs. Phelps' representative, who was a slight woman, invited Norman to stand, and stood alongside him while talking to him, demonstrating his strength and her vulnerability. The message got across: Norman would not be happy if he was as comparatively weak as this lady was, and someone was violent toward him. This resourceful lady, Mrs. Frank, went on to stress that Norman should make a new future for himself, and give up his present attitudes and behaviour. Mrs. Phelps did not want to see him go to prison, but he had to accept responsibility for his actions, by learning to say No when confronted with potential offending situations.

Norman's father spoke next. All those who report on FGCs (Family Group Conferences) say that one of the most powerful influences on offenders are the voices of those near and dear to them, speaking about how their behaviour has hurt them. Norman's father expressed sorrow to all the victims for his son's actions. His wife had actually worked in the bar where the theft had occurred, before the Chongs bought it. He himself had been a customer there since, respected the Chongs, and could hardly face them for shame. He thought he and his wife had managed to teach Norman good values when he was young, and he was very disappointed now. He had strictly prohibited any violence toward females, by example as well as by precept, and he was truly shocked at Norman's violence toward Mrs. Phelps. The family would accept whatever the court and the conference decided. Norman had to make major changes, although he had not been a problem at home. His father felt he had chosen some wrong friends, but this did not excuse him.

Norman's mother spoke then. She also expressed sorrow to each of the victims. She felt something was wrong with her boy, but she had seen some positive change since this whole process had begun. She felt hurt as a mother, deep inside herself. She was especially upset at his violence toward Mrs. Phelps, and challenged Norman to think how he would have felt if anyone had done that to any female in his family. She hoped God would help all her family, and especially help Norman; she asked for forgiveness for Norman, who was a "big boy who often acts like a little boy."

At this point, Norman was invited to speak. He began by saying he had not expected to get bail and felt very lucky to get it. Then he said how much he appreciated the letter from Mrs. Phelps. Norman said many things had moved him to understand better his responsibilities and what he had to do about them. He had prayed for the strength to acknowledge what he had done and ask forgiveness for it. He spoke of how he had wavered from his family upbringing and Christian background. "I am responsible for my actions," he said clearly, "And nobody else. I did things to put myself in prison, and I have to be responsible for them, and accept whatever you decide."

Norman was grateful that Mrs. Chong had come, and assured her he had never meant them any harm, even though he had caused them harm he now realized, and that they had nothing further to fear from him. He then said to Mrs. Frank that he was so sorry Mrs. Phelps was not present so he could tell her the same. Far from taking revenge toward any of them, he wanted to make amends as best he could. Norman's Dad promised to keep him away from the store premises.

At this point they turned toward solutions. Norman had no income, but steps were to be taken to restore his benefit and help him get a job. As soon as he had an income, he would commence payment of $700 compensation to the Chongs. Since Norman had said one reason for offending was his lack of income, efforts to remedy this would be a further insurance against temptation. Norman expressed a desire for spiritual renewal, so the Conference recommended re-involvement in his church group, which would also rebuild his self esteem and provide him with more acceptable friends. All agreed on forbidding contact with one particularly troublesome friend and Norman himself requested a curfew to help him discipline himself! A counselling service was recommended, and Norman was encouraged to pursue further education, all provisions to be under the supervision of a community corrections officer. Finally, Norman agreed to write a letter of apology to Mrs. Phelps. Several people said they had thought of other solutions earlier, but were now very happy with these. A prayer and handshakes concluded the evening.

Norman's letter of apology is as remarkable as Mrs. Phelps' letter to him:

> Dear Mrs. Phelps,
>
> I wrote a letter to you before, but I could not find you or contact you, so I have decided to write a new letter to you about how I feel now. Yesterday I had the privilege of meeting a friend of yours. I thought at first it was you, but she was there on your behalf. She spoke to one of my family about how you felt towards me. She said you had forgiven me a long time ago.
>
> I could not believe what I just heard. Here was someone who never knew me, but knew I had committed a terrible crime toward them, yet she forgave me. I am sad that I could not tell you in person how sorry and ashamed I am for what I did to someone as warm as you. You are someone I truly admire. I wish I could turn back the hand of time and go back to that day and help you with your bag to the top of the hill, instead of snatching it from your hands. I would have had the chance to know you, and talk to you.
>
> I am so sorry for hurting you. I know in my heart I have changed for the better. I have also turned back to my scriptures and prayer to help me, and it really does work.
>
> Thank you. Norman — —

I have often quoted that remarkable line in Norman's letter, "I wish I could turn back the hand of time and go back to that day, and help you with your bag to the top of the hill, instead of snatching it from your hands." Offenders taken through the standard court process, victimized themselves over and over, do not come to that conclusion! Conferencing offers a remarkable opportunity in healing relationships, creating awareness, and building community anew.

A Bike Theft

Many of my favourite stories are from Terry O'Connell, a career policeman from Australia, whose values are almost a clone of mine, and whose eloquence and dedication to Conferencing are formidable. When Terry visited Toronto, I hosted him for several days, so I got to hear his favourite stories several times. Even so, I apologize if the details are hazy some years after his visit with me. But the substance of these stories, and the spirit, is true.

Probably because of its geographical proximity, New Zealand's Conferencing legislation intrigued some people in Australia, and amazingly enough, the Australian police picked it up. Police around the world are disgusted with many of the same failings in our justice system as I am. They too want more justice for victims, more effective response to offenders, and more community involvement.

In this case, the main disciple of the new methods was a police sergeant from Wagga Wagga, Australia, with a 30-year history in policing and a long record as vice-president of the police union for that whole area of Australia. Not the first place I would have looked to find a charismatic leader of new steps for healing justice, but God is much more imaginative than I.

Sometimes people ask Terry, "What do you do when a young person offends time after time, despite all you can do with Conferencing?" Terry's answer is, "I would still use Conferencing. I would do it for the victims."

Personally, I would have been tempted to point out that the criminal justice "revenge-by-institutionalizing" approach fails 60-80 percent of the time, yet we still clamour to use it more and more. One good Family Group Conference cannot unmake twenty years of abuse, neglect, and closed doors in the life of a young person; so perhaps the failure is in adequate follow through and prevention in the whole community. But Terry prefers to focus on the impact on the victim, and I like that too. Here is a story he tells to prove his point: that victims are the really big gainers from Conferencing.

We think of bike theft as a minor crime. It's common, the amount of money involved is not large, and there is usually no violence involved. But this story illustrates that any crime is a violation of personal space, which causes pain and trauma to victims. A family with four girls kept a bike on their screened porch. One night someone broke into the porch and stole the bike. Terry didn't think it was a big deal, being used to bigger events in his years of policing. But when he phoned the family in a routine inquiry about the incident, the mother conveyed that indeed it was a big deal.

All the children felt threatened and violated — not just by the loss of the bike, but by the thought of a thief coming into their home to take it. The oldest girl kept talking about it, and couldn't stop worrying about it happening again. The second girl was having nightmares, the third had gone back to bedwetting, and the littlest one wouldn't sleep in her own bed at night. Terry said, "We'll have to see what we can do about all that." The family gladly agreed to a Conference, and met there as perpetrators two young boys who were so scared themselves they aroused the motherly instinct in even these young girls, who had felt so frightened.

The twelve-year-old girl, who had been very frightened and upset by the incident, cried for the boys who did it because "they were just like the boys down the street, and I was sorry for the lives they had led." One common outcome of Conferences is that victims find the bogeymen they had imagined are frail humans as vulnerable as they are. The power victims have in a Conference restores their own sense of pride and control over their own lives. This was so much so in this case that when Terry called the mother of the girls after it was over, she reported with amazement and enthusiasm, "You know, all the girls felt so good afterwards, and they are all back to normal, only better. They're not afraid, they're excited about what they learned, and they feel great about the whole experience. It sounds crazy to say it, but it turned the whole thing into one of the best experiences of our lives!"

What a perfect definition of transformative justice. As my mother used to say, life is about turning "irritation into iridescence." That's what one Family Group Conference did for two young boys, four little girls, and their parents.

Women's Institute Trashed!

This is one of Terry's great stories, and in this case I am assisted by an article from an Australian newspaper, the *Boggabilla Argus*. Boggabilla was one of the towns where the Australian police piloted the new Family Group Conferencing they had learned from New Zealand. While in New Zealand the method is done through the courts, in Australia it has been initiated, developed, and handled largely by the police. Each method has its pros and cons, but at their best, both are wonderful.

Boggabilla is a fairly typical small town in its area, with underlying tension between the White residents and the indigenous people. These were severely aggravated when some indigenous youth broke into the Women's Institute one weekend and caused a lot of damage. The Women's Institute was the icon of middle-class White society in Boggabilla, and the youth poured kerosene on the new carpets, set some records alight with a wall heater, and generally did their best to trash portions of the place.

The police were able to identify the four culprits quickly, and a family group conference was called soon, which included the children, their extended family, and many members of the Women's Institute. The WI women were sceptical before the Conference whether anything really would be accomplished by it, but afterwards, they were singing its praises. Not only did the children and their family participate actively, take full responsibility, and agree to participate in a collective cleanup; the incident enabled people to talk about some of the underlying causes of tension in the community.

Further outcomes were that the WI invited the police to use their building for future Family Group Conferences, and invited the initiating policeman to speak about Conferencing at their annual gathering! Terry always ends this story by having the audience guess the age of the four offenders: they ranged from eight down to two!

A Graduation Party that Got out of Hand

Most of us are familiar with high school graduation parties, and know that all kinds of things can happen there. This one happened in a town in Australia. The story, again, is from Terry O'Connell. Someone planning the event got creative, and included a scavenger hunt competition in the fun. Groups of youth were given lists of things to collect, and the group that got back to home base first with a complete collection would win.

Car wash signs were on some of the collection lists. In their eagerness to win, some of the graduating young people did considerable damage to one car wash in particular and minor damage elsewhere. Next day the town's papers were full of the usual headlines about how our youth were going to the dogs, and where was it all going to end. In short, the town was up in arms and wanted something done NOW by the local police.

So Terry set out to investigate. Given that there were 180 youth in the graduating class, he tried first investigating by standard procedures and concluded that there were about 180 prime suspects. If he proceeded as usual, he might narrow this down a little and bring someone to trial in a year and a half or so. So being Terry, and being even more creative than the folk who designed the scavenger hunt, he decided on a novel approach. He went to the primary victim, the owner of the vandalized car wash, and asked for his story. After he heard it, and allowed him to vent both the facts and his anger over them, Terry asked an unusual question, seldom posed to victims in our system of justice, "So what would you most like to happen out of all this?"

The car wash owner was somewhat taken aback by this query. Who ever asks victims what they really want? After a moment's pause for reflection, however, he replied, "Well, I want my signs back. And I want those kids to repair the damage." He paused again, and then added with even more feeling and clarity, "And I want them to understand they must never do anything like that again." Those requests are typical of victims everywhere, when they are given the chance to ask for their wishes: reparations and learning by the offender so that no one else suffers again what they did.

Terry thanked him and was about to go, when the owner turned to a man who had been sitting over in the corner while they talked. The owner said, "Before you go, I think you should hear from him." The surprise witness, a man named Ben, told an even more moving story. Ben had been unemployed for a year. He and his wife had a baby, and he had done everything to find a job, but with little education and a bad job market, nothing had opened up till last week. The car wash owner was doing a promotion, and had hired him to help with the anticipated increase in business. Ben and his wife had been ecstatic!

But now, with this damage, and with the signs gone, the sales promotion and his job were nowhere in sight. He was furious at those kids, and deeply depressed. Terry looked him over and said simply, "I'd like you to come with me, and we'll see what we can do."

So Terry and Ben went off to the local school. They didn't have a room large enough in the school for what he had in mind, so he held it out on the playing field. He invited the whole senior class to join him there, and he explained to them that they had a problem. They already knew that, and they were all attention, but had no idea what was coming. Terry said, "There's somebody here who really wants to meet you." Then he put Ben forward, and invited him to tell his story.

Given this chance, Ben held forth eloquently. It's not often that someone gets the chance to confront a whole group of people who have just done them so much harm, and he wasn't going to lose this chance. He told how he had had to drop out of high school, and hadn't had the opportunity they had to get that education. He told how rough it had been, trying to get regular employment, but how hard he had worked at it. He told about his wife's pregnancy, and how it had been marred by the incessant struggle for a dependable job. He mentioned how very hard it had been getting the things they needed for the new baby, and how thrilled they had both been when he saw the ad for the car wash job, and got it. Then he explained how their exploit had destroyed his job, and what he thought of them, kids who had had so many chances he hadn't, and who didn't think anything of destroying his one break.

By the time he finished, there were a lot of uncomfortable young people looking at the ground and stirring uncomfortably. Terry brought the meeting to an end quickly, "So you want to do something about this? You select three spokespeople, and all of you come back here with your parents and families tonight, and we're gonna sort this out."

That is exactly what they did: all the victims, all the culprits, and their families met together, a massive group. The amazing thing about these processes is that numbers help, they don't harm. Communities include all those affected, and an event like this affected just about everybody in that town, so a lot of them turned up. The victims told their stories, and the class and their families responded with their apologies and ownership of responsibility. How satisfying for the victims! How much better for the offenders to take responsibility and face those they had harmed than to go through an obscure process where everyone was victimized and no one made clear to them exactly how what they had done had hurt real people!

The outcome was that the youth not only repaired all the damage and paid for what they couldn't repair. The families agreed to promote the business, and did it so well that the owner of that car wash doubled his business, and was able to hire more new help than just Ben! All those who had experienced damage were delighted with the process: the youth and their families learned so much, and were proud of their ability to respond appropriately. Moreover, a process that could have taken many months in court was resolved in two weeks!

It sounds like a fairy story. So many stories of Family Group Conferences do, but they are true and they are real. The magic doesn't always work quite that perfectly, but the potential is there, and when we use our tired old "justice" processes, fundamentally flawed by their focus on revenge, instead of healing, we are missing a great opportunity for transformation and community empowerment.

But for most of us North Americans, indigenous ways are strange and limited to their communities, and New Zealand and Australia are off the map of our real world. So does healing justice exist in North America, in our urban cities? Indeed it does: read on, for the next section is full of true stories of transformative justice processes in Canada and the USA.

Canada and the USA Practice Transformative Models

Canadian Mennonites Lead the Way: Story of a Rampage

No, the Mennonites didn't rampage. But they found a new way to respond to a rampage. This story comes in part from Howard Zehr's account of it in *Changing Lenses*, but also partly from my memories of hearing Dave Worth tell it from his personal experience. For this is a story of how two Canadian Mennonites from Kitchener-Waterloo made history in 1974, and how my friends Dave Worth and Mark Yantzi created a made-in-Canada approach to justice, that has gone around the world.

It all began on May 28, 1974, when two young men from Elmira, Ontario, pled guilty to vandalizing 22 properties in one neighbourhood. Mark Yantzi was the probation officer assigned to bring a pre-sentence report. While working on that, Mark attended a meeting talking about a Christian response to shoplifting. The meeting got Mark to thinking about how wonderful it would be if these rampaging young offenders could meet their victims. Dave Worth, co-ordinator of Voluntary Service for the Mennonite Central Committee, insisted on pursuing Mark's wild idea with him.

Strongly encouraged by Dave, Mark took the risk of proposing to the judge that the offenders meet their victims, and arrange some way to pay them back. The judge immediately said that was impossible. But when time came for sentencing, he too had thought further about it, and he ordered exactly what Mark had suggested!

Mark and Dave took turns going with the two young offenders to each of the homes of the twenty families who still lived in the neighbourhood. Because this was a first effort, there were no fancy phone appointments made, and no preparation. Mark or Dave would walk baldly up to the door with the two boys, ring the bell, and the boys had to say basically, "We're the people who did all that damage, and we're here to talk about it." What a challenge!

Amazingly enough, even this simple, rough-and-ready approach to meetings worked wonderfully. Victims had a chance to say what they felt directly to the offenders, Mark and Dave helped make the meeting safe for all parties, and after relieving feelings, virtually all the twenty victims worked out with the boys what kind of restitution made sense to each of them. Over the coming months, these restitutions were completed, and so the first court-ordered victim-offender reconciliation in the world took place.

I say the first such court-ordered meeting, because as many of our stories show, victims and offenders often have healthy instincts to meet and sort things out. Strangely enough, lawyers, police, prosecutors, and insurance companies all tell them to keep apart, so this natural instinct is usually frustrated. Actually the official attitude is not so very strange, since if victims and offenders got together more often, most of these professionals would lose a lot of work and status. But in 1974 it was not only not frustrated — a creative judge responded to the daring of Mark and Dave and helped begin a whole new approach, one which included and responded to victims, and one which held offenders responsible directly to the people they had harmed.

Dave Worth tells a story about another victim-offender meeting, this one taking place in the home of the victim, because the wife was ill, and found it difficult to leave their home. Many victims prefer a more neutral setting, but what matters is that the setting be acceptable and safe to both victims and offenders. In this case, John and Sally had experienced a break-in where trivial things were stolen and some damage done. They had a collection of valuable paintings, and Sally had some expensive jewellery, none of which had been touched, so they assumed the thieves were "casing the joint," and would be back later to do the real raid. As a result they lived in terror, especially as John had to go on business trips and Sally with her poor health was alone in the house.

When the two young offenders were caught, and were just kids, John and Sally were astounded and relieved! These were not the stereotypical crooks of TV show lore. They were just kids, and the more the kids talked, the more John and Sally realized how needless had been their fears, based on images of big professional crooks. The theft of little things was because these kids didn't know what was valuable, and had no way to peddle it anyway. The act was random, not deliberate, and there had never been any intention to return.

Meanwhile, as John and Sally were learning, so were the young offenders. They both came from very poor homes, and they assumed that people who lived in a fancy house (to them) like John and Sally were totally different from them. In particular, they assumed such well-off middle-class people had no troubles and no problems. But there was Sally reclining on their couch and obviously suffering from serious health problems. And there were John and Sally spinning out all the worries they had had from the kids' thoughtless act of breaking in.

So that meeting brought home to both parties the common humanity of the other. That is what victim-offender meetings do at their best. They bring us into community with one another. We may not like all our neighbours, and we certainly won't like everything they do, but we do begin to recognize the truth of a wise teacher who said that my true neighbour is the Samaritan from the group I don't like. Victim offender reconciliation brings us into community with the people we least recognize as neighbours.

What About Sex Offenders?

Mark Yantzi went on to spend most of his career building on this experience, and in a different way, so did Dave Worth. Both have made immeasurable contributions to the field of healing justice. Our next story is by Mark, from his book, Sexual Offending and Restoration. Mark has spent years in the very challenging field of sexual offences, maintaining the impossible balance between working with offenders and working with victims. Over the years he has staffed support groups and counselled family members dealing with every aspect of sexual offending; the most amazing thing is how little publicity there has been about the work of Community Justice

Initiatives, where Mark and others do this cutting edge and desperately needed work.

This story is about dealing with one of the ultimate challenges: neighbourhood panic over a sex offender moving to the neighbourhood! Because Mark's work is known in his wider community, a woman we'll call Sue phoned him for help. She told Mark that a pedophile named Bob had been released from prison, and was living in her neighbourhood.

The neighbours were all talking about it, different rumours were going around, and Sue wanted to know what Mark thought they could do. She had already called the police, who wanted to help her, but felt hemmed in by requirements of confidentiality. So who was going to protect the children of Sue and her neighbours? Sue knew Bob's name and address, and the phone number of his parents. She also knew he had served six years in prison, and been convicted eight times of sexual offences.

Sue assumed Bob had been convicted on eight different occasions, over the years, but in fact although he had eight convictions, they had all occurred in one period, and he had pled guilty to all at once. Both situations are serious, but Bob's record was not as chronic as it first appeared. Sue assumed that Bob would inevitably re-offend, and asked Mark what she could do.

Mark offered to contact Bob and arrange a meeting between Bob, his family, and some of the concerned neighbours. Mark promised not to reveal which neighbour had contacted him, and he and Sue came to an understanding on just what he could and could not share, to ensure her feelings of safety. When Mark called Bob, Bob was surprised at how fast the neighbourhood grapevine was working. He had only been out five days, but he understood the concerns of the neighbours, and agreed readily to the meeting, to which he was invited to bring support persons. Meeting at the agency building ensured safety for all, and the neighbours were reassured by the presence of two police whose role was to share legal information as well as a sense of police protection. Mark and another agency worker provided security for all by their presence as experienced mediators in such challenging situations.

In preparing people for the meeting, Mark emphasized the need to confront issues, but to do so constructively. He also sought for some balance in numbers, although when eight neighbours wanted strongly to come, this became somewhat skewed. Bob agreed to this increase, and came with his parents and one church friend. Then ten neighbours turned up; two of whom had received only the shortest of preparation! However, it was too late to back out now, and Bob shrugged when informed of the additions.

Mark and his colleague outlined the simple ground rules: only one person to speak at a time, agreement at the end on what would be confidential and what would be shared, and respect in communications. After introductions, each of the neighbours stated the key questions or issues that concerned them. Then Bob read a prepared statement that responded to many of these. He thanked the neighbours for approaching the matter in the way they had, and he told some about his offences and history. He said he had had some treatment in prison, and was planning to follow up on this in the community. He had set up a daily accountability system with his pastor. He was most concerned for the impact of all this on his parents. He had hoped to live with them for awhile, but if his presence would damage their relations with their neighbours, he didn't want to hurt his parents further by doing that.

The neighbours began to affirm that Bob's parents should not be hurt further by any of this, and some said that they would stand by their children whatever they did, so they respected Bob's parents for standing by him. This led to further dialogue about Bob's history, and some were relieved when they found all Bob's victims were known to him, so he had not preyed on strangers.

The police stated how difficult they found situations like this, and how much they felt caught between their desire to protect neighbourhoods and their obligation to respect confidentiality and the rights of ex-offenders. They were impressed by the open and positive way both neighbours and Bob were handling this. The school principal said she had been having calls from parents, and the whole group got involved in discussing how to diffuse general fear and provide appropriate information without denying or increasing risk. They felt the whole situation offered an opportunity for some healthy community education about sexual offending, and the fact that most of it was by people known to us, not strangers. The meeting closed on a positive note.

No magic in this story, but when one considers the violence and terror that are often evoked by such situations, maybe the above is kind of magical. When a community can recognize that even a pedophile and his parents are part of their community, and find ways to include them in its planning, transformation is taking place.

An Albertan Community
Comes Forward for an Offender

This is one story where I managed to get in on one of the closing chapters myself. It's a wild but true story, told by my friend Darrel Heidebrecht, who heads the Man to Man, Woman to Woman prison visiting program sponsored by Mennonites in Alberta. A young man I'll call Al fell in love with "Jenny," a girl from a more middle-class family, who felt Al was not good enough for their daughter. The young couple persisted and married in the face of her family's opposition, but Jenny's family continued to dislike Al and treat him as second class.

Jenny and Al went to a party one night where Al had too much to drink — he had something of a drinking problem. The situation was compounded because one of Jenny's old boyfriends began making up to her, and she, annoyed at Al's drinking, encouraged him flirtatiously. Al and the other fellow squared off to fight it out, but Jenny stepped between them, just in time to receive a hard blow that knocked her down. She ended up going to the hospital and a much upset husband left her in hospital, returning home himself, fuzzy in his thinking, and angry at the whole world about everything.

While he was thinking over his grievances from the night, feeling bad about his role in the debacle that ended in the injury to his wife, he was looking for someone else to blame. Of course there never is a shortage of other people in our lives to be angry at. In Al's case, his Dad and one of his uncles had had a dispute about some inherited property, and Al's whole family felt cheated by the uncle. Al decided he was going to settle this once and for all. He got out his shotgun, went to his cousin's house (the son of the offending uncle), and forced his cousin to come with him. They were going to see the uncle and straighten it all out, Al insisted.

Thinking like a drunk, Al suddenly decided that he couldn't leave Jenny in the hospital for this exciting event, so he headed for the hospital where he had left her, to pick her up before taking them all to confront his uncle. Of course when he arrived at the hospital, he couldn't leave his unwilling cousin alone in the car, so he compelled him to come in with him, at gunpoint, and the two of them appeared in the hospital entrance with Al's loaded rifle, demanding to see his wife!

Hospital security called in an RCMP officer, who tried to talk Al down. But Al became belligerent and demanded the RCMP officer hand over his gun, which he wisely did — but now Al had compounded his other felonies by disarming an officer of the law! Nevertheless, from here on in, he became more sensible, and instead of going on to his uncle's, he drove home, and even called the police to surrender, and gave them further directions when they got lost in trying to find his house.

This bizarre story is too strange not to be true. Al never intended violence or serious harm to anyone, not even his uncle, and his peaceful surrender when he began to come to his senses showed his more usual sense of responsibility. But in the course of that evening he had committed a number of very serious felonies including kidnapping his cousin, threatening many hospital officials with a deadly weapon, and disarming the RCMP officer. Even without a previous serious criminal record of any kind, in conservative small-town Alberta, Al was looking at a substantial federal sentence in prison.

Enter a miracle: Al had a Sunday school teacher who remembered him as a spunky but innocent and good little boy. Jerome and another M2W2 volunteer called Darrel for advice on what to do, but a lot of their plan was their own idea entirely. They put up a petition to support Al in the local post office, asking the community to sign up to say they didn't want to see Al's life pushed down the penitentiary road by this one disastrous incident. They got 47 signatures, just from posting it there.

A second miracle was Jenny's response. Without excusing Al's behaviour, she came forward acknowledging her responsibility for having flirted with her old boyfriend, contributing to his violent response. Far from taking this opportunity to bail out of the marriage, Jenny confronted her family and told them their attitude to Al had got to change. Now was the time to rally together: marriage was for keeps, and Al was part of their family now too. Amazingly enough, they accepted responsibility for their part in the whole history too, and came to Al's support as well as Jenny's!

The impact of all this was that the court, amazed at the outpouring of community support for Al, sentenced him to two years less a day, with a recommendation for early parole: provincial prisons instead of federal, and a far shorter stay. Al got paroled after nine months, with full support from Jenny. I came into the story on a speaking tour of Alberta. In each town M2W2 sponsored an evening with entertainment, volunteer awards, food, my talk, and usually a local speaker talking about their involvement in the program. In Rosemary, Alberta, the centre of this story, the local speaker who preceded me was Al. In moving but simple words, he got to thank the community who had supported him, and in the social afterwards, Jenny added her own warm thanks. Al has stopped drinking, Jenny's family has accepted him, their marriage is stronger than ever, and a community came together over what could have been a disaster: sounds like a fairy story, but transformative love is stronger than any other magic I know.

"I'm Healed Now": VORP with Violent Offences

Dave Gustafsen is another Canadian Victim Offender Reconciliation pioneer, but his work began years after Dave Worth and Mark Yantzi had developed VORP. Dave Gustafsen's pioneering was in whom he included. A common myth about most alternatives is that they are okay for dealing with choirboys chewing gum in the sanctuary, but more serious offenders require the usual heavy, regressive measures. The result is that the best alternatives tend to be tried with only the mildest of cases, and victims who suffer the greatest traumas continue to be subjected to the failing revenge methods. Dave Gustafsen set out to prove VORP could be used on the most serious situations.

As a result, with the encouragement of British Columbia Mennonites, and some funding from Canadian federal Corrections, Dave set out to use VORP in Canada on cases where people had lost family members to murder, or experienced rape from a repeat rape offender. Not an easy challenge! But Dave brought to it a mixture of powerful commitment, spiritual sensitivity, and excellent therapeutic skills. He applied them all to this task, and developed a VORP program that was recently evaluated, and in which every victim who had experienced the program over the years said they would use this method again. Here is a story of why.

Miriam was around 50 when the nightmare happened. Sleeping alone in her apartment, she heard the terrifying sounds of an intruder breaking in. Worse yet, this intruder was not bent on simple robbery. From the beginning, he attacked her, clearly bent on rape. He was much younger than Miriam, but as in many rape cases, age differences don't matter; the rapist is dealing with power issues and usually with violations of his own in the past that contribute to his script, and the victim's age, appearance, and status matter little.

Miriam struggled as hard as she could, despite the violence of her assailant and the danger that resistance might make him still more violent. In the melee that happened on her bed, one of them knocked the clock-radio, and the radio began to play. All through the horror that followed, as Donald succeeded in raping her, the radio played on, a macabre touch in this eerie night scene.

Miriam was completely traumatized by that night. One of the minor effects was that she could not stand to hear a radio playing. Radio sounds brought back to her all the trauma of that brutal, degrading attack, and they were more agonizing to her than fingernails on a blackboard. Through the years that followed, she sought many kinds of therapy, but nothing gave her relief. Shock passed, but grief never went away. Her radio phobia and many other aftermaths of the horror she had experienced continued. Donald was caught, and tried. Miriam had to testify, and Donald denied responsibility. His testimony made Miriam seem partly responsible for her own rape, and the trial outcome left Miriam feeling even more soiled and dirty, even though Donald was convicted and went to prison for many years. Miriam was not the only woman he had raped, and other cases came out more unambiguously, leaving Miriam feeling even more wronged. Wasn't she as innocent as those other women? Like Lady Macbeth, only without that lady's real guilt, Miriam could not wipe the feeling of guilt and shame from her, no matter how many sessions of therapy she went to.

Eight years passed, and Miriam heard of Dave Gustafsen's VORP program. She contacted him, and Dave began his wonderful work. Dave visits victims and asks them if there are any questions that are vital to their healing, that they would like to ask the person who did this to them, if they could feel entirely safe in asking them. With that vital question, Dave taps the first of the five victim needs: the need for answers, many of which can be provided only by the offender. Given enough support and safety, virtually every victim answers yes to that question. Then Dave helps them to think through what questions they need to ask, and how they want to ask them. With their permission, he videotapes the victims asking the questions.

Following shuttle diplomacy, Dave takes the video in to the prison, and shows it to the offender. Just as with the victim, Dave does a lot of supportive, maturing therapy with the offender, helping them think through what they need to say for themselves, and how what they say will affect their victim(s). When the offender is ready, Dave videotapes the offender answering the questions, and back he goes to the victims. In a few cases, an exchange of videos, which may continue several times as the exchange deepens, is all that is needed or wanted. But usually the videos satisfy both partly, while also preparing them for a face to face meeting.

In the case of Miriam and Donald, the two decided they wanted to meet, and Dave felt they were ready for it. Dave is extremely careful in his proceedings not to damage either party in the handling of these highly delicate meetings. But in order to spread the message, he occasionally gets their permission to tape the meetings, and share the tapes, with both parties understanding fully what they are agreeing to. In general when people discover a wonderful remedy, they want to share it with others, and this is the case with the Langley, BC VORP program. Donald and Miriam wanted their story to be shared, so that it could help others.

I have actually seen the video of part of this incredible meeting, a meeting in which the two talk about many important things, including the anguish Miriam suffered, and the fact that Donald had a pattern of raping older women. Donald stated openly, clearly and powerfully that his testimony had been a lie, and that Miriam was totally an innocent, wronged party in that rape scene. Miriam felt a sense of cleansing like nothing had given her for years. But the powerful part of the story to me is something Dave Gustafsen tells about the trip back. Miriam had come by another means, but Dave was bringing her back from the prison in his car, to her home. He had been listening to the radio on the way, and so had not turned it off. After a minute he realized to his horror that the car radio was playing. Being an extremely sensitive person, he was distressed by his allowing this to happen even briefly, and reached up quickly to turn it off.

Before he could do it, however, Miriam, stopped him in the act of turning it off. With shining eyes, she said, "No, it's all right. It doesn't bother me any more. I'm healed now." The answered questions, the recognized wrong, the melted terrors in facing her assailant — all these things had healed places deep in her heart that all that therapy over eight years had not been able to touch.

Genesee County Justice: A Modern Miracle

We turn now from Canadian stories to stories from the USA. Many people might think that a country gone mad with incarceration, a nation with 1,800,000 prisoners, a country that shares with Russia the dubious distinction of the highest incarceration rate in the world, would have no stories of healing justice. Yet as in all countries, the paradox exists that while incarceration rates are usually growing, and the penal system becoming more archaic and inappropriate, new seedlings of the future are springing up everywhere too. The USA has over a hundred VORP programs, and Europe has even more. So it is important to remember that Americans are not all in lockstep unity with the mad race to incarceration. An exciting San Francisco Conference in 1998, "Critical Resistance, The Prison-Industrial

Complex," challenged the whole philosophy of penal incarceration. The organizers aimed for 500 participants, and ended up with 3000! All our stories show this other side of American character; but nowhere is this feisty, miraculous resistance to the massive incarceration of racial and economic minorities better exemplified than in Genesee County, an unpretentious area of upstate New York.

Genesee County Justice deserves a book for itself. In 1981, a rightwing candidate was running for sheriff, and a group of people who felt his directions would be destructive got together to oppose him. They needed someone to run against him, and Doug Call volunteered. They needed a platform, and they ran on a proposal to implement victim offender reconciliation that would respond to the need to prioritize victim needs for a change.

To everyone's amazement including theirs, Doug Call won, on their platform, so they had to figure out what to do about it! Unlike many politicians, they did carry out their election promises, with roses. Unlike most victim offender programs, they decided to work especially on violent cases, since these are where victims suffer most, and these are where public costs are highest for long incarcerations and expensive trials. They became one of two model programs in North America (the other is the Mennonite program in British Columbia just described) doing quality victim offender reconciliation with violent crimes.

From there, it is a twenty-year story of stunning success. To have Sheriff Doug Call taking the lead in such an initiative has been key: healing justice is coming from a direction that is normally obsessed with blind punishment. Dennis Whitman works as community service and victim/witness co-ordinator to "keep the local jails empty." Their joint campaign on this is so successful that in times when prison building and overcrowding is epidemic, Genesee County makes money renting out empty jail space to neighbouring counties!

But does it work for victims? Indeed it does. Above all, the Genesee County program shows what can be done for victims when their true needs are prioritized from day one throughout the process. The Mission Statement of Genesee County's unique Criminal Justice System says:

> The Mission... is to promote the public good and safety by seeking solutions to crime which preserve life, protect property, hold those who violate the public trust accountable, and give standing to victims. This is accomplished through:

Community participation
Crime prevention
Education, and
Monitoring and assessing the criminal justice system.

The statement goes on to stress that it is "accountable to the offender, victim, and the community-at-large." It sounds so obvious that justice should be just that, and yet how unusual that approach is!

While US justice systems have gone mad with skyrocketing incarceration rates, Genesee County has maintained its unique and terribly useful approach.

Tim and Amy Coursen: Victims Take Charge

This story (Evers, 1998) started like many others. Tim Coursen and his wife Amy Miller woke up to strange noises in their house. She stayed upstairs with their five-year-old daughter while Tim went down to investigate. He found two intruders and gave chase. As they fled, one of the intruders threatened him with a utility knife.

The after-effects were profound. Their daughter began having nightmares. Both parents struggled for sleep, hearing menace in every creak in the house at night. When they heard that the intruders had been captured, Tim and Amy requested a meeting with them. The older of the two, Jason, agreed to the meeting reluctantly. Bruce Kittle, the mediator, warned the Coursen family not to expect too much of the meeting as Bruce seemed immature and closed off.

But when Tim told Jason of his experience of that evening, his reaction, his pain and his subsequent paranoia, Jason opened up with his perspective. He and his pal had not been thinking of the people in the house, just their search for "stuff." The Coursen's daughter reacted strongly in the meeting, and her fear reaction got across to Jason what he had done to an innocent child. They agreed on restitution by Jason, with work in a local homeless shelter plus repairs around their home, and later repeated the process with the other offender.

Tim and Amy felt that although neither of their offenders "got it" completely, the process they went through face to face honoured and respected their needs, while the court process left them out and kept them vulnerable. The meetings helped the family in their recovery. This is a story repeated again and again: whatever the impact on offenders, well-conducted meetings are a support to victim healing, and restore power to them by recognizing their wrong. From having their own life space violated, they are now given a significant place in the life space of the offender, and this experience restores their sense of balance, and of self-respect.

Confronting the Demons

A Texas program focussed entirely on victims has a waiting list of 300 victims wanting to meet their offenders. About half are the loved ones of murder victims, and another 25 percent are survivors of violent crimes: attempted murder, muggings or sexual assaults. So much for the myth that transformative justice doesn't work for victims of violent crimes, and that they wouldn't want it! Dave Doerfler, director of the Texas program says that victims have discovered within themselves the need to meet the person who caused them so much pain. Doerfler's program has months of preparation in which victims have many kinds of opportunities to express their grief and anger: structured grieving.

Some advocates for battered wives and for victims of sexual violence argue that such meetings may roll back the progress toward recognizing the seriousness of these crimes. But as long as the seriousness is recognized in some appropriate way, and advocacy and control are included with transformative meetings, there is more healing in such meetings than in the power down court system that isolates victims as well as offenders. As for offenders, many of our stories show the powerful impact meeting a real victim and hearing and seeing their experience through their ears and eyes can have on them.

Michelle C. is another victim who took charge of her own life. She was so traumatized by abuse as a child that she had her tubes tied to be sure she never violated a child of hers. Her father and several older brothers beat her regularly. One of the brothers, Robert, abused her sexually. A few years ago, Robert was sent to prison. At first Michelle believed the story that he was sent away for drunk driving but Michelle discovered he was actually in prison for violating another child!

The statute of limitations had expired on her violation, and there was nothing that could be done legally to help Michelle, within our retributive system. But she wrote letters that went in his files, and through a healing justice program requested a meeting with him, since she lived in fear of his coming out and contacting her outside. She went into therapy and gained the courage to confront him. The mediation service gained Robert's consent to a meeting with Michelle, although he still denied having victimized her. But when they finally met in the prison, Robert broke down and admitted his guilt. More than this, he gave her vital information on the extent and duration of the abuse, details which she had suppressed, and which were a help in her further healing.

Their agreement prohibited him from contact with her, and required that he get sex offender treatment, and help pay for her therapy. Michelle walked out proud, happy, and relieved. In confronting her demons, she had relieved her own fear, advanced her brother's chances of growing toward responsibility, and done much to prevent anguish for other child victims. Results like these are not guaranteed, but without transformative approaches, they are impossible.

The Richmond Unity Walk

Dick Ruffin's great grandfather Edmund Ruffin fired the shot at Fort Sumter that started the American Civil War (Henderson, 1996). Edmund Ruffin was such a true believer in the cause of the Confederacy that when the war was finally lost, he wrapped himself in the Confederate flag and shot himself. Dick Ruffin was brought up steeped in pride in his ancestor's passion for slavery, secession, and agriculture. The humiliations of the South were burned deeply into his subconscious and into his values.

An unlikely beginning for Dick to become head of the Moral Rearmament movement in the USA and a leader in one of the most innovative steps ever taken to heal the terrible alienation that that history has left between Blacks and Whites. Yet as he grew older, Dick Ruffin became aware that his great-grandfather had never grasped that Black Americans were human beings with lives and feelings just as real, diverse, deep and profound as those of White Americans. A whole new vista opened for him, and he wrote an article in the Richmond Virginia newspaper trying to describe this new understanding. Much of that understanding evolved from his participation in the Richmond Unity Walk and all that led up to it.

Richmond, Virginia, was equally unlikely to be the site for a creative act bridging the Black-White barriers in the American south. Richmond was proud of being the capital of the Confederacy, and proud of its many statues on Monument Avenue, each one to honour some Confederate hero of the Civil War.

Yet individuals in Richmond, Virginia began laying the groundwork for transformation in the '70s. For many years I have said, "Individuals can and do make a difference. Every change I have succeeded in could have been lost had one or two of us dropped out; and every change I have failed to

achieve might have made it with one or two more shoulders to the wheel."
Nor can we predict who those individuals may be. In Richmond, Virginia,
part of the change was electoral, when in 1977 Black Americans became
a majority of the City Council and Henry Marsh III became its first Black
mayor. With Whites still in control of the economic sector, polarization
threatened. But a number of individuals determined to build bridges over
the chasm.

Cleiland Donnan, a White businesswoman rooted in the community,
began reaching out to Black residents. When she invited a Black couple to
her home for the first time, she was anxious, and again when she invited
Black friends to her exclusive club. Through these friendships, she began
to understand the legacy of the anguish of slavery. She saw how self-righteous
and wrong her arrogant assumption had been that she was entitled to all
her privileges, and Blacks deserved their deprivations. Collie and Audrey
Burton, Whites who had organized the voter registration drive that helped
create the Black majority on City Council, had bridging of their own to do.
They managed to reach out to Joyce and Howe Todd, Whites high in the
city government whose values seemed very alien to theirs. Dr. Paige
Chargois, an African American Baptist minister reached from the Black
community, promoting dialogue across races among youth, and organizing
a dialogue between the White Junior League and the Coalition of a hundred
Black Women.

Out of these trailblazers, "Hope in the Cities" was born, which sponsored
forums from 1991 on. From all of these came a Conference in 1993,
called, "Healing the Heart of America — An Honest Conversation on Race,
Reconciliation and Responsibility." Hundreds of people came from over
50 American urban areas, and twenty other countries.

A highlight of the Conference was the Richmond Unity Walk. Over
500 people walked in 95 degree Fahrenheit heat, stopping at key sites
along the two-mile route. These sites honoured the suffering of all people
from the heritage of racism and oppression and division. Confederate War
sites, Native American suffering, and the tragedies of slavery were all
acknowledged in one mighty vista of the universality of suffering, when we
are divided from one another.

The walk began with a Native American ceremony. An actor recited
the words of Patrick Henry over freedom versus slavery, and then an actress
re-enacted the suicide of a slave who hurled herself into a well after losing
22 children to slavery. Flowers were dropped on the harbour water where

so many slaves had perished in the "middle passage." This occurred in the shadow of a monument to a Confederate soldier, and the shadow of common grief came through to all. The walk ended with each walker writing down to burn whatever might stop them from carrying forward an honest conversation on race, reconciliation and responsibility.

The impact of the Richmond Unity Walk across America has been profound. But locally one remarkable event occurred. Arthur Ashe, the famous and distinguished Black tennis star, had grown up in Richmond, Virginia. As a child, he had been denied access to the city's public tennis courts because of the colour of his skin. When the Richmond Walk occurred, Arthur watched plans for it with interest from his deathbed, for he was dying of AIDS, contracted from a blood transfusion.

In 1995, it was proposed that a statue to Arthur Ashe be erected on Monument Avenue, already graced with so many White Confederacy heroes. Debate was hot among both races over this mix: even Blacks questioned the propriety of this combination. A hundred and eighty people spoke at the public hearing on the monument to Ashe. But Arthur Corcoran on behalf of "Hope in the Cities" spoke for reconciliation, and urged the city to be more concerned with a process that would enhance racial understanding and peace, than with the precise site outcome. He concluded, "Let us use this opportunity to develop a process by which we may embrace the triumphs and tragedies of our common history in a spirit of humility, repentance, and forgiveness."

With little difficulty the Council unanimously recommended that the statue to Ashe be accorded a prominent place on Monument Avenue. In the groundbreaking ceremony, Mayor Young said that this event would bury the history of racial conflict in their city.

A remarkable story, but how is this a story of transformative justice? Justice is not just about someone who stole ten dollars in the street. Justice is about Native and Black babies dying because we have not provided them with the bare essentials of life. Justice is about job discrimination by race. Justice is about the heritage of slavery, and of workers dying of black lung disease. Justice is about education and health taken from the poor. Justice is about the many ways in which we destroyed whole tribes and communities of indigenous people. And until we come to terms with these injustices, the charades that pass for justice in our court system are petty games of children. So Richmond is a powerful act of transformative justice applied to some of the underlying injustices which link both distributive injustice and street crime. The Richmond miracle shows that when we are willing to bridge, we can find new keys to transformation.

Our next chapter takes us a step further into process. For one of the key magic potions of transformative justice is the magic of forgiveness. Forgiveness is an essential ingredient of any transformation, but forgiveness of large harms requires an act of will, which is spiritual. Those who catch the spirit of it sail with the gale of the Holy Spirit. Let's see how it works.

Chapter 6

That "F" Word:
Where Does Forgiveness Come In?

Forgiveness has been our biggest challenge throughout human history. One of the earliest stories about it is in the Old Testament, in the book of the prophet Hosea. Hosea lived about the seventh century BC, and like most prophets, he preached a lot about the unfaithfulness of the Israelites to their God Jehovah. I used to think all those Old Testament passages about a jealous God and a people who were always setting up false idols and bowing down before graven images were hopelessly dated and irrelevant. But I have come to recognize that the commandment about not worshipping false idols is the most contemporary of all.

What is it but worshipping a false idol when we violate the needs of our families for the commands of corporations? What is it but worshipping graven images when we put the value of stocks, shares, and money above the agony of homeless brothers and sisters in the street? We are the Israelites of today, and new cars, television sets, designer clothes, wasteful restaurants, and fancy vacations are among our graven images and golden calves.

What does all this have to do with transformative justice in general and forgiveness in particular? Quite a lot! We cannot experience transformative justice till we are willing to let go of our particular graven images. And a part of letting go is both giving and receiving forgiveness to others caught up in this seductive illness, as well as others who have hurt us in other ways (Henderson, 1996).

The Bible certainly talks a lot about revenge. But Hosea is one of the earliest prophets who understood another side of the picture: in spite of our hoarding the divine gifts at the cost of our brothers' and sisters' survival, God is willing to forgive us. We only need to forgive others in order to be able to experience that wonderful gift. Hosea tells an amazing story, and scholars disagree over whether it is meant literally, or only as a parable of the divine love and forgiveness. But most believe that it is both: that Hosea did indeed love and take a woman who was or became a harlot, and that he found the divine power to forgive her, and redeem her from the fallen state into which she had slid. In this experience, he saw that that is exactly what God wanted for his Chosen People of Israel: that though they had been in harlotry, he would redeem them, forgive them, and take them unto Himself again:

> When Israel was a child, I loved him, and out of Egypt I called my son. The more I called them, the more they went from me; they kept sacrificing to the Baals, and burning incense to the idols. Yet it was I who taught Ephraim to walk. I took them up in my arms; but they did not know that I healed them. I led them with cords of compassion, with the bands of love, and I became to them as one who eases the yoke on their jaws, and I bent down to them and fed them...
>
>   My people are bent on turning away from me, so they are appointed to the yoke... Yet how can I give you up, O Ephraim! How can I hand you over, O Israel! ... My heart recoils within me, my compassion grows warm and tender. I will not execute my fierce anger. I will not again destroy Ephraim. For I am God and not man, the Holy One in your midst, and I will not come to destroy (Amos 11).

The recognition that we are called to forgiveness goes back and back and back through all history, along with the temptation to take vengeance into our own hands, over the many injustices of life and our fellow dwellers on this planet. All of us wrestle again and again with these kinds of questions:

"If I forgive, am I CONDONING the wrong?"
   "If I forgive, am I being disloyal to my dead child?"

"I want to forgive, but how can I feel forgiving toward someone who did that?"

"Why should the world expect me to forgive what was done to me, and do nothing to stop that person from doing it to others, but get all worked up over correcting other wrongs that don't seem very big to me?"

"I thought I had forgiven, but then something happened that brought it all back, and I fell right back where I was before I had tried to forgive; was my forgiveness real?"

These are advanced questions, with no easy answers. Forgiveness is rightly a topic for whole books in itself, and has fascinated me for years. I believe forgiveness is one of the most fundamental lessons we are called to practice in this life. But this is not a book about theology or just about forgiveness: it is a book about stories, stories that transform. Forgiveness is a key power in such transformation, so let's hear some of the great stories about it, and then have a brief look at whether they answer any of the questions above.

But first, why in the title of this chapter did I call forgiveness "the F word?" I learned that from Wilma Dirksen, the amazing Mennonite woman whose daughter was murdered and who leads a project and edits a magazine, *Pathways*, to help victims find healing in something other than endless unsatiated revenge. Wilma says we do a lot of damage to victims by telling them they have to forgive.

It is not for Wilma or me to tell a murder victim (for the murdered person is not the only "murder victim"; their families are murder victims too) what they must do, especially if I have not walked their path of pain fully and deeply with them. So murder victims feel re-violated by superficial friends who, without journeying with them to the depths of their grief, preach the word "forgiveness" at them. It is in protest at this sanctimonious preaching that some murder victims call forgiveness "the F word."

We have to tread carefully to avoid that sanctimoniousness, for grief is deep and profound and healthy, and it ill behoves those of us who have not walked in it and have not given our utmost to right its wrongs to preach forgiveness to its most wounded travellers. So without preaching, let's hear some stories of people who found healing in the forgiveness journey. We begin with stories of personal violations that are not physically violent. The vast majority of life's wrongs are in this category, and they are far more challenging than society acknowledges. But the challenge of physical violence and even murder is something else, so our second section will look at that. Finally in this chapter, we look at how groups can forgive the congenital violence of ongoing racism and even genocide. We conclude by taking a glimpse at the gift to be found in walking the path of forgiveness, after our loss of innocence in violation.

Forgiving Our Personal Violations

The sense of being taken advantage of, of having our kindness and generosity exploited, our trust violated, and our rights trampled upon, outrages every one of us. We begin with some stories where that is the key problem. We will move later to stories of heroic forgiveness which seem Herculean to the beginner, but we hope the stories in this section will remind us that every one of us can walk the path of forgiveness. All it takes is the resolve to take that first step, and keep walking.

An Old Quaker Story of Neighbours

This is an old but true story of two Quaker farm families in New Jersey who were neighbours, and belonged to the same Quaker Meeting (Crowe, 1995). Their farms adjoined, separated only by a stream. The younger farmer decided to divert the stream where it flowed through his land, to irrigate the land better. The older farmer visited him to explain that he was angry, for his land badly needed this diverted water. The younger farmer refused to give in, and after the manner of Friends, the issue was brought to the Meeting for care.

The local Meeting was unable to find a solution, so it went on to the Quarterly Meeting and then the Yearly Meeting. The longer the issue remained unresolved, the worse relations became between the two families. Finally, they had stopped speaking altogether.

Then one evening a visiting preacher stopped at the older farmer's home, asking for lodging for the night. The family was honoured, and enjoyed the wise presence of their guest. In the course of the evening meal, the farmer told the story of their difficult neighbour, and asked for advice. The preacher responded, after a thoughtful pause, with these words, "More is expected of some of us than others."

The farmer went to bed pondering those words. Next morning, he assembled a basin, a towel and soap. He walked to his neighbour's home, and knocked on their door. The young farmer's wife was startled to see their "enemy," and so early at that! The visitor asked to see his antagonist, and the wife replied he was still in bed. The visitor still wanted to see him, and proceeded upstairs to the bedroom. Determined to carry out his mission, the older farmer declared, "Friend, I have come to wash thy feet."

Later in the day, the astonished younger farmer brought his whole family over to visit. The relationship had been restored, and in a new spirit of co-operation, a solution was found. These two men eventually established a new Quaker Meeting in their area.

"More is asked of some of us than others." What a wonderful escape from the self-righteousness that mires us into entrenched conflict positions! Every one of these stories of forgiveness exemplifies people rising to those challenging words, "More is asked of some of us than others."

Organizations Can Do It Too: A Thrift Shop Story

The Board of our charitable organization, the Circle of Friendship, was being faced with a seemingly impossible set of demands from a former employee who had left us with bad feelings. This was the most challenging issue facing us at our Annual Board Meeting. Kathleen was an educated woman with a Master's degree in social work, who had been hired by our previous Director, Robert. The financial difficulties we faced had finally forced us to let Robert go and hire Jenny in his place. Jenny was a former volunteer who lacked professional training, but had the abilities we needed and was both willing and able to work for a minimal salary till we could recover financial stability.

Robert had felt some understandable anger at being let go, and had passed his anger on to Kathleen. The two of them had also discussed Jenny, who Robert saw as taking away his job by willingness to work for a substandard wage. He warned Kathleen that Jenny would find some excuse to get rid of Kathleen.

This set the stage for conflict between Kathleen and Jenny. Kathleen balked completely when Jenny suggested minor changes in the report forms used. The problems were exacerbated because our main office was in the North and Kathleen's field office base was a thousand miles away in the deep South. Fortunately Jenny was due for a field trip south, so she determined to try a face to face meeting with Kathleen to build a relationship and solve the incipient problems. They included Marie and Reg Thomson in the meeting, two dedicated volunteers who organized large-scale donations of clothes for the needy families we served in the area. The meeting went well and the outstanding issues, forms and all, seemed to be resolved. But as often happens, the underlying issues were not addressed because no one was willing to speak to them, and some were not even aware of them.

A few months later another crisis developed. Kathleen fell ill for awhile, and after she returned she refused to submit any work reports, and became so openly insubordinate that after due consultation with the Board, Jenny felt she had no choice but to fire her. Kathleen had also been keeping an eye on a thrift shop we were running there. At about this time, Kathleen closed it down, saying we had not paid sufficient rent for it. She moved all the clothes and books and equipment to the house of her mother, who had recently died. She also alleged we owed her 50 dollars in moving costs, plus ten dollars a day storage, a wholly outrageous amount for storage — even had we authorized it — in this very poor rural area where rents were extremely low.

This was the situation that confronted us at the Board Meeting. Jenny had consulted a lawyer, who got a very hostile reaction from Kathleen, and made no further progress. I came to the Board Meeting knowing nothing more than what I had read in formal reports. But I also came fresh from reading an exciting article in Fellowship magazine about a remarkable businessman named Arthur Friedman who decided one day to run his business wholly on trust! He told his employees to ask for as much money as they felt they were worth, to take cash as needed, to work the hours they felt appropriate, and only do the jobs they felt should be required of them.

Friedman found his employees rose magnificently to this challenge, and he even treated bad accounts in the same friendly manner: he would write threatening to cancel the bill after a certain period! If the account was unpaid, he first wrote them commenting that he was interested they had decided not to pay his bill, and would appreciate their taking a moment to tell him why. Time after time, when people tested his trust, he rose to the occasion by trusting them, and they rose in turn, by responding to his trust.

Inspired by this example, I couldn't help thinking that the logical solution to our problem was to trust Kathleen to do the right thing with the clothes. By venturing out in trust with her, we could hope to revive in her the spirit of concern for the poor that was part of her original motivation for going to work for us.

The first people I met at the Retreat Centre where our Board Meeting was being held were Marie and Reg Thomson, the volunteers who had helped to collect so many of the clothes at the Thrift Centre. They were by now personal friends of Kathleen's, but also close to Jenny and to our new President, Mildred. The Thomsons were rare and wonderful people. Reg's idea of a fun hobby was going around buying defunct TV sets as cheaply as possible, repairing them, and distributing them through the Thrift Shop as windows to the outside world for the impoverished mostly Black families in the rural isolated areas we serve.

In discussing the problem with the Thomsons, I explained my idea and showed them the article that had inspired me. They loved the article, the idea, and the whole vision behind both. Far from being worried about the gifts they had lovingly laboured to gather, Reg explained that his philosophy was, "A gift once given is given. You don't question it, for that's not giving freely." There was no way Kathleen could use the mountain of clothes of all sizes for herself, even had she been so minded. Why not trust her to do the right thing with them, to get them to the poor in some way? Reg became so enthused about the idea as we discussed it that he was soon explaining it better than I could, and adding his own ideas.

By this time Jenny, Mildred, and another Board member had arrived, and we included them in our brainstorming. They expressed some skepticism, but Jenny especially was warm to any peaceful resolution. Marie Thomson now felt free to tell Jenny that back of Kathleen's difficult behaviour was a statement she had once made to Marie; "I'm not taking orders from any secretary." Jenny took this with great graciousness, and was glad to understand more of Kathleen's resistance to her. Back of it were generations of Blacks with greater education and qualifications having to work under less qualified Whites. Jenny could understand and accept this.

The rest of the Board arrived later that evening, and our meetings began next morning. So eight of us sat around the breakfast table, and Mildred introduced the difficult subject. Mildred and Jenny gave an excellent summary of the whole history of our difficulties. Going through it revived angry feelings, as each unreasonable act by Kathleen was recited. As someone less involved, I struggled to listen for the underlying message behind the whole story.

When Jenny and Mildred had finished the history, I was invited to present my ideas. I began by saying it was most important that Jenny and Mildred felt the full support of all of us in whatever course we took. It must be clear that we all sympathized fully with the difficulties they had experienced, and that we respected the way they had coped with these. I felt it was essential that we try to find a course we could agree on with consensus instead of voting. After all, what use is it to try for reconciliation, while putting one another down in the way we reached the decision?

I continued, "I've had some practice in trying to hear the underlying message in a group discussion. What I keep hearing here is a very frustrated person playing a game — and the essence of the game is to provoke and antagonize. As long as we responded with anger and counter-moves, the game player could only win. She was getting the rise out of us that she wanted."

When Jenny had first heard the proposal Friday from me, she had said, "But that would grate on me, giving the clothes to her!"

My response was "Exactly, Jenny! As long as she knows she can grate on you, she will go on finding ways of doing it. But if we can make clear that nothing she can do will grate on us, because we are giving up the hostilities approach, then she too will lose interest in finding tactics to irritate." Jenny caught onto this as a revelation, and was big enough to grow with it.

As I presented the idea Saturday morning, everyone was ripe for it. No one wanted a bellicose resolution, and we were beginning to get caught up with enthusiasm for this new creative approach to our conflict. Almost immediately there was a subtle shift from, "What should we do?" to, "How can we carry this idea out in the right way?"

In the course of discussing the hows, we felt it would be best if someone could convey the message to Kathleen in a friendly way. A letter should go from the Board, but should someone go with the letter? If so, it was clear it should not be Jenny or Mildred, toward whom Kathleen nourished so many unhappy feelings.

Reg spoke up and said, "We've always been close to Kathleen, and Marie and I could drive up and see her, and bring her the letter." As Marie agreed with him on this, and everyone was enthusiastic and grateful, Mildred added that of all people to carry such a message, the Thomsons were ideal since they were close to Kathleen and had also given so many of the clothes. They further offered to go that very afternoon, a two hour drive each way, and return by evening with a report to us, so that possibly the whole sad episode could be finished before our weekend Board Meeting was over.

Two questions remained to be settled: the 50-dollar moving charge that Kathleen was demanding, and the writing of the letter. We also needed to see about reclaiming our books and assets from the Thrift Shop, which included a tape recorder, camera, and other relatively valuable property of ours, that Kathleen was holding. At this point, we felt that the group had been so generous, I would have been willing to put up the 50 dollars personally sooner than see the plan come to grief over this. Reg made the same offer before I could speak up.

But Jenny said, "No, Kathleen made that charge when she was working for us, and it is a routine part of her employment that we pay all such charges. As long as she produces a slip showing she paid that, we should definitely refund her out of our money." So another potential contentious issue was resolved with astonishing ease. The spirit was gathering momentum!

Normally Mildred as President would have written the letter, but I knew that after all she had been through with Kathleen, she might have some difficulty phrasing it in the spirit we had discussed. To my surprise, she asked me to word the letter for all of us. But before I was sent off to tackle this challenge, Mildred said, "I just want to add that Kathleen had an uncommonly hard time with a major operation, and the death of her mother, in the past few months. I lost my own mother recently, and I know what a hurdle that is." So Mildred, who as a dedicated volunteer had suffered so much from a lot of unreasonable behaviour by Kathleen, ended this session on a note of deep human solidarity with Kathleen, for a common human trauma they had each experienced in their own lives.

The sense of mutual love and support in our group was so real you could almost touch it at this point. They sent me off to write the letter without letting me so much as move my dishes to the kitchen. There was a spirit of joy and warmth, which grew from a large challenge, responded to in an even larger spirit.

My draft was approved immediately, and the Thomsons were sent on their mission with all our blessings and prayers. They returned that afternoon to relieve our suspense with a glowing report. Kathleen had read our letter, and her first reaction was whether we didn't really want the clothes back?

"No," responded Reg, "As we said in the letter, Kathleen, all of us have complete confidence that you will dispose of them in the spirit of our shared concern for the poor who need them." Kathleen immediately said she would give the clothes next day to a community group we all respected. She returned all our other things, and was happy about clearing up the 50 dollars, and the spirit of our whole letter.

Kathleen and the Thomsons went out together for a hamburger, chatted about old times, and agreed to get together for Thanksgiving. Finally, as they were parting, she added, "When I get my things together again, I think some time I will write in and adopt one of the families our project helps." Reconciliation like this was beyond our fondest dreams. I believe the step we took was valid regardless of the response it evoked, but Kathleen's warm response gave all of us a deep sense of the growth we had gained as a group and as individuals: growth in unity, in understanding, and in the power of forgiving, trusting love. As St. Francis put it so well, "For it is in giving that we receive."

A Chocolate Mint

With stories coming of murder victims forgiving and the one above of a farmer washing the feet of his opponent, some of you may be thinking all this is out of your league. Such heroic acts seem beyond the ken of normality. So here is a story from my life, one which happened to me, and which certainly influenced my future development. It is a modest chocolate mint sized story from my own experience.

My career in the field of criminal justice has been blighted by two traumatic job losses, when I was the head of major agencies I had founded or built up from disastrous conditions. The second story happened in 1990. I had been working for three years to build from a shattered shell a strong agency willing to respect and empower clients, and to speak out on crucial issues affecting them. My Board and I had built a strong Advocacy Committee, had spoken out to the press again and again, and I had managed in hard times to build the beleaguered budget up 50 percent so we could almost afford to meet the thousands of needy clients who walked through our doors.

My Board had invited me to include clients in every aspect of the agency's business, not just as lowly clients in an agency totem pole. A number of my inherited staff supported me in this, but others wanted to go back to the safe old days when a client was a client was a client, and only got beyond the waiting room as a statistic in some "helping" office. People in the Provincial office were jealous of our success, and angry at our radical positions on issues. So although I was not fully aware of it, our work was actually being plotted against both within the agency and outside it. My Board chair, as events began to unfold, said that this whole thing sounded like a wild paranoid fantasy on my part, so many people were plotting against us in general and me in particular — except it was real. Not only was it real, but I was so far from paranoid fantasies that in my naive faith in the goodwill of those around me, I anticipated very little of its coming.

The issue that gave our opponents a chance to run wild was Joe Fredericks. Joe was a lifelong sexual offender toward children, on the rare occasions when he had lived outside of institutions. Moreover, Joe had openly told me these facts about himself. Joe was one of 10,000 clients who walked through our doors, and it was only thanks to his offer to work on our Advocacy Committee that I met him. He wanted to speak about the need for treatment for people like him, and the need to educate kids to be warned about sexual predators. It sounded good to me, and it was not easy to find offenders who wanted to work on the broad issues behind their situations. Most of them felt the odds against them were so heavy, they only wanted to escape individually from their burdens, and integrate into mainstream society as far as they were able.

So I was delighted that Joe wanted to speak out and work on such important issues. But Joe didn't want to stop there. He also wanted to tell young people about who he was, what he had been through, and the things they had to look out for. It sounded interesting but tricky. However as I was talking with Joe, a Catholic youth group approached me which had been running an "Inner City Awareness Program." They wanted to revitalize it and improve it, with a strong component about criminal justice.

The two needs seemed to fit perfectly. Inner City Awareness Programs after all are not for visiting the flowers in the park: they are for learning about the tough realities of inner city life, so those who participate know what they are walking into. But just to be extra sure, we took into consideration two other factors. All the youth in the program were thirteen or over; Joe's sexual impulses had been visited on kids eleven and under. Secondly, whenever the groups visited our agency, at least two other adults were present at all times, usually three: a mature staff-person of mine, the class teacher, and the Catholic Program Co-ordinator.

Joe presented about four times to different groups visiting our agency, and our staff-person added a presentation on his experience with the system. The group also visited a local jail, to complete their introduction to the world of criminal justice. Evaluations of those sessions always gave Joe's presentation high marks as memorable, sincere, and valuable. In fact to this day no one associated with the program itself ever complained about it or considered it anything other than a very worthwhile experience, beneficial to the youth and to Joe himself. For once in his pathetic life, he was able to contribute something positive to the world! Joe himself was the eleventh child in a multi-problem family and spent his childhood in abusive foster homes and even more abusive institutions, being molested himself.

Then came summer. School was out and the sessions were over. Joe visited me once, asking for something else to do but I couldn't come up with anything that concrete. He disappeared for some weeks, but I hardly noticed, as my life was so full that I barely knew who he was. I had no legal responsibility for him and, except as he was my brother in Christ, no moral responsibility either. All we had done was above and beyond the call of our multifarious duties.

The next thing I knew was a news bulletin. Joe was wanted for the disappearance and death of Christopher Stephenson, an eleven-year-old child from Brampton! I was shocked, but knew Joe so slightly that it never occurred to me how much this event would impact on my life. The press was looking for a scapegoat beyond Joe, parole was looking for anything to divert attention from them, and my opponents were looking for an issue. The result was that our little program began to be featured as a major part of the scene. I, who had always handled the press so well, was denied the right to speak to them on behalf of the agency, because it was my reputation that was on the line. A young reporter from a major local paper, Stacey Hall, made the issue of Joe's involvement with my agency her cause!

The Board sensibly enough appointed their chair as our press representative. Steve was an ideal choice except for one thing: very busy in court, he was unavailable for most of the press' calls. This situation only maddened the press more, and made them feel we were hiding something. I couldn't talk to them, and Steve was seldom available. Stacey wrote articles distorting the situation, attacking us more clearly all the time. The paper even editorialized against us! Yet they had never been given our experience of the facts. My Board had probed every moment of Joe's involvement in every aspect of the agency, and had solid information showing how harmless it was. Finally, to my relief, the Board agreed I could meet with Stacey, as long as Steve, the Board Chair, was present as well.

Steve was an early-bird and so was I. To meet our busy schedules, we set a breakfast meeting in my office, and I made homemade pastries to show my goodwill, and my lack of animosity despite her attacks. The meeting went well. Backed by Steve, I told the story from the beginning. Toward the end of the meeting, Stacey asked a question. "Don't be embarrassed by this. Joe called one of his psychiatrists at one institution Mom. Is it true that he called you that?"

I acknowledged that he did, and explained the background. After he had been accused, before I knew whether he was guilty or not, he had begged for visits from me, and I had visited him from time to time in the jail. On one occasion, as I stared at a tattoo on his arm with the words "I love Mom" inside a heart, I thought of the irony of such a tattoo on this man who had never known a mother's love. His mentally challenged mother had rejected him at birth, and none of his family had ever responded to his desperate reaching out to them.

As I looked at that tattoo, which I had never seen before, I could almost anticipate the request coming. A moment later, it came. "I have to ask you something. It sounds kind of crazy, and if you say No I understand. I expect you will say No. But it would mean so much to me if you could — would you and your husband consider adopting me?"

It was a crazy request from a man in his 40s only eleven years younger than I was, a man accused of a notorious murder, a man who had nothing going for him. But I had always been a risk-taker and I didn't want to hurt him with an outright rejection, so I said I would discuss it with Ray and get back to him. I relied on my sensible husband to say No, but to my surprise, Ray's reaction was, "Legal adoption makes no sense. But if he wants to regard us as family in the way our friends are Aunt Marge and Uncle Dick to our kids, that seems fine." But Joe had taken this modest offer far beyond its intent, and had added fuel to the fire by calling the agency and asking through some of my hostile employees for his "Mom." So I gave this background to the reporter, and the meeting ended on such an amicable note I felt we had defused the attacks successfully.

The paper next day was another shock to my system. The article's title screamed: "'He Calls Me Mommy,' Says Director." Catchy, as headlines of articles are meant to be, and of course, not written by Stacey herself — headlines are written by higher-ups, and are often inaccurate reflections of article content. But what damage they can do, as this one did! The article itself was still nasty enough; although it had a few palliatives from the many facts we had given her, it was clear Stacey had used our trust and abused it to continue her attacks. My homemade food sat ill in my own stomach. Betrayal of hospitality may seem a small thing in such a large scene of horrors, but betrayal of trust given, especially trust given to someone who has already hurt you, is never a small thing.

The title was brutally offensive in two ways, beyond the betrayal of trust in the whole article. The title implied that I had bragged about the parental aspect of my relationship with Joe, a highly unprofessional, inappropriate and silly thing to do. The fact was, I had simply replied honestly to Stacey's probing question, and put the use of the word "Mom" in context. To say "Yes," honestly to her question about it was a very different thing than to initiate proudly the statement, "He calls me Mom."

Secondly, there is a vast difference between the words Mom and Mommy in our culture. Mommy is an affectionate diminutive used for the most part by very young children, expressive of a highly dependent relationship. Mom is used by adults in many contexts. The distortion from Mom to Mommy was a huge one, and deeply offensive and shocking to me. I felt that, little consideration as Joe might deserve from any of us in this situation, given what by this time I knew he had done to Christopher, and given the ways in which his naive use of Mom to my staff had endangered my own position — nevertheless, the use of the word Mommy was grossly unfair to Joe. He was incredibly immature in many ways, but the idea that he would use a word limited to very young children demeaned him falsely.

I was furious, but there was nothing I could do. I was bound always by the directions of my Board, who had less press experience and sophistication than I did. As the situation worsened, their controls on me, while well meant, became stricter, and their opinion was that we should not challenge this article. Although in retrospect I would have changed our whole press approach in many ways, I am still not sure my approach would have been any more successful than theirs was — the dice were loaded against us. In any case, we didn't challenge this lethal article, and it played a major part in all the disasters that followed.

The dissidents on my staff spent hours organizing a vicious petition against me, with so many kinds of libel and slander, mutually contradictory in many cases, it was nauseating. Yet by using work hours to strong-arm signatures from the many naive new people we had just hired, with our increased funding for which I had worked so hard, they got signatures from about half the current staff and some departed disgruntled people. The new staff had had little chance to really know me, given the size of our organization and the number of hours it took me to deal with the crises from high need staff and the funding challenges, let alone the endless Joe Fredericks probes by Board Committees and others.

It still shocked me that so many would sign such a vicious letter, but I later learned a couple of things that explained it a little. First of all, the full absurdities of that long and contradictory letter, which accused me of everything short of sex crimes myself, were probably not included in the petition to fire me, which was bad enough, but was at least short enough that a sane person could sign it. Secondly, the approach of the dissidents had been typically bullying: two or three of the three leaders would get one person who had not yet signed into a room and plague them until they signed. One Black person who had refused to sign said they kept telling her how racist I was, which was the more crazy since I had devoted much of my life to the struggle for racial justice. But any argument would do, just so they could get another signature.

None of the complaints were brought to me or to the Personnel Committee. They waited till I was speaking overnight out of town, and hand delivered the vicious letter and petition to the homes of each Board member! There was something peculiarly ugly and intimidating about this intrusion into the homes of my Board, let alone the violation of my personal procedural rights. The whole experience was the more excruciating to me because I was so dedicated to not abusing my power over staff. I spent endless hours dealing with the emotional needs of staff in crises, my door was always open to them, and I was almost always the last to agree to manager requests to discipline staff in some way. I refused raises for myself, preferring to recommend that any resources go to raise lowest paid staff. I insisted on the rights of staff accused of anything to be present and to have full input into the accusations. The cruel letter would have been even more devastating to me if I had not learned from previous work situations that you cannot please everyone, and that the larger an organization, the more distorted truth is likely to become.

Nonetheless the attack had so many signatures and was so well orchestrated that my Board had to take it seriously, and I went through a hellish period, unable to do my job properly, and uncertain of my future. After exploring the facts fully and putting me through an agonizing hearing, including several sessions where, unlike accused criminals, I was not allowed to be present to correct misstatements in any way, my Board acquitted me. However, they tried to placate the opposition by refusing to dismiss any of the ringleaders, and on my own suggestion, they put a very competent neutral external administrator in charge for two months, during which time I was scheduled for a much needed three week vacation visit to our daughter in Scotland.

This was not enough to satisfy our Provincial opponents, who had been hand in glove with the dissident staff. The day I flew to England, the Provincial agency passed a motion to seize the agency, using an obscure clause which was intended only for financial malfeasance, changed the locks, hired security guards of their own, and grabbed our accounts! This was no small matter, since it left my Board helpless, with staff under Provincial control, me away, and our money in the hands of the opponents, who had just acknowledged that unlike our solid financial situation, their Board had wasted an inheritance of several million dollars over the past ten years!

The outcome of it all was that with the press loving this, my reputation was further smeared on front pages and major TV before I even knew it had happened. My Board waged a gallant struggle, in which I joined them on my return, for months, but I was the meat in the sandwich. I had to watch helplessly, as we were rejected by the courts until we had finished pursuing a loaded process which had us appealing to the Provincial Board against the Provincial Executive. Their Board were hardly likely to rule for us against their own Executive and Executive Director.

By the time it was over, we had wasted our energies on a process which made even the worst criminal courts seem just, and the loyal half of my staff had almost all been forced out. I had just hired seven ex-offenders for most of the new positions, and except for one in a temporary position, they were all eliminated ruthlessly, which seemed especially hypocritical for an agency supposedly there to serve ex-offenders. Apparently, "serving" did not include respecting or including. I was later to hear my appointed successor testify at the inquest into Christopher's death, "No, we at SJ (a pseudonym) Toronto would never allow a client to call himself a volunteer now. We might let them take out the garbage or something like that, but they could never call themselves SJ volunteers."

This was the wonderful world to which my opponents and the press had brought us. After the Provincial agency fired me, having got rid of my Board for refusing to do so, I had to pay about $30,000 in legal fees, mostly to defend myself against the attacks my own agency — which should have protected me — had set me up for. My dream job, a job I had worked so hard for and endured so much to make a success, had gone up in smoke. But most painful of all, I had had to watch the suffering of my husband and family, the anguish of my loyal Board, and the pain of the dismissed loyal employees. I knew that every one of them were suffering because they had been loyal to me, and had trusted me, and believed in the things I had stood for. Being helpless to prevent the suffering of others who suffer for being faithful to you has to be a supreme anguish, and I had a powerful dose of it.

The head of the Provincial agency was a particular challenge to me. A very bright man, George had a lot of common values with me. We were both strong reformers who stood up for prisoners' rights, and we both had good rapport with the press. I had dreamed of working well with George, and whenever I had gone to Kingston where he worked, I tried to meet with him and talk about common goals. Nevertheless, we differed in our ideas of how to treat people, and George had become furious with a number of people in the SJ Society, persuading Boards to get rid of them one by one.

The last he had eliminated, the previous Director of SJ Ontario, had been close to me, and I had helped Harold deal with his very traumatic and very public firing — almost an execution. George and the other staff he had lined up against Harold celebrated the Roman-games-style open event with refreshments and joy in the back of the room. George hated me for having supported Harold, although my support had been almost entirely emotional, and after the event, and I took no part in the debate or politics before.

Nevertheless, when George was finally appointed Executive Director of SJ Provincial, I went to his office, reached out and shook his slightly reluctant hand, promised my loyal support, and gave him my personal congratulations. I even offered to help him get a valuable educational grant, which he had blocked our agency in getting earlier. A year before, because I wondered if his jealousy of me were related to my having published six books and George having published none, I had offered to work with him on co-authoring a book on a topic of mutual interest.

Memories like those, and like George's weak but more kindly sidekick Bob drinking my coffee five days before the seizure, my guest in the office he was about to strip, sat ill with me. I had a lot of forgiving to do of George, Bob, and the dissident staff, and I worked hard at it. I even wrote letters of forgiveness, letters that were the harder because I knew that my opponents never had admitted, nor were ever likely to acknowledge, any of their cruelty or any wrong on their part. They had even thrown a party to celebrate, after stripping my office when they invaded! My letters did not deny my pain or my sense of right and wrong, but they offered all I could, my willingness to proceed in goodwill, and a desire to do no further harm in this wreckage of a situation.

So I felt I had done the hard work when, several years later, the inquest into Christopher's death finally arose. It had been delayed by Joe's legal appeals. As long as his appeal for a different legal conviction and sentence were pending, the inquest could not be held. Joe was not denying guilt, just the nature of the charge and his mental status. Happily for the press and their following public, which by this time had put Joe in the category with serial killers, although Christopher was his first and only murder victim, Joe was murdered in prison after about two years.

The murder, which came just after a magazine article demonizing him further had appeared, occurred in a prison shop with obviously inadequate protection for such a high profile child killer. The Warden in charge of the prison was quoted in the press as saying words to the effect of, "Good riddance to bad rubbish." Given that he was in charge of protecting many prisoners like Joe, I wrote and asked for an inquiry. While I was the last person to believe we could trust press reports, I felt that if the Warden who should have protected Joe had made such remarks, he should be relieved of duties, which required him to protect the lives of other Joes. My letter was never answered. However, the death of Joe enabled the inquest to proceed.

I give all this background partly to show the number of hurdles and blockades on the road to social reform, particularly in the highly charged area of criminal justice, and partly because the severity of work traumas tends to be underestimated. Newer research and articles are beginning to recognize how much pain unemployment and work stress in jobs bring; but the incredible anguish of the kinds of vicious political workplace assassinations I experienced twice still tends to be minimized. I was actually helped by the fact that I had been through a different but somewhat similar workplace firing some years before, over my human rights stands. I had lost my innocence there, but resolved to learn from it. Indeed I had learned, and the hard lessons of the Bail Program and my spiritual work on it helped me enormously in dealing with the SJ Society.

Never have I claimed that the workplace traumas I have experienced are in the league with the murder of one's child, or some of the other colossal traumas described here. But workplace traumas are far more serious than is generally understood. Canadian Mental Health Association lists unemployment alone as one of the major causes of depression and mental health breakdown, even without the traumas associated with personal attacks on one's integrity and value as a person, which are part of major workplace conflicts.

My own anguish was augmented by very public and brutal attacks on myself, and on all Board and staff and friends who dared to be loyal to me. There is a very special suffering in seeing those dear to one suffering because of oneself. The brutality of my treatment was expressed by the fact that three people who had recently drunk my coffee and pretended to be friendly guests invaded my office while I was on a much needed holiday in England, stripped my spiritual posters and personal pictures from the walls, and never allowed me back in to get them. I had to try to remember and name what was mine, including personal items such as letters from my daughter, which were never returned to me.

The public attacks were so vitriolic that years later on a call-in show in Alberta a caller from Ontario attacked me on this old issue. A decade after the original events, a *Toronto Star* columnist covering an unrelated issue devoted a whole column to a brutal personal attack on me, based on a very distorted version of the old story. Although originally Joe was only one of 10,000 clients, a person I barely knew, I was drawn in by the search for a scapegoat from a peripheral figure to a very central one in this tragedy.

The traumas also had a greater impact on me because I put so much stock in working to make the world a better place, rather than for money or status. They were in a very real sense my loss of innocence, my loss of the simple faith that if I did my very best to bring kindness and justice everywhere, the world would pay me back in kind. As a dear friend of mine, dying of brain cancer, used to say to me when we co-counselled, "Everyone's troubles are big enough for them." I hope this background enables readers to understand that, in this incredibly painful situation for the Stephenson family, there was so much pain and suffering to go around that it touched my life deeply too. In short, my experience with the SJ Society was traumatic enough to leave me some good forgiveness challenges.

The inquest was yet another ordeal to get through, long after it seemed I had surmounted so many. I had gone on to a new job and career, was building a new life, and we were struggling to recover financially from all we had been through, when the inquest opened it all up again, and dumped a new and larger financial load. One of the best law firms in Canada gave me rock-bottom prices, but nevertheless legal representation for a full week is no small cost. And I had to know that for a week I would be sitting in court with George and possibly Bob and possibly Sally (my appointed successor, whose testimony above has etched itself into my memory).

I would also sit with Christopher's bereaved parents, who understood nothing of my role, because all they knew of it was from distorted press reports. I knew their grief was greater than mine, but I wished they could understand that I had tried to prevent their sorrow, and I had experienced nothing but abuse and pain for my efforts.

So I had prepared myself for all the big challenges, and indeed that week was one that changed my life. I prayed the perfect prayer, more powerfully than ever before, because of my desperation. I prayed not that my truth would emerge, or that any of my opponents would learn anything, or that the press would be fair for a change, or that the costs would be minimized in any way. The prayer I prayed was that I could be given the grace to be and live love during that whole week. And although I did not fully attain that large dream, with God's grace I received enough power so that ever since when people say they see something in me, I know it has come partly from the experience of living in the Light for one deeply challenging week.

I was prepared to sit in a hostile courtroom in the presence of George, Bob, and Sally, and of many other bit players in the scene. But I had not expected all of what did meet me. When I walked in that first day, I was greeted by my wonderful lawyer, Marlys, and by her very capable student. They were saving a place near the front, where I was safely ensconced between the two of them. They even secured me a cup of tea. I felt wrapped in a cocoon of their protective caring, even before they did anything legal! I have always said that my definition of a good lawyer is one who is not only capable in court and all its preparation and knowledge and articulation, but who also demonstrates caring in visiting clients in jail, returning calls promptly, and interpreting in human terms the gobbledegook that passes for legal jargon and procedures. Marlys was such a lawyer, with trumps. Her support for me was part of God's answer to my prayer to be freed up to live love.

Nevertheless, supported as I was, I was not prepared for the fourth person in our little row, just on the other side of Marlys: Stacey Hall, the fledgling reporter who appeared to me to have pinned her enterprising career on a series of sensational attacks on me and my agency! Her career success appeared to have been gained at the expense of my career and my dream job. We had never talked since that dreadful article, and all that had followed, nor had she stayed on the story to gloat after it was all over, but that didn't matter a lot. Once we began rolling over the precipice, I had not devoted much thought to her, and it had never occurred to me that I might be called to play an active part in living forgiveness toward this bit player in our tragedy. I knew she had never intended harm, but I also knew her lethal attacks had played a major part in this colossal tragedy. So when I first saw her, and found her reaching across eagerly to greet me, I was almost struck dumb. This was NOT in my script for the terribly challenging week ahead!

But it was clear from the beginning that it was in her script. She was very young, and every bit of body language and the few words she said showed she wanted in her way to make peace. If I had not known before that she had never expected our whole shooting match to come down from her little peashooter, I knew it now. Yet I struggled with it that first day, and my body language was no more than reluctantly civil.

Our lawyers were busy making peace on more fronts than one. They were of course more easily able to be friendly to Stacey — in an inoffensive way to me. They were also close friends of the lawyer struggling for the rights of the Stephenson family, and both sets of lawyers were trying to help the Stephensons understand that I was not part of the enemy. Yet could they speak to the woman who had "adopted" their son's tormentor and killer? What a challenge for them! The Stephensons were at a new crisis of their own, for after verbal promises to pay the huge costs of a fulltime lawyer for themselves at the inquest for six months, the government had reneged, which would leave both the Stephensons and their law firm bankrupt!

Knowing the enormous capabilities of my lawyer Marlys, their lawyer wanted our support for their cause, and I had no difficulty authorizing Marlys to spend any reasonable amount of her time for me in working for their just demand to have their legal costs covered. So peace was being waged on multiple fronts. I didn't blame the Stephensons for their very natural failure to understand my role adequately. I just wanted to do what I could to bring healing nearer to their lives.

But this thing with Stacey — how on earth could I be expected to act in a peaceful and forgiving spirit toward that little reporter who had done so much damage, especially with that one terrible article, after I had reached out in so much trust and told the story so fully and so warmly? I prayed about it that first evening, and all I got back was the simple call to forgiveness: no exceptions. Bit players were part of it too. I sighed, and told my divine advisor I'd do my best. I knew by now that emotions are not the measure: forgiveness is a series of acts of will based on goodwill, based on the call to "Do good to those that hate you, and pray for them which despitefully use you, and persecute you" (Matthew 5:44). That had been part of my favourite text when I was a child, and I should have known God had something up the divine sleeve when I fell for that passage!

So I gritted my teeth, and approached Stacey next morning before court. She was eager to be approached, and made it easy. I knew I could not make peace without confronting any of the issues, so I expressed some of my disappointment at that article and the damage it had done. I was prepared to acknowledge, had we got that far, that by itself that article and her other work could not possibly have brought down an organization, had we not been part of a long pathological organizational history in the SJ Society.

But we never get that far. Each conversation moved us a few inches forward. Stacey met me more than halfway. She defended the reporting, arguing that the editor had cut out a lot of the good stuff, and that she had not, of course, chosen the title. We didn't agree, but it was obvious that she was sorry for the pain I had gone through and overwhelmed by her part in it, even though the magic words "I'm sorry," were not spoken. And she did let me get out of my system directly to her my distress over her article, which diluted some of my pain. I had had so little chance to express to any of my antagonists any of my feelings about the many injustices I had experienced in this whole crazy scene!

So things began to mend between us. The next day she rushed up to me and started telling me how much better the article she had just written was (from my viewpoint) than the one they had printed. She didn't want any new wounds between us. In fact, I had barely noted her latest article, and found it reasonable in the present context, and said so. But I was touched by her anxiety lest she wound me further and damage my tenuous faith in her capacity for fairness. It was increasingly clear to me that she was more vulnerable to me than I to her, at this juncture. This reversal of power toward the victim, who holds the power to choose to forgive, is a strange and wonderful factor in many forgiveness stories. And yet it is so hard for us victims to let go of our grudges for wrongs that can never now be reversed! The amazing truth is that in letting go we are not saying wrong is right; we are simply freeing up everyone to move forward, integrating into each of our lives some learning from the mutual tragedy.

By the end of the week, Stacey and I were talking fairly easily, and during one break, she offered me a chocolate mint. Now I was on a diet, and candy was one of those addictive things I was trying to stay away from. More significantly, it felt to me as if, by taking that chocolate mint, I would be accepting a symbol of the fairness of all that had gone down. I rebelled inwardly, and for a few crucial seconds, as I stared down at that chocolate mint, I said, "Come on, God! Are you seriously asking me to take one chocolate mint in exchange for the future of a whole agency; for the fact that high need clients will not be served there for years to come; for the lost jobs of over a dozen people; for the anguish of my Board and me; for all the lies and misrepresentations and cruelties and costs to all of us?"

The message I got back was short and simple, "Yup, that's the deal." I reached out and took that chocolate mint, and said "Thank you," quite sincerely to Stacey. Although emotions are not something we can depend on in great forgiveness stories, in this case, the bells and whistles went off for me and have never stopped tooting. I knew I was healed of any remaining animosity for Stacey, and that that was healing for her. That chocolate mint was a truer communion wafer than any I have ever had in any church or religious setting. It was a mint of forgiveness asked for, given, and received gratefully. To this day I never feel anything but warmth when I think of Stacey, and I see that chocolate mint, and taste the sweetness of its forgiving power. Most of my forgiveness experiences have been hard, one-way sledding uphill, with opponents not playing their part very well. Stacey taught me the incredible spiritual power of the two-way forgiveness game.

There are two little postscripts to this story. When I was on the stand on the last day of that incredible week, and felt God's presence with me all the way, it did not stop the press from interpreting my testimony in varied ways. Stacey's article was the most understanding and sympathetic of all, nor did that surprise me. By this time, I was honestly beyond caring much what any of the press said about any of this, but her article, showing that she finally got the spirit of what I had been trying to live, was an affirmation of the healing that forgiveness had brought to us.

The second postscript was that she phoned me one night that weekend, and began, "Ruth, if I had any part in hurting you, I just want you to know I'm really sorry." If! The word offended me again. Of course she had had a part in hurting me, and the if set me off again for a moment. But only for a moment. I tuned in again to the gigantic peace I had had since the chocolate mint bells and whistles had been going off, and I responded from my heart.

"Stacey," I said in a voice that was tender and warm, "It is all — really and absolutely — all right. I don't want you to worry about it any more. I'm all right, and it is all right, but thank you for calling." Those words felt absolutely true for me. They were not a denial of the pain and tragedy.

They were a statement of the spiritual "all rightness" that comes to us when we venture out in forgiveness.

What about Violence and Murder?

The above stories of forgiveness are challenging, and open the doors to a glimpse of a strange peace to be found when we forgive even unrighted wrongs. Now we are going to up the ante some more, and tell stories of forgiveness of physical violence and murder. In doing this, I want to stress that murder is the exceptional circumstance: only one percent of prisoners are in jail for any form of homicide. Most of those homicides are within the family or immediate circle of the victim. Murder by strangers is very rare, and not what the criminal justice system deals with, except about one in five hundred times. But it is murder by strangers that most people think of as the unforgivable act, and physical violence as the great terror. So let us look at whether people, including some people who were fairly ordinary to begin with, have ever found a way to practice forgiveness in cases of extreme violence. Most of the stories concern family members of murder victims, who have to struggle with the fear of being disloyal to their loved ones if they forgive. Yet as each story portrays, these people have found a higher loyalty, and a way to show deeper honour to their lost loved ones.

"Yes, Jack, I forgive you"

Anyone seriously into applied Christianity has to be into adventurous forgiveness. Catherine Marshall, whose books on Christian living have had a profound influence on our times, tells one such story in her book *Something More*. She told this story directly from the words of Harvey Smith, a family friend who experienced it. Harvey moved to New York City from Georgia in the 1950s, to attend Columbia University. Harvey met a young man named Jack in one of his classes. A broken home followed by a stint in the American navy had left Jack an unhappy person, lonely and confused. Unaware of the depth of Jack's disturbance, Harvey invited Jack to share his basement apartment with him.

But as Jack's drinking and temper tantrums became more and more difficult, and as Jack refused to go to a counsellor, Harvey soon realized he was over his depth. He decided to choose the safest course: rather than try to persuade Jack to move, he would move out himself, leaving their apartment to Jack. He sought a room nearby so he could still befriend Jack.

When Harvey told Jack, on a Thursday morning, of his decision to move, the reaction was worse than he had anticipated. Harvey had become Jack's only hold on life, and it felt as if that one prop were disappearing. Jack pleaded, then raged. Harvey restrained Jack physically when Jack struck out at him. When the whole thing seemed to be over, Harvey went over to the mirror to attend to a cut on his nose. Behind him, a snarl alerted him to Jack's having seized a heavy hammer. Harvey was still not frightened — his greater size and strength and his own control could handle the situation. He grabbed the hammer from Jack and kicked it under the dresser, but as he wrestled with Jack he felt a series of heavy blows on his back. Then he glimpsed a knife in Jack's hand! Summoning all his strength, he managed to shove Jack out the door and lock it, but not before he had received more blows in his front chest.

Trying to call for help, Harvey realized his voice was not normal. He was sickened to see blood oozing out of his sweater, and realized he had been stabbed! As he struggled for consciousness, a knock on the door told him the superintendent had heard his cry. Harvey managed to open the door, then collapsed. The horrified superintendent ran for the police, without thinking that he was leaving Harvey vulnerable to whoever had assaulted him.

Jack reappeared, standing over his helpless victim, and Harvey realized there was nothing he could do to stop his finishing the job he had begun. But Jack was repentant, and sickened by his work. He dragged Harvey to the bed, pleading for forgiveness. As he begged for forgiveness from the friend he had stabbed so viciously, Jack raised the knife to stab himself. Harvey summoned a reservoir of strength from somewhere, reached up and grabbed the knife and threw it away. Then he heard himself saying, "Yes, Jack, I forgive you." He realized dimly that this was not the superficial man Harvey speaking, but a person called by all the Christian training he had received in his life.

For a week Harvey hung between life and death, nearly dying more than once. As he suffered horrifying pain, as he lived in fear of early death, as he wondered how anyone could do this to a friend, Harvey wrestled with the meaning of those words he had uttered. He realized forgiveness was not a facile thing: it was costly. It became even more so when he heard that Jack was taking advantage of Harvey's fingerprints on the hammer to claim self-defence! Jack was claiming he had had to knife Harvey to defend himself against Harvey's first attack with the hammer. Could he forgive this slander of his very Christian character, too?

Harvey came to the awareness that forgiveness was not about feeling good toward Jack. It was not thinking Jack's conduct — any of it — was justified. Forgiveness was something he had to do; an act of will and of conscious choice for goodness. So at a more finished level, Harvey, lying there on his hospital bed, chose the path of forgiveness. A week later his doctor said to Harvey, "You're going to get well." Harvey said he had known that, and much of it was owing to her care.

"No," she said, "You were so ill, it could have gone either way till about a week ago. You've been at peace with yourself since then. If you had held on to any hatred at all, it would have sapped too much energy for you to have survived."

Harvey's case was a clear illustration of the price we pay for holding hatred and revenge feelings inside us. They destroy the holder far more than they can the object of our fury.

A Lifer's Story

Stories of amazing forgiveness abound. Like everything else in life, "whatever we seek with our whole hearts, we find." Being fascinated by the call to forgiveness, I encounter wonderful stories of it unexpectedly in all kinds of places. As I was writing this chapter, I went to a planning meeting for the next International Conference on Penal Abolition. One of our speakers for the weekend, Ken Logan, was a lifer who was just released from prison after over twenty years inside for murder. Ken was still shaken by the newness of life outside, but with simple eloquence he told this story of his encounter with the family of the man he had killed.

Ken served much of his time in Collins Bay. Many years ago some very creative inmates there began the Olympiad: an event inside the prison, which organizes Olympic athletic events for handicapped people from outside. It is held each year, and the prisoners raise all the money for it, arrange all the permits with administration, and host this incredible event of community across two worlds of rejected people. Every time I see the video on the Olympiad, tears of amazement and joy flow at this living demonstration of the power of community.

The Olympiad is not the heart of this story, but it plays a part. After years inside, Ken was struggling to put his life together in a more meaningful way. He was involved in a number of positive activities, including a Lifers'

Group, which is close to a number of outside volunteers I know. In the course of this, he became very involved in the Olympiad, and finally one year became the inmate Chair of the event, which led him to do a lot of outside outreach and correspondence.

In this capacity, Ken wrote to a childhood friend of his, an old schoolmate who had become the minister of an evangelical church. Ken's letters about the Olympiad and its cause were moving. What Ken did not know was that the secretary of that minister was the sister of his murder victim! She and her family were still stuck in bitterness, hatred, and revenge, and it was dividing them and adding to their suffering. It also left them mired in self-blame for the "if onlys," agonizing over whether this one or that one could have done something to prevent the tragedy. As Ken's letters came in, she and the minister began talking about it all and praying about it.

The minister didn't need to point out that the man who was so obsessed by the needs of the handicapped for community and inclusion was not exactly the same man who had killed her brother. Since Ken did not know that his letters were reaching so close to the heart of this crucial experience, he could write as he was, and the church secretary was more and more moved. Prayer did the rest. I have always said I preferred addressing religious audiences because whatever their specific theology or affiliation, at bottom they are "stuck with the gospel," and the gospel of all faiths includes the call to forgiveness.

Being "stuck with the gospel," the church secretary, Sarah, took the first giant step along the path. Forgiveness is not an emotion; it is a commitment to a path of goodwill action. Sarah's first step was a letter to Ken, telling him who she was and how she came to be writing. This led to a modest correspondence, tentative and cautious for both, but beginning to open doors.

The doors were still just slightly ajar when the Olympiad came. Unknown to Ken, Sarah, her husband and their children all decided to come to the event. The first he knew of it was when a strange woman walked up to him in the middle of the already incredible event, threw her arms around him, and said, "Jesus has already forgiven you, and I do too." Identifying herself, Sarah began a healing series of hugs from her whole family, all of whom repeated similar words.

Although this happened years ago, Ken remains overwhelmed when he talks about it. Imagine what it would be like to be organizing the biggest event you have ever come close to dealing with. Then add in such an unexpected meeting with the people you had most dreaded meeting for years, had most emotion about, and such magical words of forgiveness! In spite of the demands of the event, they sat down and talked about what had happened that long ago night of the murder. The unanswered questions were answered; the healing built by sensitive sharing.

Forgiveness is an act of giving and an act of receiving. Often one party plays the forgiveness game better than the other does, but there is still a lot of healing in it. Most of my forgiveness games have been played without much help from the people who wounded me: they still will not acknowledge the harm they did me, any of the wrong on their side, or say those magical words, "I'm sorry." That is the hardest kind of forgiveness to give, to those who will not acknowledge their wrong. Yet even that has healing in it. In other cases, the wrongdoer begs forgiveness, and the victim refuses to give it. Again, there is still healing to be gained from one-way steps toward forgiveness. But when both parties are playing their parts to the full, as in Ken's experience, what power there is!

The immediate impact on the family was that most of their tensions over the historic tragedy melted. They became a stronger, tighter family unit. They found healing for themselves in giving forgiveness. The gift was so complete that they said they would like Ken out of prison now and wanted to help him.

The long-range impact on Ken was profound. Although his management of the Olympiad showed he had made a lot of personal and spiritual progress already, it was nothing to the growth that lay before him now. He had continued to hate himself for what he had been and done. The words and reality of forgiveness from the family of the man he had killed made him feel that if they could forgive him, he needed to forgive himself. Forgiveness does not mean condoning, by anyone. It means recognizing that we are not just one evil or good act: we are whole persons. We acknowledge that something we have done was very wrong, but we need to learn from that and move on from it, integrating that learning into who we become. The family's heroic gestures of forgiveness freed Ken from a stuck place in his life, and enabled him to accept himself, and blossom into the person he is today.

Moreover, it made him determined to do well, to honour their gift. "I wanted to make them proud of me," he explains. This is an amazing by-product of the winds of forgiveness in many stories I have heard. Bernie Pinet, former head Chaplain of the Canadian prison system, tells a story of a woman whose son was murdered. She began visiting the man who had killed her son, and telling him that he had to make something of his life, or her son's death would have been in vain! The killer was still stuck in his problems, addictions, and vicious circles for a while. But the persistence of the mother of his victim overcame his resistance. She hounded him into growing. He has pursued treatment and education and new paths inside. When asked about the dramatic change in himself he attributes it all to the mother of his victim, who would give him no peace until he changed, saying repeatedly, "If you don't make something of yourself, my son's death will have been for nothing!" How much more powerful and satisfying a path than primitive revenge this great woman found.

So forgiveness, freely offered in impossible circumstances, frees the giver and the receiver. Far from cheapening the significance of the wrong, it builds a monument of heroic love to honour the suffering, using the power of the pain to build a bridge of love in community.

Story of an Adoption

This is an old story, one I found in my sister's file on "Forgiveness," years ago when I was preparing a sermon on that topic. It comes from newspaper articles in *Parade* (May 3, 1959) and *Guideposts* (September 1976). It began six days before Christmas in 1958. Little Craig Ellerbusch was coming out from kindergarten. He went to the school crossing, and he followed the direction of the school crossing guard, but the speeding car came so fast the patrol boy had to jump himself, in order to escape death. Craig had no chance. His father arrived in time to see his crumpled, curly-headed body in the middle of the road, being loaded into an ambulance. He died that afternoon.

Max Ellerbusch had never been religious the way his wife Grace was. But that night Max prayed as almost everyone does at such a crisis. He wailed the cry of Job, over the emptiness and injustice of life. Of their four beloved children, Craig had been the most cheerful, optimistic, bubbling with love of life and of everyone around him. Craig's death took Max back to the death of his two sisters from scarlet fever. Their death had taken the love and joy from his mother, and Max had grown up in a dismal home. It was Craig most of all who had given him back faith that there could be joy in this world. And now — what a mockery!

"If such a child can die, if such a life can be snuffed out in a minute, then life is meaningless, and faith in God is self-delusion." These were the bitter thoughts of that first terrible night for Max Ellerbusch. By next day, the police had arrested fifteen-year-old George Williams as the boy whose car had killed little Craig, and who had then sped away. Max's rage was distilled and directed toward this teenager from a broken home, at a time when broken homes were rare and meant more hopelessness than they do today. Max phoned his lawyer asking that the boy be prosecuted to the limit. By that evening, Max's despair had reached as low as it could go. Pacing the floor, weary beyond belief, he prayed, "Oh God, show me why!"

Then with the suddenness of a flash of lightning, a great gift came. We Quakers call it an opening. Most religions speak of it as a mystical experience. All the sickness went out of him with a great sigh, and instead he was filled with more love and joy than he had known in his whole life. The Light of that experience melted away the anger, grief, and rage that had filled him. He felt carried to another plane, and on that plane, he was given a chance to learn the greatest lessons of life. He understood why Craig had had to leave them, and that Craig had learned those lessons of life already, and was ready to move on, while he, Max, was just beginning. The understanding he had could not be put into words, for it was beyond the intellectual realm, and yet he tried to express it.

Max understood that life was like a grade in school, and the one lesson we are here to learn is love. His wife looked at him, as he walked in the bedroom, and she saw how dramatically he had changed. Max tried to find words to tell her: "Tonight Craig is beyond needing us. But there is someone else who does need us: George Williams. Maybe there will be no Christmas gift for him at the Detention Home, unless we send it."

Grace looked at him blankly at first. She was a woman of faith, but her faith was deeply tried, and now her agnostic husband was telling her things beyond what anyone of her church had ever said. She was momentarily baffled and overwhelmed. Then she burst into tears. "Yes," she cried, "that's the first thing that has been right since Craig died."

The Ellerbusches never turned back from the vision God had given them. They sent homemade cookies to George Williams and to his mother in her home, for Christmas. They asked their minister to visit them, and talk about their dream for responding to this tragedy. They found George and his mother deeply appreciative and responsive. Eighteen days after the accident, Max Ellerbusch stood up in Juvenile Court and said these words, "To add more hatred and sorrow to what already exists in the world would make me feel my son had died for nothing. But if we can help this boy to make something of himself, Craig will not have died in vain." George turned pale, and George's mother wept, as Max Ellerbusch offered George a job after school in the plant Max managed, a welcome into the Ellerbusch home, and full support in pursuing a college education.

The magazine picture in *Parade* shows a beaming George Williams holding in his arms the three-year-old little sister of the child he killed. The follow-up article twenty years later tells of how the two families remain linked, and of the fact that George has made a good life for himself out of the incredible love which Max and Grace Ellerbusch were inspired to share. Love like that can come from only one source, for to love those who have wounded us that deeply is truly Divine.

My Son, My Son: The Story of Azim Khamisa

On January 21, 1995, Azim Khamisa, an investment banker of San Diego, California, received a call that his 21-year-old son Tariq had been killed in a robbery attempt while delivering late-night pizzas to earn money for his university education (Karim, 1998). Azim went through all the stages of grief, rage, and hopelessness, but soon centred on the need to understand and deal with the causes. He found this peace in a retreat time in his beloved mountains. His life, so centred on this beloved son, now seemed void of meaning. As a Muslim, he knew he was called to compassion, mercy and forgiveness. He was reminded of a verse, that "Righteousness requires us to spend of our substance, out of love for Him, for your kin, for orphans, and for the needy" (Surah 2:177). He saw that all children are orphaned by a society that puts so many at risk of gang involvement and other traps.

The murderer of his son was a fourteen-year-old juvenile, slated as the first to be tried as an adult in California in a felony case. Azim did not wish to interfere with the legal process, but he wanted to make a significant gesture. He invited Ples Felix, the grandfather of the murderer, to his home! Azim made the amazing statement, "I realized change had to begin with myself."

Although our world would have seen them as mortally opposed, these two men were big enough in their spiritual vision to realize that a single moment of irresponsibility had shattered both of their worlds, and that their joint shock over this event could be a bond. Azim said, "From the beginning, I saw victims at both ends of the gun. America was robbed of two children on that fateful night." The two men agreed to work together to try to change teen violence.

After many months of searching, they decided to establish the Tariq Khamisa Foundation, in memory of Azim's beloved son. Ples Felix, the grandfather of his murderer, sits on the Board! The purpose of the group is to involve young people in discussions of gangs and violence. The two men reached out to ten local schools, and organized violence impact forums, which included a videotape discussing, among other things, their own tragedy. The sessions explored peer pressure as well.

Azim comments on his experience that only by acting to save others could he appropriately memorialize the life of his beloved son. Azim's history of community service and involvement paved the way for his ability to transcend his deep personal tragedy in such a wonderful way. Azim received national recognition for his work, and has appeared on NBC's *Today* show, and was featured in leading US magazines and newspapers. Azim and his wife are pleased that their example is giving a more correct image of the stance of the Muslim faith toward forgiveness. Azim and Ples both received an award from the San Diego Crime Commission. Azim's inscription reads, "For teaching the world that the heart sees what the eyes cannot."

"I'm Going to be the One that Shoots Him"

I met Maxine in Washington, DC, at a Conference of CURE. Her story illustrates that you don't have to start out on the forgiveness trail to get there. CURE is the largest prison reform group in the USA, lobbying for decent conditions and rights in US prisons. The amazing fulltime work of Charlie and Pauline Sullivan on an annual budget of about $30,000 for their salaries, office, travel, and conference, is one of the most heartening stories in the spiritually impoverished world of criminal justice.

I heard Maxine tell her story to a group at the Conference, and I was so moved by it that I had lunch with her later to get it straight. Nine years before we met, Maxine's only son Herbert was murdered in his car, as part of a robbery. They apprehended his killer, a ne'er-do-well drug addict, and he was sentenced to what sounded like many years in prison. But when Maxine learned that this disgusting wanton murderer could walk out on the street in as little as eight years on parole, she announced, "I'm going to be the one to shoot him when he walks out of there." She went out and bought a handgun, to express the sincerity of her words.

Moreover, dwelling in understandable bitterness, Maxine organized other victims into a revenge oriented crime victims group. They met, they expressed their anger, they lobbied, and they wallowed in their pain and anger. She was an effective organizer and leader, and the group appeared to go well for many years. The only thing that wasn't going well was her own life. Locked into revenge, Maxine felt she was getting deeper into her nightmare instead of emerging from it.

As the time neared for the first parole possibility for Ted, the killer of her son, Maxine became more and more upset. But instead of wanting to kill him, she found herself more and more obsessed with the desire to meet him! The court process had answered none of her anguished questions, nor given her any healing. She began asking friends and officials about a possible meeting, and she began reading about mediation between victims and offenders. Virtually no one encouraged her — officials especially and the kinds of crime victim friends she had drawn around her, all felt it was a crazy idea, more likely to re-wound her than do anything else.

But in spite of them all, Maxine felt drawn toward the meeting idea. She contacted Mark Umbreit, whose work in victim-offender reconciliation is well known. Mark also cautioned her about the dangers of such a meeting to her perilous equilibrium. But under careful conditions, after correspondence with her, he agreed to fly East to New England from his work in Minnesota, to mediate the session. He did some preparatory work with the offender to be sure he was reasonably ready for such a challenge.

Maxine was so far from wanting complete reconciliation that she stipulated there should be not one but two tables between her and Ted at the meeting. She did not want by any chance to touch the hand that had pulled the trigger to kill her son! Nevertheless, the meeting went well. Ted was getting treatment for his addiction, and beginning to understand enough so that he could respond to the depth of her grief and anger. While not perfect, the meeting left Maxine feeling differently about things. She left, deciding not to intervene either way in Ted's upcoming parole hearing.

Ted was denied parole, but when the issue came up again a year later, Maxine decided she wanted another meeting. This time there was only one table between them, and the conversation went deeper. Maxine asked Ted about her son's last moments. She had to know, whatever the news was, good or bad. This is a common need of murder victims: strange as it may seem, they often need to know from the only person who can tell them about their loved one's sacred last moments. Ted answered her honestly, and the answers were not pretty. He had shot her son in cold blood, then reached into his dying body to take his wallet and strip his arm of its watch. When she asked if her son was involved in a drug deal or anything else shady, because of the bad neighbourhood, Ted shook his head and said, "No, he was completely innocent. He was just at the wrong place at the wrong time."

Maxine raged back at him, "No he wasn't at the wrong place, he had a perfect right to be there. It was you who were at the wrong place at the wrong time!" Ted agreed in shame that this was so. This opportunity to vent one's anguish over injustice directly to the wrongdoer is one of the unique opportunities of such meetings. While in general mere venting of anger is no longer perceived to be a healthy outlet, expressing clearly to those who have hurt us what is wrong in their behaviour does satisfy a basic need to set the record straight and have our wrongs recognized.

The session went on, and as it deepened, Ted took courage in hand toward the end and asked Maxine for her forgiveness. The word forgiveness means many things to many people, and a lot of people think it means an emotion of warmth toward the other person. I've said that I think forgiveness is a commitment to a course of action of goodwill, and so in my sense Maxine was clearly on the path of forgiveness. But she searched within herself and came up with this astounding response, "Ted, there is one thing I want from you more than anything else, and can't have, and that is my son's life back. And there is one thing you want from me that I can't give you: my forgiveness. But here we are working together to try to make something decent come out of this horror, and I think that's pretty good, don't you?" And she reached across and took his open hands, underneath his bowed head.

When I last heard of this pair, Maxine was tutoring Ted in life-skills, to be sure he didn't come out, relapse into drugs, and do any more harm to some other family. Looking into Maxine's eyes, one could see that while her life would always be changed by the tragic death of her son, she had found a new meaning, much more satisfying than that gun.

Can We Forgive the Murder of a Family?

Everyone's challenges are big enough for them, as my friend Irene said often to me. But there is something of extra horror when a whole family is wiped out. We are afraid to ask ourselves, "Could I deal with that?" Here is how one couple dealt with that precise situation.

This inspiring story comes from the July 1990 copy of the Mennonite periodical *Accord*, entitled "Story of a Reconciliation." The same magazine talks about how a 1988 survey of victims and offenders by Dave Gustafson found both groups wanting to meet with the other party. The principal story however concerns Steven Kinney, who was sentenced to life imprisonment for murdering his wife and her two children. The father of the murdered children, and his new wife, initiated contact with Steve Kinney.

After a lengthy correspondence, Herb and June Simpson decided they wanted a face to face visit with Kinney. June remained a bit skeptical about Kinney, and felt a face to face visit would ascertain whether he was truly sincere in all the pages he had written. Herb Simpson, the father of the murdered children, believed the pages spoke for themselves, but he felt a visit would round out the vital experience for all of them.

The couple was visited by a parole officer, who validated the Simpsons' motivations, but wanted to make sure Steve Kinney would not use this experience to bolster a plea for release. But the spiritual journey of the Simpsons inspired even the parole officer, and by the end of her visit with them she was a supporter of their request. Conditions of the visit were no media, and the presence of Kinney's social worker as a mediating presence.

The social worker met them at the prison and spent a full hour briefing them. She mentioned Kinney's limitations in fitting into the prison environment, and her doubts that he had fully grasped emotionally the seriousness of his crimes. As Herb Simpson began talking about their victim support group and the things they had experienced and accomplished, Kinney listened. But after a few moments, Kinney interjected, "You know, I'm really nervous." Herb Simpson said they were too, and Kinney said he was trying to be prepared for severe criticism from them. Herb turned to June and said this was her cue.

"Is that what you want, Steve, for me to really hurt you? Why didn't you just walk away? And why did you kill the children — wasn't your argument with the mother? Don't you realize I would have been a good mother to those children? They would have gone to music lessons, sports, college..." Both June Simpson and Steve Kinney were on the verge of tears. But Steve just nodded and let her go on.

"Billy's fourteenth birthday was very hard on my husband. And Christmas is so tough. Have you any idea what an emotional wreck my husband was at the start of all this? Our marriage will never be the same. We've survived, but the scars are there." After Kinney absorbed all this with difficulty, he tried to explain his thoughts at the fateful time of the murders. They shared how they all still wept for everyone involved.

Kinney mentioned he had pictures of his wedding to the children's mother, including photos of the children that June and Herb had never seen. Steve Kinney said he understood they would not want to see pictures of him, but would they like to see pictures of the others? They would, and they did. Kinney gave them two snapshots of the children from his album, for which he had negatives.

At the end of the visit, June gave warnings about no press, no comments, and that she wanted a report from Steve Kinney about his experience of the day. He agreed to it all, and added that he realized she would have made a good mother to the children. Then Herb Simpson told Steve Kinney how much their correspondence had aided his healing.

As they were leaving, the social worker remarked, "You are so forgiving." Yet Herb Simpson did not feel they had done anything remarkable, just followed a very natural series of steps. "It's the answer," replied Herb Simpson spontaneously. The couple went out to a restaurant, celebrating the amazing experience. June, who had been most reluctant, furious, and skeptical, now didn't want it to end. A visit she had thought she could only endure for an hour had gone on for two, and they were still savouring its healing quality afterward. The Simpsons were learning that the path of reconciliation with the tormented killer of their children was the most creative memorial to their lives that they could build.

Murder Victims' Families for Reconciliation

There are a plethora of amazing forgiveness stories from the wonderful group "Murder Victims' Families for Reconciliation." Their stories have a common flavour and a common wonder, but each is different, as each life is unique. Every member of the group is a victim of murder; including their Executive Director, who even became a state legislator to resist the intrusion of the death penalty in his state. Some are victims of state murder (capital punishment), but most are victims of individual crimes, and the two sets of murder victims work together in common cause and total harmony. They see that murder is murder, whether perpetrated by individuals or the state, and that revenge begets more revenge.

Rev. Bernice King, daughter of Martin Luther King, Jr., says of the group: "MVFR is one of the most important organizations in America, because its members have moved beyond revenge, retaliation and retribution, and are today setting the very highest standards of forgiveness, compassion and non-violence... Having lost my father and grandmother to gun violence, I well understand the deep hurt and anger felt by the loved ones of those who have been murdered, yet I cannot accept the judgement that their killers need to be executed." Reading that statement, and watching a videotape, which includes a longer speech by her to the same effect, I cannot help thinking how very proud of her her father must be.

It is hard for those of us who have never faced challenges as deep as those of these MVFR members to comprehend how they can find the strength not just to forgive, but to radiate peace and beauty in their faces and their lives. There is a power greater than the superficial fixes of consumerism and boxed-in living we too often limit to a tight inner valued circle, while ignoring the needs of wider humanity beyond. MVFR members have all tapped into that power, and it shines from them.

The book *Not in Our Name: Murder Victims Speak Out Against the Death Penalty* is a powerful witness by this remarkable group. The photos in that book tell the story of the transformation of each of their lives, for it radiates from their faces. One that particularly baffles my comprehension is the face of a woman who is a leader in community peace and yoga groups. She sits in a leotard with a shining face, looking much like meditation and yoga leaders are expected to look. Below is her story: she spent seventeen years on death row, during which time her husband was executed for the crime neither of them had anything to do with. After seventeen years, their innocence was confirmed and she was released, a widow of state murder, and having spent all those years in death row isolation. How could such a person escape bitterness? She said that only finding a deeper power enabled her to keep her sanity in all those unspeakable, unjust years on death row. Truly MVFR members are onto something very powerful.

A Steelworker Discovers Forgiveness

Bill Pelke does not look the image of someone on a reconciliation trip. A well-built steelworker, Bill was unprepared for the shock that met him when his wonderful Christian grandmother was brutally murdered by a gang of girls. Bill's dad had been trying to get her to move out of her home where she lived alone, because he was worried about safety issues. But Bill's grandmother loved her home and trusted people. The gang that killed her was after money, and killed her to be freer to loot the house.

Finding her butchered body with many knife wounds on her dining-room rug left an indelible, brutal memory for Bill and his dad. When Paula, the fifteen-year-old leader of the gang, was arrested, Bill and his dad attended the trial and were hoping for the death sentence. But when it came, something else came with it that changed Bill's life forever, and has influenced many others around the world.

As the death sentence was announced for Paula, Paula's grandmother burst into heartbroken sobs. Instead of experiencing the satisfaction he had expected, Bill felt a deep discomfort. Here was a grandmother who loved her grandchild just as his grandmother had felt about hers. That moment haunted him for four months. As he thought about it one day, he saw in his mind's eye a lovely picture they had of his own grandmother, but with a difference: she too was weeping. Bill knew in that moment that she was weeping because this was not the course that wonderful Christian woman would have wanted or did want. Another amazing thing happened to Bill then and there. As Bill became aware that he needed to take a new path, a strange path with unknown steps toward forgiveness, he realized that he was in touch with his grandmother again!

This is something person after person in that group tells. As long as they are on the revenge road, all they can contact, all they can see, is the butchered dead body of their loved one. But as soon as they turn toward forgiveness, they are reunited with the spirit of their living beloved. They have got beyond the act of death to the truth of the immortality of all that is spiritual in each of us.

So Bill began taking his first tentative steps on the new forgiveness path. He tried to tell reporters that he wanted to get Paula off death row. Strangely enough the US press, which loved to wallow in statements of revenge, weren't interested in his new views. Bill began working any way he could to get Paula's sentence changed from death to life. The US press remained indifferent, but interestingly enough, the Italian press picked up on it, and invited him at their expense to do a tour of Italy telling his story!

Having seen how united Europeans are in repugnance at the archaic barbarity of the death penalty, this does not surprise me as much as it did Bill. He accepted the offer, and the European press carried his story so widely that some American press picked it up from there! So the ice was broken, and Bill's campaign began to gather momentum. He also wrote to Paula, and told her of his forgiveness, and that it was part of his love and devotion to his grandmother. I have seen a video of Paula's comments as well as Bill's on this whole experience, and I have heard Bill speak publicly about how it has changed his entire life.

Eventually, Bill was successful, and Paula did get removed from death row. But what sticks in my mind most from that video is the look in Paula's eyes and the sound of her voice as she says; "I don't understand it at all. I don't understand how Bill Pelke can want to meet me, how he can forgive me after what I did. But I do understand just one thing: I think if there had been a Bill Pelke in my life before this happened, it never would have been."

"I am here to speak for life"

Suzeanne Bosler was the daughter of a Brethren minister. Her father was truly a minister of the gospel of peace, for the Brethren Church is one of the three historic peace churches in America. Suzeanne remembers vividly her father saying one day, "If anyone were ever to murder me, I would not want that person to be executed." Suzeanne had cause to remember that story, and devote years to honouring those words.

One day Suzeanne heard her father answer the door of their modest home and she heard sounds that did not sound normal. Going to see what was happening, she saw a man stabbing her father repeatedly. Suzeanne rushed to his aid, and the assailant, who had already severely wounded her father, began stabbing Suzeanne. Very quickly she too collapsed bleeding on the floor. Among other places, he stabbed her in the head, causing brain damage that left her speech and other faculties impaired for months to follow. But now he rushed around their home, looking for articles to steal. For theft had been the underlying motive for these savage attacks.

It is interesting to note that several of our stories of violence were perpetrated solely for theft. These stories remind us that the violence of telling marginalized groups and individuals that they must obtain wealth to be valued, and depriving them of most means of doing so legally lights a fuse under a bomb of potential violence in our society. This truth does not condone the ugly brutality of violence for theft, but it does remind us that the violence of obscene wealth and desperate poverty spawn many of the evils that rightly horrify us.

As Suzeanne's nightmare continued, the assailant twice checked his victims to see that they were dead. Suzeanne held her breath, and he believed her dead. Her father was indeed dead, although Suzeanne did not yet know that. At last the assailant left the house. With her last remaining strength Suzeanne managed to crawl to the phone and summon help. Her father was dead long before it arrived, but Suzeanne survived despite her grievous wounds and the shock of the whole experience. The assailant was arrested and charged, and I have seen a tape of Suzeanne's testimony at his sentencing. She described for what seemed like ten minutes exactly what had happened, a scene of such unprovoked violence it makes me shudder just to remember her words. But she closed her testimony with these words, "We are not here to talk about that today. We are here to speak about the fate of James —, who has been convicted of this crime. I am here to speak for life, for his life, and for my father's life, for my father stood for forgiveness and reconciliation, and never for revenge." She went on to plead for the life of her father's killer and her own brutal assailant.

The video continues with the Judge's sentence, commending her mildly and ambivalently for her attitude but saying the state could not be so forgiving, and sentencing the killer to death. Suzeanne burst into tears for the killer of her father, and perhaps also at the horror of a State that values its own machismo power more than the pain and pleas of the actual victims of a crime. She went on to fight years to get her father's killer off death row, and recently finally won that struggle. In the course of those years, she was threatened with contempt of court for daring to speak out against the death mentality of the US courts and the revenge mentality of all our courts. But Suzeanne stayed true to her father's life and witness, and to the faith that they shared.

When she was unable to meet with her father's killer in prison, she asked for and managed to arrange a meeting with a group of prisoners who had all committed murder. She carried her message of both pain and reconciliation to them, and that group and she comforted one another, and took steps along the healing journey together. Suzeanne helped them understand the anguish they had caused, but she also helped them know that forgiveness and reconciliation are possible. They witnessed that although the courts were stuck in vengeance and violence, these individual perpetrators of murder were open to growing beyond it. Suzeanne Bosler brings a witness to her father's faith to all the darkest corners of our society, and her life is another shining light in Murder Victims' Families for Reconciliation.

"Our own heart gets changed"

For many years I wanted to meet Marietta Jaeger, a woman who is a summa cum laude graduate in the school of forgiveness. She and her family were camping when a nightmare happened to them, a nightmare so bizarre it goes beyond our worst fantasies of terror. As they slept unsuspectingly in their family tent in the American Midwest, on a family holiday trip, someone sliced a huge flap-cut in the tent, and abducted Susie, their youngest child.

Thus began a horror which went on, and on, and on, and changed the lives of every one of them. For a month the family stayed in the area, hoping for news of Susie. Local police and authorities and townspeople were all very kind and supportive, but the uncertainty, as well as the fears, drove the family nearly crazy. Toward the end of that first month Marietta, not yet on the forgiveness path, said, "At that point, if he had returned her unharmed, I would have wanted to kill him for the pain and anguish he had inflicted on my husband and other children."

But Marietta was a devout Christian, and God had other plans. As she prayed from the depths of her broken heart, she kept getting the message that she was supposed to forgive him — she always assumed correctly that it was a man who had done this. Marietta, like Saint Theresa of Avila, had a sense of humour in her conversations with God, and she finally said, "Look, you keep telling me to forgive him. Nobody else thinks that makes sense — my family don't, the police don't, even the local priest doesn't. But since you're so set on this, God, I am willing, but I don't know how. This is your idea, and you're going to have to bring it off. All I can say is, show me, and I'll try to do what I can." Willingness to be made willing — it was a huge step along an unknown path, which would lead Marietta into a whole new life.

So every day, Marietta began praying for her daughter's unknown abductor, as best she could. At first all she could manage was, "Dear God, let one good thing happen to him today." While this soul-changing work was going in Marietta's heart, events kept tormenting them. There are always false clues, false hopes, false discoveries of what could be your child's body. The family oscillated every day from hope to despair and back to the tortured nothingness of not knowing. No easy terrain to be travelling while praying for good things to happen to the unknown author of all their torment!

After a month, the family returned home, a step that was as painful as remaining had been. To return without Susie was a terrible defeat and separation. But Marietta went on step by step with her prayer journey. As the year passed, a good ending seemed less and less likely, and publicity died down, as did the investigation. However, as the anniversary of one year from the abduction neared, a reporter decided to do a piece on this sad story without any ending. Miraculously, the reporter quoted Marietta correctly, when Marietta said, "I would give anything for just one conversation with the person that did this."

One year to the hour, Marietta's phone rang. It was still tapped by the police, and the voice that was on the other end claimed to have her daughter with him, claimed she was alive. He appeared to have called to torment Marietta further, but out of the year of prayers, following orders from beyond herself, Marietta turned his agenda around in words I have heard on that remarkable tape. She asked, "How can I help you?" What words from the mother of the child you have stolen! The murderer was stunned, and began to cry.

This opening led to an incredible, long conversation between the two. Although he was still not being honest, he began to open up. Above all, he stayed on the line so long that the police were able to identify his voice and person. He was a young man who lived near the campground, and whom the police had interviewed, but felt they had inadequate ground to hold, and released. But they had had enough questions about him that the long tape and some of his comments on it led them right to him.

Through that unique conversation, the murderer of Marietta's child was arrested. A strange ending to a year of prayer for his welfare, one might observe. That year enabled Marietta to relate to him in such a way that he was stopped in his terrifying pattern — for it came out that he had killed three other children before he kidnapped, raped and killed Susie. Marietta was not satisfied with his capture, although of course she was relieved that because of her prayers for forgiveness, she had been able to stop his homicidal pattern by leading the police to identify him. Marietta wanted to visit with him, to tell him of her forgiveness.

Marietta says of her communication with her beloved daughter's kidnap-killer:

> In God's eyes he was just as precious as my little girl. He had dignity and worth. I had prayed for him every day. I was able to speak to him with respect. Our own heart gets changed. How important it was for him to experience the love of God. My prayers had come to fruition in me. He was taken aback

by it... He wept. I felt desperate to help him. He said, 'I wish this burden could be lifted from me.' I finally came to understand that God's idea of justice is not punishment, but restoration. I do not see Jesus as someone who came to punish us. I asked the FBI to give him the alternative of the promise he would not get the death penalty, and he confessed then to four murders...

A few days after his arrest, this tormented man hung himself in his cell, and Marietta made this amazing statement, "I was as grieved by his death as I had been by my child's." For his death left unfinished business, and Marietta went on to devote her life to the unfinished business of forgiveness. When she and her family were driving west a year later, they stopped in the small town where it had all happened. Marietta wanted to pray for peace for all of them, including her child's murderer, in the cell where he had hung himself. The jail had been closed down in the meantime, and turned into a modest local museum, open just one day a week, but they "happened" to hit the day. The curator, when Marietta explained her errand, agreed to leave Marietta alone in the small cell, to pray there for awhile.

As Marietta was praying for healing for all concerned and especially for the tormented man who had ended his destructive life in that cell, she was suddenly aware of the presence of Light. I have often commented, and so have many others, on the relation of light to mystical experience. For me it is not a physical sensation quite like a light bulb — I know one is spiritual light, the other physical, and yet that spiritual light is real and, as Marietta's experience shows, can be shared by others sometimes. What was so incredible about Marietta's experience was that it was transmitted: her host down the hall called, "Who turned on the light down there?" In fact, no one but Marietta's prayers had touched any source of Light.

The same video that tells the story of Bill Pelke and Paula shows Marietta, with her piercing blue eyes, visiting, along with the mother of the murderer, the graveyard where both Susie and her killer are buried. The two mothers grieve together, and bring flowers together to the graves.

Marietta's story is told in her stunning little book *The Lost Child*. When I finally met Marietta at a Conference, I was amused to hear the persons introducing Marietta say, "Marietta just wants to be introduced as someone who hopes there is cheese popcorn in heaven." Nothing pompous about Marietta Jaeger, but for 30 years her life has been devoted to sharing her story of reconciliation. Her adventures in Christianity carried her further into civil disobedience for peace, from having been a much more conventional housewife. The Light Marietta's prayers have turned on, as she walked the path of impossible forgiveness, has shined in my life and many others, lighting the way to hope in this world so often weighed down with the despair of hoarded wrongs.

Forgiving Racism and Genocide

It is hard to say whether the murder of a loved one, or the systemic violence that results in lifelong discrimination and many instances of genocide against one's whole community are hardest to forgive. But each has its own challenges, and I have put the forgiveness of racism and genocide in a category by itself, because it has some special horrors to deal with in the forgiveness path. For one thing, racism continues, and even genocide in many areas of this world. As a result, there is not the universal recognition of wrong that the family survivors of homicide experience in the stories above. For another, we members of the majority group generally lack the empathy to grasp the enormity of the experiences of racism and even genocide.

I have read much about the Holocaust, and about the experiences of indigenous people and Black people in North America. All these groups despair of ever being understood. Holocaust survivors often keep their story to themselves, because the society around them does not want to grasp the truth that such things could really happen. We know the Holocaust did happen, but we don't want to think about it, because its reality forces us to realize that we too have the potential to sink to such execrable depths.

So our society forces many survivors to keep their deepest reality to themselves, and go on through life without the degree of healing that could come from a community that shared and validated their grief and their wrong. That is one reason why so many courageous survivors have written their stories, and founded museums and other memorials to the Holocaust. They are fighting an uphill battle for true recognition of their wrong, and I admire the courage of the Jewish people who do this in truth-telling, just as I have compassion for the many who have retreated into despairing, sterile silence.

The continuing history of racism in North America is as ugly in its own way as the Holocaust. It allowed the deaths of countless Africans on the slave ships, under slavery, under Jim Crow and segregation, and the genocide of millions of indigenous people. It continues today under conditions of health and life that swell infant mortality, alcoholism, suicide, and violence in these oppressed groups. Job discrimination, housing discrimination, personal attacks, are all the fare of every person of colour in our society at one time or another. The hardest part is, they never know when they are being attacked for their race, and when they are being rejected or attacked for something really objectionable about them.

One study of Black youth matched delinquents and non-delinquents for many characteristics. The study found that the main difference was that those who managed to avoid delinquency recognized that most of the rejections they had experienced were because of their race. Those who retreated into the path of delinquency toward which our society not very subtly pushes many minority youth, believed there was something wrong with them that led to the hate stares and other rejections they had experienced.

So how do you forgive ongoing discrimination, racism, and even genocide? You certainly don't condone the attitudes or behaviour. But retaliating with violence of your own eats away at your own innards, even if it doesn't end in death for some. This is too big a topic for this book, but we tell two small stories below that hint at some of the answers. Laughing at the opponent is one: we laugh at the devil and gain power over him. The other is found in a love larger than any human love can imagine.

The Purifying Water of the Fire Hoses

How do groups live forgiveness, groups that have experienced racism, discrimination and oppression for generations, and who continue to feel the heel of the oppressor? How do you forgive ongoing wrong on a broad scale? William Sloane Coffin, in his autobiography *Once to Every Man and Nation*, tells this story of his visits to Black churches in Birmingham during the height of the civil rights struggle there.

Daily the dogs and fire hoses of the great American justice system, Alabama style, were being turned on these Christians who were just asking for minimal human rights. Sloan writes vividly:

> Like the later teach-ins to oppose the war in Vietnam, these services would last up to three hours, not because they were scheduled to, but because people wanted it that way. Like nothing else in their lives, these services told those attending who they really were as children of God, and what God's world

was all about. They were also good reminders to me that going to church was less a means to an end, than simply a necessary consequence of trying to live a Christian life. The Blacks who went to church every evening in Birmingham were not there because Christianity had been tried and found wanting, but because Christianity had been tried and found difficult.

"Do they hate us?" Abernathy would ask.

"YES," would reply a couple of thousand voices.

"And do we hate them?"

"NO," the chorus would answer.

"Not even when they curse us and say all manner of evil against us?"

"NO!" — a little louder.

"Not even when they wash away all our sins with the purifying water of their all powerful fire hoses?"

"NO!" This time there would be laughter too.

"That's right," Abernathy would say, his face one broad smile. "Because our lives are not in the weak hands of those who hate us, but in the almighty hands of God who loves us!"

"That's right, Preach! ... Amen!" would come from all over the church. Then when Ralph had finished draining the bitterness from every heart, someone... would start, "He's got the whole world in His Hands." Everybody would join in, singing and clapping, and loudest of all on the inevitable verse, "He's got Bull Connor in His hands."

I could not resist quoting Sloane's account word for word, he has captured so perfectly the power of this astounding approach, where the weak become strong, and the strong become inconsequential, except as souls to be loved and transformed.

Forgiveness and the Holocaust

But can forgiveness apply to acts of genocide such as the Holocaust, and such as White men giving smallpox-infested blankets to Indians to wipe out whole tribes of unsuspecting indigenous people?

Years ago I heard the great writer Elie Wiesel speak. He grew up in concentration camps, and his face was a marvel, a précis of his life. As he spoke of how rescue came too late to save the innocence of children like him, the lines of anguish were there, lines that came from learning the depths of evil to which human beings and societies can sink, at an age when no one should have to encounter it. But overlying those grief lines etched into Wiesel's face were triumphant lines and a sparkling joy which came from having used his anguish to lead the cause of oppressed and suffering groups of refugees in many parts of the world. Wiesel's face was the first I saw that told the story of the power of really deep forgiveness; forgiveness of the greatest crimes imaginable.

Gene Knudsen-Hoffman discusses this challenge in a *Fellowship* article in March 1993, called "Victims and Victimizers — Mutual Sorrow, Mutual Suffering." He suggests that every victimizer has been a victim and is acting out fantasies of repressed rage. Personally, I find this an insufficient motivation to forgive. When I try to forgive based on understanding my opponent, I start wrestling with the rights and wrongs of our exchange, and the opponent comes off worst in my perceptions, so my rage only increases. I think we have to forgive because God made us for loving, and damned up love destroys our inner works. Knudsen quotes several Rabbis who say that forgiveness is a release from the past, which does add up for me. The power of unmerited forgiveness is a force that cleanses all in its path.

A number of articles on the Holocaust and other traumas point out the power of post-traumatic stress syndrome. I wonder if some of its damaging capacity is in our holding onto terribly destructive emotions of hatred and bitterness that don't allow us to move beyond the past. Mary Craig, whose book *Blessings* is the most profound book I have ever read on the subject of grief and healing, tells a true story from Ravensbruck concentration camp.

An unknown prisoner wrote this prayer on a torn scrap of wrapping paper, and left it by the body of a dead child:

> Oh Lord, remember not only the men and women of good will, but also those of ill-will. But do not remember all the suffering they have inflicted on us; remember the fruits we have bought, thanks to this suffering — our comradeship, our loyalty, our humility, our courage, our generosity, the greatness of heart which has grown out of all this, and when they come to judgement, let all the fruits which we have borne be their forgiveness.

Whenever I am tempted to feel that "more is asked of me than of some others," I remember that awesome prayer, and am humbled.

Happiness after the Loss of Innocence

It is tempting to continue this chapter for much longer, the stories are so numerous and so inspiring. I have omitted so many stories equally inspiring. Who is to say whose story of forgiving a great wrong is the most significant? The fact is that forgiveness is far more common than we realize, if only because our bodies, hearts, minds and spirits are not strong enough to endure a life lived on the cancerous fuel of continued hatred.

Some years ago I wrote a piece called, "Happiness after the Loss of Innocence." In it, I spoke of how we often say after some personal tragedy; "I'll never be able to be happy again." Indeed, after our first great loss of innocence, when we learn that we can give of our best and finest to the world and it does not pay us back in kind, we are usually convinced that we will never know the innocence of childhood joy again. We take an attitude toward God and this world God has given us of, "If you won't play my way, I'll take my dollies and go home," and we continue life on this sulky path.

But the loss of happiness from our first great loss of innocence is partly true. The joy of a child who has never known injustice has an innocence about it that is charming, wonderful, and pure. One day after I had been through several major cataclysms, plodding through them with God's therapeutic forgiveness medicine, I commented spontaneously on the gorgeous countryside. We were travelling in my brother-in-law's car, and the natural beauty was augmented by beautiful classical music on our car radio. What came out of my mouth, surprisingly enough, were these words, "The older I grow, the more happiness I find in such things."

Remembering my peaceful farewell to happiness some years before, I was startled, and realized that my pleasure in temporal things was actually deepened by knowing how vulnerable they were. Also, having come through the depths of pain, shock, grief, and forgiveness, and knowing they would come again, it was as if the pale pastel of childhood were enriched by the dark hues of deeper experience. A pastel world had become a full-hued rainbow of gorgeous colour; a string orchestra had burst into a many-toned symphony complete with woodwinds, brass and percussion! I realized that when we walk the path of forgiveness through our tragedies, we can find on the other side of those barriers a deeper joy, of the full symphony of life and loving.

The powerful path of forgiveness is the fuel behind transformative justice. As long as we cling to our wrongs, the world around us remains stuck, and our communities are mired in burning grudges, some more merited than others, but all destructive. I have never met an offender who was not the victim of many injustices. If we expect them to deal maturely with their injustices, we need to use processes that enable all of us to do just that. The path of forgiveness heals those who take it, and offers healing to others who witness it or receive it. Transformative justice starts with the power of forgiveness, and its magic is found in that power.

But transformative justice also includes the recognition of wrongs, which makes forgiveness so much easier. Collective recognition of wrongs, followed by freely offered forgiveness are the two sails that enable the ship of transformative justice to sail forth on troubled waters, bringing strength to community and renewal to all. Part III looks at how each of us can transform two great challenges. For we can transform both our revenge-based justice system, which heals neither victims nor offenders; and the chasms of distributive injustice, in which hungry children cry while others indulge in consumer waste that fails to satisfy the deep spiritual yearning of us all. The greatest story of transformative justice is that you and I can play a part in it, here and now.

PART III

KEY CHALLENGES IN TRANSFORMATION

Chapter 7

Transforming
Our Penal Justice System

There are three basic tools in any social change effort: direct action, community education, and lobbying. Direct action includes demonstrations, letter writing, petitions, phone calls and meetings with officials, all by the general public. It also includes changing policies by officials, trying new model programs, and abolishing old practices that seem wrong.

Claire Culhane was a great Canadian activist in this area, who practised direct action of all kinds. She visited prisoners across Canada, and demanded reforms from prison administrators again and again. She wrote letters tirelessly, to prisoners, families, general public, newspapers, and officials. She demonstrated. One time she stood outside a prison for hours just so an isolated, brutally beaten prisoner in segregation could see her there, a lonely but indefatigable one woman support group. No wonder her biographer called her, a "one woman army."

When barred from the system for her truth-telling, Claire wrote a book called *Barred from Prison*, and travelled across Canada pedalling it. When they refused to reverse her exclusion from British Columbia prisons, she revised it as *Still Barred from Prison*, and pedalled that across Canada. When after some years a court finally ruled in her favour, and she regained admission to her own province's prisons, she put out a third revision, *No Longer Barred from Prison*, and off she went across Canada again! No one can illustrate the power of direct action for penal change better than

Claire. But as her book tours also illustrate, she mixed in plenty of public education, and her letters to officials certainly mixed in lobbying.

Lobbying is aimed strictly at politicians, and tries to get them to pass legislation that will move things ahead in the way you think they should go. In the US Civil Rights movement, people lobbied for laws that would outlaw segregation. The tobacco lobby lobbies for greater freedom to promote tobacco to young people and other vulnerable populations, lower tobacco taxes, and less health restrictions. Lobbying can be good or bad depending on who is doing it with what purpose. But all lobbying is aimed at getting what you want straight from the legislators.

The glue that links these two is public education. In my opinion, public education is the most basic and powerful tool of all. If we can get the public to understand what we understand, if our facts are true and our values are sound for a good community, then actions will follow, and laws will follow, in a true democracy. So although a blend of all three techniques is useful, I believe community education is the most essential, and I will focus on it in this chapter. It is true that key legislation can sometimes create changes that carry public opinion with them. Examples include the US Civil Rights Bill, some of the restrictions on smoking in public places, and the New Zealand act making Family Group Conferences the way to respond to all juvenile offences. It is also true that courageous demonstrations can change the world: witness the Gandhian movement for Indian independence, the amazing acts of South African school children for freedom, and the peaceful revolution in the Soviet Union which melted that dictatorship.

Nevertheless, I am going to focus most of my attention here on how we can communicate the truths of transformative justice to the general public. People spend far too much energy moaning about how we are always preaching to the converted. In fact, to influence the general public we have to reach four groups:

- The Converted
- The Sympathetic
- The Neutral
- The Hostile

Let's look at how we can reach each of these groups, and conclude with a list of practical suggestions which you can do, to help build more transformative justice systems, justice systems which will allow and encourage the kind of stories and outcomes which fill this book.

People often ask me, "How can you hope to change the justice system in the directions you talk about it, when the public is so hard-line, and against it?" My response is that the public is not against what I am talking about, and I have done about three hundred call-in shows on radio and TV to prove it. With a handful of exceptions, I get a really friendly reception, and even in those cases, there are more friendly callers than even I expect. We will come back to this point when we talk about how to reach those who are neutral, and those who are hostile to transformative justice.

But a second point I make is that what the public says depends on the questions you ask. If you ask the general public, "Do you believe that juvenile delinquents who repeatedly offend should be released to the community?" most of them will say, "No!' resoundingly. But if you ask that same public, "Do you believe that young people from deprived backgrounds who have committed non-violent crimes should be dealt with in the community?" most will say equally firmly, "Yes!" Yet we are describing the majority of offenders in both questions. It depends on what kind of spin you put on it.

So I have concluded that the questions you ask are more important than the answers you arrive at. There are no good answers to trick questions like these:

- How long since you stopped beating your grandmother?
- How many years in prison should shoplifters get?
- Should we televise executions?

All of these questions presume things we don't want to presume: that we've been beating Grandma, that shoplifters should go to prison, and that we should execute people.

Similarly, there are no bad answers to questions like this:

- How can we involve the wider community more in healing justice processes?
- How can we offer more support and healing to victims of crime?
- What can we do to narrow the gap between rich and poor, and ensure that all children have the essentials of life?

These questions presume we want to move toward a more caring community that includes victims, offenders and community in healing both crime and distributive injustice.

So when I am asked to go on a TV show, I usually try to find the question they are addressing, and if it is a bad one, I suggest they change it, and if they won't, I don't appear. One of the reasons I organize conferences and workshops is that we can name good questions to address, and focus social attention on the questions that will move us forward.

Let's look now at how we approach these four key groups, and focus them on the forward-looking questions. We begin with the so-called "converted."

Preaching to the Converted

My friends in social movements are always complaining, "There we go: preaching to the converted again!" It's true we don't want to limit our efforts to talking to people who agree with us completely. But the "converted" include a lot of people who never lift a finger to improve the justice system. Nearly all ex-prisoners, their immediate families, and many victims know that the revenge approach to justice fails miserably, and that prisons are cesspools of injustice and waste. What would the world be like if every one of them devoted their spare time, money and spiritual energy to the cause of transformative justice?

An economic historian did a study of agrarian reform. He found that not a single "reform by grace," in which some kind person gave justice, survived 50 years. In contrast, 50 percent of "reforms by demand," in which the oppressed group demanded and obtained relief, survived at least 50 years. This fact underlines the need to include ex-prisoners and victims and their families in the struggle for transformative justice. You can't give a person freedom; they have to take it for themselves. So when we are preaching to converted "consumers" of our retributive justice system, we are persuading them to put this particular cause high in their priorities, and empowering them to participate in their own liberation.

Another interesting fact is that university courses inside prisons are among the very few positive forces strong enough to lower recidivism, because they give prisoners something so powerful, it overrides for many the sucking whirlpool of degradation and institutionalization. That powerful force is the understanding that the prisoner is not the sole author of society's problems, and that their incarceration is part of repeated social patterns over the centuries in which penal systems are used to enforce social barriers. When the prisoner understands that, a fifty-pound weight falls off their back, and they have the knowledge they need to be part of a movement to change the root causes of what has happened to them. No wonder they find better life directions from that than obliging the authorities by continuing the crime-police-courts-prison cycle. Two of the finest criminology professors in Canada are ex-offenders, who have gone on to educate generations of students about the real story on prisons and retributive justice!

So an important thing we can do is preach to the converted. Involve prisoners, ex-prisoners, victims, and their families in the cause of transformative justice. Give them important parts in the organizations we have for change. Speak to them about the issues. Treat them with the dignity they deserve, as key players on the road to transformative justice.

What about the other converted, the fifteen or twenty people who are most concerned to transform our justice system, and who come out to all our forums? We need to honour their commitment, celebrate their participation, and use those forums to plan together the next steps we can take for creating transformative justice. Most of the great changes in this world were led by a few people. I have often said, three people are a group, six are a movement, and ten are a mass movement. It's not far from the precise truth.

Enrolling the Sympathetic

Lots of people know there is something wrong with our justice system, but they satisfy their discomfort with it by helping one prisoner, righting one wrong, or donating a few dollars to one of the mainline justice service groups. All these acts are commendable, but we have to find ways to lead these people further. In talks and writings, we have to point out that while they are helping one prisoner, a thousand are being brutalized. The combination of individual stories of oppression with statistics about the overall picture is powerful. We also need to educate them on how the history of prison reform is one of repeated failure, because you can't reform a system designed to fail.

In all our efforts, we need to help the converted and sympathetic find small, winnable steps, but not stop at them. Always keep leading them deeper to social analysis of root problems, while validating their involvement and achievements as they walk with us toward transformative justice. In planning the ninth International Conference on Penal Abolition (ICOPA), we recruited about fifteen people prepared to work on the conference, but many of them had little background on penal abolition. So we introduced an item at the beginning of each meeting in which I shared some writings or thoughts on some aspects of penal abolition, and we discussed this for half an hour. What fun! People enjoyed the meetings more, and what is more, our unity became deeper as we understood the underlying issues better as a group.

Winning Over the Neutral

The neutral are probably the largest group on many issues, including the criminal justice system. Ambivalent might be a better word than neutral. All of us, even we penal abolitionists, can get worked up about some kinds of offences and wax quite angry. For me it's Nestlé's continued complicity in killing off a million babies a year by promoting baby formula to mothers who can't afford enough of it to keep the babies alive and/or do not have clean water and enough fuel to prepare the formula in the first place. For others, it's sex offenders, or someone who broke into their home. Our conclusions about what we want done to these offenders may vary, but anger against what we regard as destructive crime is natural. On the other hand, we have all pardoned offences of those nearest and dearest to us, and plenty of right-wing hard-liners waxed sentimental about not wanting Nixon to go to prison, because he had suffered enough.

Of course questions worded one way or another will push the neutral onto one side or another, but the majority of the population hates crime, and wants it stopped. But they also may dimly suspect that there is something wrong about the proportion of minorities in the penal system and the neglect of victim needs. There are several keys to getting the neutral on our side:

- We have to persuade them that what we do about criminal justice matters
- We have to provide them with more accurate information about crime
- We have to convince them that the present criminal justice system does not meet their objectives

If we can do these three things for a substantial portion of the neutral, we will advance the cause of transforming our justice system enormously. The first point may surprise you. People certainly get hot and bothered about crime, don't they? Yes, presented in the simplistic way opportunistic politicians do, they do. People watch TV shows that portray courts and police in utterly unrealistic ways. But organize a forum for people who experience the actual system to present, and droves stay away. Write books about the real issues, and they are hard to sell to the wider public. Ministers of Corrections in our province are chosen from the ranks of MPPs who don't matter much, but need to be given an unimportant job where what they do won't make much difference.

Similarly, liberal groups forming networks for social change talk about linking feminism and economic justice and antiracism and environmental issues, but they nearly always leave out the criminal justice system as an issue. So our first job is to persuade all these groups that what we do in criminal justice matters, and has a huge impact on all these other issues, and on our daily lives. People in many countries and many areas live behind walls of self-imposed security, because instead of creating economic justice, we have, through our criminal justice system and economic system, created a social class completely motivated to steal from the haves. They are also well trained in how to do it by the prisons of this world. Similarly, one of my public education pamphlets is called, "The Penal System, Linchpin of the Corporate Agenda," to show how vital the penal system is to the maintenance of social inequality.

So how do we persuade the neutral majority, right-wing or left-wing, that the criminal justice system matters? One way is to network with other issues ourselves, and be a broken record on the importance of transforming the criminal justice system. I have been actively involved in most of the above causes, and more, and wherever I go, I constantly remind my friends in those movements that unless we change our destructive, racist and classist criminal justice system, we cannot win on their issues. We need to promote the issue of transformative justice in other people's settings: if they don't come to us, we can come to them. People are more willing to listen when you do them the courtesy of coming out to their locales and listening to their concerns as well.

Further, as we will discuss more with neutralizing the hostile, we need to validate their just concerns, and convince them that solutions are possible. If you think that the only people concerned about our justice system are "soft on crime" and unconcerned for victims, you don't want to listen to them. So I always emphasize that victims and their needs are as important to me as offenders and their families: that we are all part of one community, and the healing of each is bound up in the healing of all. I also validate the pain and recognize the wrong of victims of crime, and the natural social fear of crime. When you have done that, then people are more interested in hearing the good news that the seedlings of transformative justice are already working in little communities of hope all over the world.

Secondly, we have to correct the misinformation the public has about crime. The media have a natural bias, as well as a bias based on who owns them. The natural bias is that they believe the public is only interested in the exceptional, extreme, sensational bad news story. That's why Clifford Olson and Paul Bernardo have had more press in Canada than all of the 90 percent of non-violent offenders in our prisons put together. Given a steady diet of Clifford and Paul and their few peers, the public comes to believe they are surrounded by violent criminals, and they cower in their homes, and wax furious at the thought that prisons aren't holding people long enough.

Tony Doob and Julian Roberts did classic research in the early '90s showing that the public overestimates the percent of violent criminals in our prisons by seven times: instead of ten percent violent offenders, they believe the federal prisons are 70 percent full of violent offenders! Doob and Roberts also presented research on judges and sentencing, in which they presented fairly typical real cases for sentencing. They then asked the public to choose the sentence, and on the average, the public consistently gave lighter sentences than the judges did. Yet a majority of that same public stated that judges were too soft on crime! Why this contradiction? Because the media tend to choose cases where judges have given comparatively low sentences, present the crime negatively without any of the extenuating circumstances known to the judge, and attack the judge.

So how can we correct these misimpressions? First of all, every one of us can seize every opportunity to emphasize certain key points, in casual conversations, in speaking, in teaching if we teach, in letters to editors:

- 90 percent of offenders are non-violent, and only about one percent are in for homicide of any kind
- Community alternatives to prisons are cheaper, safer, more effective and more beneficial for all concerned than prisons
- Victims are as dissatisfied with the present penal system as is everyone else, but there are alternatives that include them and satisfy their core needs

Secondly, whenever conversations focus on the dangerous few, and questions are asked about Clifford, Paul and their few serial killer counterparts, stress how exceptional they are, and turn the issue back to the typical penal population. I often say, "No penal abolitionist I know wants to turn out Clifford and Paul, but this handful of rare individuals are the pinup boys of a system that uses them to justify costly, destructive responses to the 99 percent of prisoners who are not like them. Ninety percent of prisoners are in for completely non-violent offences. Let's get back to discussing the small thieves who are the bulk of the penal population."

Thirdly, support the few groups like our Rittenhouse, A New Vision that devote themselves to disseminating correct information about criminal justice, and take every opportunity to inform yourself more. Evil thrives in ignorance, and the evils of our criminal justice system thrive on the separation of prisons from the rest of us. Breaking those barriers casts the light of firsthand contact on the false beliefs. More of this later, when we come to specific actions you can take.

Finally, in dealing with the neutral we need to help them understand how counterproductive the revenge approach to justice is, an approach which disempowers all those most affected by it. I love the impossible true quote from a lawyer who thought nothing wrong with telling a researcher, "I never explain anything to my clients. They wouldn't understand it, anyway." That sums up the experience of victims, offenders, their families, and stray witnesses.

I seldom go to court but when I do I sometimes observe some other case being run through, and as the bewildered faces affected by it leave the courtroom, I go out in the hall and say, "Do you understand what just happened?" The answer is no, so I translate into real human experience the courtroom gobbledegook that just happened. But day after day people are being ground through this system without me there to translate.

Fortunately, the present system is our own best ally in this education process. Regardless of what the TV shows and the mass media say, most people have themselves encountered it either directly or through a neighbour or relative, and they know it didn't work for them. All we have to do for most of them is listen to their story and then tell them that their experience was not unique, but typical. We can build on the system's failure in their lives to a broader understanding of its failure for our whole society.

Neutralizing the Hostile

Strange as it may seem, our opponents are not necessarily the hardest people to reach. Some Japanese systems of fighting use the force of the opponent in one's own cause. The conversion of St. Paul to Christianity is only one of many instances when the strongest opponent becomes the strongest convert. Our opponents have two important things in common with us:

- They believe the criminal justice system matters a lot
- They believe the present system does not work at all well

Beyond that, we have large differences. They want to try more of the punitive approach that has never worked, and throw good money after bad, while we want to move toward a healing approach that includes all those involved in creating solutions.

Nevertheless, we can build on our common ground. Conflict resolution training teaches us always to listen to the other person's underlying feelings and validate them. Actions may be right or wrong, but feelings can be accepted: fear, anger, love, attraction. Everyone is entitled to their own feelings, and should have them understood and accepted. When we begin by accepting the fears and angers that lie behind so many of our opponents' attitudes and behaviour, we lay the ground for being heard ourselves.

Years ago, Quakers and pacifists organized something they called "The Listening Project" in the American south. On hot topics like racism, abortion, and local pollution issues, they went door to door in pairs, and began by listening to the views of the residents. After listening, and validating the feelings and concerns of the people, they were able to respond with solid facts that laid to rest some of the fears, while still showing respect to the other party. The project was such a success they could hardly absorb all the new volunteers they got for their work! We need to do a listening project for transformative justice.

What You Can Do

All this is very well, but what can each of us do, in our own lives, which may be limited by jobs, health, by the care of babes or the elderly, or by other demands? Below are eight things almost anyone can do, without taking a lot of time, and without changing the whole course of your life to prioritize the work for transformative justice:

1. **Inform yourself.**

   Only by informing ourselves continuously can we be prepared to carry the case for transformative justice in our daily contacts, wherever we go. We can't predict when the topic may arise, but as we get the knack of being carriers of truth, we welcome opportunities to learn even painful truths, for we know we will disseminate them. But without first learning a lot, we won't be sufficiently informed to be carriers of transformative justice. Once we have gained the basic knowledge, we don't need to read a lot, but we do need to keep in touch through newsletters of relevant groups, or other good sources.

2. **Make contact with prisoners, ex-prisoners, and/or crime victims.**

   One of the reasons prisons are so distant from populated areas is that the penal system is about separating certain classes and races out and widening the social chasms. Once, years ago, I was riding in a car with a friend to do an evening program at one of the Kingston prisons, so far from Toronto. Being tired already and knowing how late we would be getting back that night, I was grumbling and saying I wouldn't ever do this again. With dismay in his voice, he said, "Don't say that, Ruth. Don't you realize that is exactly what the people who created this system want you to think and do? Prisons separate people from each other, and to defeat their purposes, we have to travel as far as necessary to bridge those barriers." I realized he was right, and I have continued to make those trips, as far as I am able, over the years.

   Moreover, prisons and prisoners can educate us better on these topics than all the articles and books put together. When you experience the bars and clanging locks and gates, the dehumanizing setting, the crude counts and demeaning treatment of prisoners and even of their visitors, you don't need a book to understand the indignity and horror of it all. Visits through a glass sound innocuous enough when I say those words, but try the reality! So contact with prisons and prisoners, or if you have a friend who has been victimized, with victims going through our legal system, is important both for the humanity of the act, but also for promoting your deeper growth and understanding.

If you can't manage to be part of a regular or occasional visiting program, there are programs that arrange to match volunteers one to one with prisoners, either for monthly visits, or even just as pen-pals. I could fill a chapter of this book with stories of the transformative effect of just that kind of correspondence on both parties. Tragically, every visiting and pen pal program I know of has a long waiting list of lonely prisoners waiting for a community volunteer willing to offer a window of community inclusion through a small bit of their time. There is no better way to broaden your understanding than through some type of direct, personal contact.

3. **Be a mole for transformative justice, wherever you are.**

When you inform yourselves both through reading and through some kind of direct contact, you are ready to be a mole for transformative justice. So many bits of conversation offer opportunities to speak truth about these issues. If every one of us who care about a more healing justice system just responds to direct openings, we could have a huge impact in creating a more informed public. Be tactful, be gentle, tell personal stories, and you can help others understand the wonderful potential of transformative justice.

4. **Join a group that supports transformative justice.**

Rittenhouse, A New Vision, the group I work through, started ten years ago with two ex-prisoners and myself. We cheered every time we got a new member. Today we have several hundred, but we are still small enough that every active member makes a big difference. Your membership may just be a token donation and reading the newsletter, but those things are powerful, and they link you to other ways to support transformative justice, and new stories and facts about it.

5. **Write one letter a month that promotes transformative justice.**

I am not suggesting you devote a whole letter every month just to this topic, but in the same spirit that you infuse it into conversation where it is relevant, you can mention it in letters about other subjects, where it fits. However, it is also very good to write letters to editors, support letters to individuals going through the present system as victims or offenders, and commendations to people acting in the spirit of transformative justice.

6. **Write your legislators your views on transformative justice once a year.**

We often think writing our legislators has no impact, but most legislators figure that every letter on a topic represents about 100 people who don't bother to write. Taking the time to explain your views on transformative justice to your legislator can have an impact, particularly because it makes so much sense, and it is fairly easy to show that. Many legislators have never heard of it, so break the silence! Better still, make an appointment with your legislator, bring along a friend who believes as you do, and tell them about it.

7. **Use transformative approaches in your personal conflicts, and any contacts you have with the legal system.**

It's no good talking about transformative justice if we don't practice it ourselves. As many of the stories in this book show, we don't have to wait for legislation to practice transformative, healing, methods in our own lives. Victims are in a particularly strong position to assert what they want instead of falling completely into the hands of the police and courts, although the system will pressure them otherwise. But even offenders who reach out and take ownership for their offence can help change the tone of the process. Given the obstacles, if your problem is potentially legal, you may have to be creative and work at it, but you can witness to what you believe. We have friends in Thunder Bay whose daughter was brutally murdered, and who have gone through devastating years of trials and anguish. But they still manage to reach out to the parents of the man who murdered their child, in spite of many situational obstacles to the transformative approach they would have preferred. Most of our challenges aren't that big, but if we keep it in mind, life's daily conflicts offer many opportunities to build a culture more ready for transformative justice.

8.   Try forgiveness in your personal life.

That brings us to the last and in some ways most important witness. Without forgiveness, every community would be a seething mass of violence. We do practice forgiveness toward our children and immediate family, or we would never stay together. But forgiveness toward the *out*-group is a concept too much neglected in our culture. I have sometimes said we are a pena-holic society, addicted to penal approaches. The way to break an addiction is to support one another in finding healthier paths that break its ties. So Bill Pelke's phone number — TO FORGIVE — says it all. If every one of us who believe in transformative justice put forgiveness that much in the centre of our lives and consciousness, we would do more to build a society ready for transformative justice than by all the speeches we could possibly make.

Everyone can forgive. It is an act of will, not a rush of emotion. It is a path and a process, not an instant high and achievement. Forgiveness is simply willing what is best for our opponent, and determining to act in goodwill toward them. It does not mean accepting continued abuse, for it includes saying No to wrong behaviour. But while it embraces restraint of wrong behaviour, it abjures giving pain back for pain received. Forgiveness is heady stuff: try it, it's challenging, but once you catch it, it's just as contagious as revenge, and a lot more freeing!

Every one of us can bring transformative justice nearer to fruition in our society. It isn't something that people like me who write and speak about it all the time can accomplish. Only as everyone who believes there is a better way takes these kinds of small steps will we bring it about. In the same spirit, let's look now at how each one of us can begin to change the terrible abuses of distributive injustice, which are destroying our world community as well as our local communities.

Chapter 8

Transforming Distributive Injustice

So how do we transform distributive injustice, in this real world that has been riddled with inequality, domination, oppression and greed for a very long time indeed? Yet for all humanity's sordid record in this regard, we have running side by side a very honourable record. Privileged people have renounced privilege to stand for social justice in every culture and every decade. Marginalized groups have risked and given their all to work together for transformation. Transformation is an ongoing process and challenge. The question is not whether transformation will be on the human agenda, but where our lives will fall in that great struggle.

Almost all writers on the threat to humanity and the environment by corporate rule have a section on how to challenge and transform the widening gap between rich and poor that comes with corporate rule. Two that do an especially good job are Goudzwaard and De Lange's *Beyond Poverty and Affluence*, and David Korten's *The Post-Corporate World*.

Beyond Poverty and Affluence is a book by two Dutch Christian economists. Bob Goudzwaard is a former member of the Dutch parliament, and both he and Harry De Lange are professors of economics, yet their book communicates clearly both the problem, and a twelve-step program for recovery. Originally published in Dutch in 1986, the book was translated into German in 1990 and into English in 1995, being updated each time and made more relevant to the wider audience. Citizens for Public Justice, a Christian social action group, thought so well of it they persuaded their donors to pay for copies to be sent to every MP in Canada!

The translator has included many current examples from Canada and the USA. Like many other analysts, Goudzwaard and De Lange point out that the economic theories of the past twenty years have led the world to the brink of disaster. Poverty is widening everywhere, the rich are getting richer, the poor getting more desperate, the environment is on the verge of total collapse, and the ownership of media and power of money put both media and governments in the thrall of the few elite corporate rulers. One-third of the world's labour force that wants desperately to work is now unemployed, and a high proportion of the rest are working in such marginalized conditions that they lack any security, social safety net, or even enough income to provide minimal food and housing for themselves and their families.

UNICEF estimates that 40,000 children per day, seventeen million per year, die from exhaustion, hunger, or lack of basic necessities. The richest twenty percent of the world's population had incomes 30 times greater than the poorest twenty percent as of 1960. By 1994 this gap had widened to 78 times greater (Korten, p. 79). Korten quotes a Forbes Magazine report, that by 1996, there were 447 billionaires in the world, and their fortunes equal the total combined annual income of the poorest half of humanity (p. 80). What does one do with a billion dollars? It would take us every waking moment of 40 years to count so far. Yet while the super-rich wallow in more affluence than they can possibly use, hunger, disease, homelessness, and desperation afflict more and more of the world's children.

Meanwhile, acid rain, the vanishing ozone layer, global warming, vanishing species, toxic chemical waste, and deforestation are rapidly destroying resources it took the planet millennia to store for all life, in perpetuity. Korten quotes China expert Carl Riskin in a 1997 *Nation* article on the severe levels of pollution in that country. A study by the World Bank, hardly a bastion of left-wing propaganda, estimates that two million people die each year in China from air and water pollution (Korten, p. 72). Yet corporate lobbies persuade governments to give a green light to the continued rape of the environment, a process that endangers the future of the children of these governmental and corporate leaders as much as it does yours and mine. For example, two million Chinese die per year from pollution's unfettered effects and a million (mostly) African and Asian babies continue to die each year because of the promotion of baby formula by Nestlés and other avaricious marketers of formula over healthy affordable breastfeeding. The amazing thing is that few people note that this genocide toll exceeds that of the Holocaust, terrible as it was.

In the midst of all this myopia, where is the hope for transformation? Reading books about the real crisis in human and world history is depressing, but both Korten and Goudzwaard-De Lange are full of hope, and of signs of the future we can have, provided we work for it!

The basic remedy proposed by Goudzwaard and De Lange is to move from a *post-care* economy to a *pre-care* economy. They speak of the economics of care, or the economics of enough. Most analysts point out that our theory and behaviour are those of adventurers on an unlimited frontier, instead of denizens of a limited spaceship. We have so despoiled our world that we are now facing very constricted limits in this spaceship, but we go on acting as if we have an infinite frontier to exploit and waste. Our present out of control priorities centre on:

- Growth
- Ever increasing production and consumption
- The idea that wealth, materialism, consumerism and amassing more and more money is the only way to be happy and fulfilled.

Not only do many writers point out these fallacies, but the remedies are not new or surprising. The economics of a pre-care society are to seek:

- Enough to supply the basic needs of all
- Full employment or adequate income for all
- The preservation of the environment for future generations and our own

If we put these first, then we will see that the search for unlimited growth in production, consumption and materialism is not only unsatisfying but also fundamentally impractical. The environment cannot sustain our cancerous escalating demands, and materialism itself has demonstrated repeatedly that it puts the profits of distant shareholders above the need for jobs or food for those more immediately contributing. Korten puts it eloquently when he says in effect that the way to break the golden chains by which the corporations hold us in thrall, is to abandon our worship of gold. When money is no longer our king, we are free to seek transformation, and give our lives to healthier goals.

Both books quote numerous examples of how transformation is already occurring in our world. *Beyond Poverty and Affluence* mentions that one-percent of the annual income of Swedish union members is designated for improvement of workplace conditions. A Dutch Union (CNV) has offered to freeze wage increases for five years in exchange for more care to the environment, the poor, and the needs of the unemployed. I-G Metall, Germany's largest union, has made a similar offer. In 1990 people from all walks of Kapuskasing, Ontario banded together to buy the local pulp and paper mill, setting aside feuds between management and five competing labour unions. The outcome has been a plant upgraded to meet environmental standards, and one of the few profitable mills in North America in the early 1990s (Goudzwaard and De Lange, pp. 103-104).

The Twelve Step program advocated by Goudzwaard and De Lange includes giving Third World countries an equal voice in the economic power bases of the world (International Monetary Fund, etc.); and re-establishing controls on corporations, whose power comes from a charter from the people. They also include challenging international trade agreements, building international consumer-labour networks, and simplifying our lifestyles.

David Korten also mentions many of these examples of beginnings, and recommendations for continuing. Korten's contagious optimism sees that we are part of a change already happening, although it will not happen automatically without further effort on our part. His "new storytellers" are key contributors to a world movement building a pre-care economy that puts human essentials and environmental respect before profits, greed, and endless growth.

They include "ordinary heroes" like cab driver Dick Falkenbury and poet Grant Cogswell, who put together a ballot measure to relieve downtown congestion in Seattle, Washington by extending an old monorail system. They spent all of $2000 on their campaign, which was mainly walking around Seattle with a plywood billboard showing a map of the proposed monorail system. The Seattle chamber of commerce and other sensible critics called them silly dreamers, naive and irrelevant. But Seattle citizens approved their proposal by a 53 percent majority, making a major contribution to creative planning and healthier living in the city (p. 226).

A much more marginalized group of Hispanic-American mothers in Los Angeles formed MELASI (Mothers of East Los Angeles), and have blocked a number of hazardous projects in their neighbourhoods. Humble villagers in Kito, Japan, organized in 1997 and stopped their powerful government from constructing a dam that would have flooded their village (p. 227). "King Tone" Fernandez, leader of a gang in Queens, New York, known for violence, drugs and murder, has turned his street skills to local economic development, and risks his life challenging former drug dealers to help him build strong, local, legal jobs (p. 229).

Then there are the environmental heroes, such as the amazing Amrita Devi and her three daughters who literally gave their lives to save sacred trees in India, three hundred years ago, establishing the "tree huggers." The struggle for the environment goes back a lot further than some of us realize! Rachel Carson sacrificed her career and reputation to write *Silent Spring*. Although she was jeered at by establishments of all kinds, 40 bills to control pesticide use were introduced within three months of its publication, and the book has become a legend of whistle-blowing on the vital environmental issues of our time (p. 232).

More amazing still are the stories of responsible people of wealth who are with us in working for a future for humanity and this planet. Jesus said it was harder for a camel to go through the eye of a needle than for a rich man to enter the kingdom of heaven, but an amazing few manage the needle trick. A group called Responsible Wealth, created in 1997, work together to educate policy makers and public about the dangers of growing inequality, and support measures to narrow the wage gap, limit influence of big money in politics, and increase taxes to themselves. To belong you have to be in the upper five percent income bracket. Members are encouraged to donate their gains from the new capital gains taxes to groups working for equity. By 1998, 125 members had given over one million dollars to such groups!

Ben Cohen of Ben and Jerry's Homemade ice cream company has led a similar group directly from responsible business. Their cause is getting the US government to take money from the military and move it to social needs. They work for more money for job creation, health care, US payments to the UN, environmental care, and world hunger (p. 235).

In short there are plenty of good news stories, but of course the press, owned more than 90 percent by the largest corporations, do not report them. Lest you think that these stories are exceptional, and still feel you are isolated in your work for social justice, Korten quotes a number of studies of the American public that show, probably owing to the corporate media stress on materialism and consumerism as the norm, that most of us live in "pluralistic ignorance." Pluralistic ignorance is something sociologists have often pointed out. An example is a church where everyone believes "the group" is opposed to card-playing, but in fact when surveyed individually, most of the members play cards and think it is fine.

Korten quotes revealing research by Paul Ray, a values researcher from California. He identifies three major cultural value groupings in the USA:

- **Modernists**: 47 percent of Americans, modernists embrace consumerism and materialism.
- **Heartlanders**: 29 percent of Americans are religious conservatives. They want to go back to traditional community and gender practices, but include in this helping others and working for social betterment.
- **Cultural Creatives**: 24 percent of Americans are committed to family, community, the environment, international caring, renewed spirituality, and feminism.

Moreover, the modernists can be broken down into three more or less equal groups:

- Modernists who play the game of consumerism, but are thoroughly alienated, and find little satisfaction in anything.
- Modernists who play the game, but yearn for deeper spiritual and community meaning in their lives.
- Modernists who really accept consumerism deeply (Korten, pp. 214-217).

When you look at this, you see that we cultural creatives working for social transformation are actually a very powerful, substantial minority, and many of our values are bolstered by people in the other groups. Although the Modernists appear to have the most power, in fact only one-sixth of Americans buy the consumer culture hook, line and sinker. The hollow core of materialism is not selling at all well!

This is confirmed by a variety of specific questions, with over 80 percent of Americans endorsing statements like:

- "We need to treat the planet as a living system" (87%)
- "We need to rebuild our neighbourhoods and small communities" (83%)

Still another surveyor, the Trends Research Institute, names the shift toward voluntary simplicity one of the ten top trends of Americans in 1997. Twenty-eight percent of those surveyed by The Harwood Group in 1997 reported having voluntarily simplified their lives and incomes in the past five years! Three times as many felt they would be more satisfied by spending more time with family and friends than by having a nicer car. More than twice as many felt making a difference to help their community would satisfy them more than a bigger house or apartment (Korten, pp. 217-219).

Transformation is indeed happening all around us. But as Martin Luther King said, it doesn't just roll in on the wheels of inevitability. We have to be part of that wonderful process. Maude Barlow quotes an 87-year-old activist who prodded Maude in a discouraged moment with these powerful words, "Fighting for social justice is not something you do once and then forget. Fighting for social justice is like taking a bath. You do it every day or you start to stink!" (Barlow, p. 112). So what can we do to be part of that wonderful process?

Seven Steps Toward Social Transformation

After the election of a very rightwing, oppressive government in my home Ontario, I was one of many who devoted myself to resistance to the destruction of all that made us a caring, happy, secure community. I began to get irritated at the many that said, "Nothing I can do will change any of this. What is the use? I might as well just give up." I sat down one day and wrote in a couple of hours, "Fifty things you can do to change Ontario today," dividing them into spiritual approaches, communicating with our families and friends, using visual messages, public witnesses, organizing, and political action. Later, I have consolidated these many paths into seven broad directions. Let's look at each of them here:

1. Tuning Up Our Individual Lifestyles
2. Using Our Consumer Power

3. Disseminating Our Awareness Everywhere
4. Transforming Our Sources of Information
5. Changing Our Political Systems to Achieve Democracy
6. Regaining Control of Corporations
7. Building International Networks for Compassion

These seven steps move from the personal level to the global. The first two focus on what each individual can do in their own home, family, and environment. The next two focus on the key issue of how we communicate truth in a society saturated with corporate controlled media disinformation. The final three move to political action and directions, for the international movement to reclaim community and a safe, sustainable environment.

1.   Tuning Up our Individual Lifestyles

One myth that helps keep all of us on the path of destruction is this one: "My one life cannot cause much harm. I am dealing with so much stress. I need comforts. So I will continue to indulge in some wastes, which enable me to work more effectively for good. When everyone else comes along, I'll be glad to drop these habits too. Now I live in a society where it is very hard to live in harmony with nature. Then it will be easy." Corporations, insofar as they have the capacity to think collectively, probably have much of the same logic; "My bit of pollution would do no harm if the others behaved. So long as they are doing it, I will too. When everyone else gets in line, I will too. But don't expect me to lead the way."

This logic reminds me of a famous quote at the end of a two-hour discussion in Civil War days between a pacifist Quaker farmer and a general. At the end of all the arguments, the general turned to the Quaker and said, "Friend, if all the world were like you, I would turn and follow after."

The Quaker responded immediately, "Then thou hast a mind to be one of the last people in the world to be good. I have a mind to be one of the first, and set the example."

It is the general's kind of thinking, collectively and individually, which is leading us to abuse and actually destroy the home God gave us all to share and honour, Mother Earth. It is this kind of thinking which causes us in the North, especially in North America, to consume vastly disproportionate amounts of the world's goods, and to cause most of the pollution and environmental destruction that threaten the future of ALL the world's children. The situation is so severe that our children may not live out their natural lives even if we all stop now. Whether we are environmentalists or not, whether we are billionaires or in dire poverty, all of us share a need for air, water, arable land, mineral resources, and forests. No amount of wealth, education, or other advantage will enable anyone's children to survive if we do not change our way of living.

So ask yourself in what ways you are living that contribute to waste, pollution and destruction. Each of us must pursue this on our own, and I am no expert, but some of the questions I need to challenge myself with include:

- How can I use cars less?
- What about international travel, airplanes, etc.?
- Can I consume less, and buy more local items when I do buy?
- Can I use fewer disposable items, and reduce, reuse, and recycle more?
- Can I re-route some of my spending to sustain the groups struggling to create the caring community?

You can probably come up with a better list than this. The important thing is to make your own list, and work on it. All these questions have to be balanced by the purpose of cars, travel, and other consumption. Below I will be advocating international gatherings, which require travel. But we do need to keep asking ourselves, "Is this trip necessary? From which choice will Mother Earth gain most?"

2.   Using our Consumer Power

The next step is also about our consumer power, but it begins to move to collective action. Yet it is an individual action, because every one of us can choose individually to buy or not buy. Moral values can influence our choices, and there is power in the choices we make. For many years, my husband and I boycotted South African goods in a world that seemed to ignore this crying issue. We had little hope that our actions would help to bring down the most viciously racist government in the world, yet in the end the actions of consumers like us around the world played a role in one of the most dramatic and beautiful liberations I have lived to see.

Similarly, we still boycott Kraft goods, based on an unsuccessful boycott call by small Canadian farmers years ago. The movement to boycott trickled out, and only rarely do we meet someone else who boycotts Kraft. But the cause has not gone away, and we do not choose to spend our dollars on a firm that has done and continues to do more than its share of objectionable actions. Consumer choices are ours as individuals, whether or not anyone joins us. As my friend Ammon Hennacy said years ago when reporters asked him if he seriously expected, with his repeated solo fasts and picketings, to change the whole world around to his way of thinking, "Well, I don't know about that. But I do know one thing: they're sure not going to change me around to theirs!"

We don't have to choose to be as visible and bold about it as Ammon was, but our consumer choices are ours to make, from our own values. We can choose to use them to support local family businesses and crafts, and not to support the multinational corporations that are destroying our world. Often the multinational corporations, because of a combination of exploitative labour, ruthless destruction of environmental resources, and a world market, can and do sell cheaper (until they squeeze local businesses out altogether). But it is worth paying a little more to sustain local economies, reduce the huge transportation of goods which adds to pollution, and witness to that great truth, "small is beautiful."

To empower a world consumer movement for co-operative communities, we need to become more aware of the many consumer boycotts now launched, and we need to broaden support for them, and add others to the list. We also need to use consumer power to sustain the best production efforts in local economies. Consumer power is one of our most important resources. We have 90-95 percent of the world's population potentially behind us, because that number is not in any way gaining from the runaway greed which divides the other five to ten percent further and further from us. That greed is making more and more of us marginal and jobless. Our consumer power is a mighty force: let's *use* it!

3.   Disseminating our Awareness Everywhere

In our daily lives, all of us encounter dozens of people. Most of us meet, over a month or two, hundreds, and some meet thousands. Many of these are casual contacts. We are not doing a fraction of what we can to carry our message to all these people. Let's consider some of the lacks:

- What would our community look like if all who believed in a compassionate community had bumper stickers, lawn signs, and office slogans on our walls that told our story? Right now, few of us use our resources fully. Every time I see a lawn sign or window sign affirming an important community value, my energy goes up. Let's re-energize the converted, and remind the indifferent and the opposed that we are a mighty tide for social justice and compassion. Moreover these messages can be phrased in a way that points out the centrality of a caring community. When I passed out leaflets for our Interfaith Vigil for Social Justice and Compassion, I used to say with a friendly smile, to the few people who wouldn't take them, "Which are you against: social justice or compassion?"

- What would our lives be like if every day each of us wore buttons telling our story? Our mobile bodies are the best free advertising space God gave us, and most of us waste this opportunity. Thoreau said, "Cast your whole vote, not your ballot only." Most of us haven't begun to cast our whole vote.

In addition to these, I initiate conversations about key issues even with strangers on buses and on the streets. A late bus reminds us of cuts to shared public transit, and what these are doing to the air we breathe, as car pollution increases. A street person's situation brings up the topic of the attack on subsidized housing, and the end to rent controls. A friendly face suggests words about the value of a caring community. Not everyone feels comfortable with such approaches, and neither do I always. But sometimes an opportunity offers, and I seize it. I talk with street people about what has put them there, and about my support for their dilemma. I include some of the key issues of our time in almost every letter I write, in one form or another, group or individual, because these key issues are what matter most. Why should we pretend that only trivia and superficiality matter?

"Not to decide is to decide," and when we fail to speak for the marginalized, the widening gap between rich and poor, fuelled by the inevitable corruption of power, continues to erode our community. Cast your whole vote, make it the core issue of your life, and you begin to use your life for dissemination in the way we need to if we are to win this struggle for the future of humanity.

Finally on this level, we need to use postering and street leafleting. The powers of wealth have media control, money to elect politicians, and control of many jobs and economic influences. God gave us our bodies, our lives, and our souls. We have to use them effectively. A Toronto movement called

Citizens for Local Democracy demonstrated the power of leafleting in subways. Ontario Coalition Against Poverty continues to show the power of postering. Poor people can plaster posters on telegraph poles and bus shelters and fences. Let's use what we have, and disseminate truth with all our lives, and all our resources.

Speaking of truth, let us be faithful to language, and not call neo-reactionary policies neo-liberal. Let's not call welfare changes that destroy lives, make people homeless, drive some to suicide, and make many children hungry "reforms." They are "*de*-forms," because they deform our community. The powerful, who are themselves afflicted with the cancer of greed, have stolen truth in language. Let's reclaim it.

4.   Transforming our Sources of Information

Everywhere I go, people are talking about media issues, media workshops, and dealing better with the media. All that is well and good, but trying to react better to the existing corporate controlled media is a little like trying to out-hit Babe Ruth. Baseball is his game, and he almost owned it. The corporate media are owned by corporations, and while we can improve our ability to cope with them on their turf, we need to establish turf of our own, where we have some hope of getting our message out, and presenting more of the whole truth of community life and values. Corporate media are not open to carrying community messages, and they are committed to selling us on the idea that buying something, buying anything, will assuage the terrible emptiness that a consumer culture of materialism and winner-takes-all leaves in our souls.

Thomas Mathiesen (1997) and others have pointed out that media shape our minds. If media doesn't cover an event of ours, we feel as if it has not happened. Mathiesen argues that the modern mass media have given disproportionate attention to a variety of "outsiders." The media identify someone or some group as an outsider, and try to convince us that they are the problem causing all our grief: criminals in the street, our youth, the poor, single mothers on welfare, drunken Indians, new immigrants and refugees, or some particular ethnic minority. Much better we should blame these marginalized folk than question those who are making the policies that leave us alienated, jobless, and insecure!

The key role television has played as a tool in bringing us to the brink of disaster is noted by many. Some of this is not intentional, some is very intentional. Our capacity to use every new miracle of technology to our destruction more than to our benefit fills me with amazement, and television is a prime example. David Korten (p. 33) quotes a 30-year US study of nine million American freshmen on 1500 campuses across the country, showing a radical shift in why college is important to them. A simple summary of the results looks like this:

Why College is Important to American Freshmen

	1968	1996
To develop a meaningful philosophy of life	83%	43%
To be very well off financially	42%	74%

Of course the insecurity forced on them by the corporate culture, which regards downsizing of jobs at all levels essential, except for those at the very top, has forced more attention to financial security on many youth. But the drop in valuing deeper meanings in life is astonishing. More striking still is that the switch in values is almost wholly correlated with hours of television viewing. Those who watched most TV before college were most likely to believe that money mattered more than life perspective! The ceaseless messages of commercials and programming, each intoning in their own way, "Buy something, buy anything, and you will feel better," have had their impact on these students.

Neil Postman says that television has "transformed our emphasis from the written message to that of the picture" (cited in Mathiesen, 1997). Since pictures define what is true and false, tabloids and punchy headlines triumph over boring factual details. Mathiesen calls it "living in a viewer society." Since thoughts require something more than a 30-second sound bite, and life issues increasingly have to be compressed into 30-second sound bites, many vital issues simply are not discussed in the media. When we walked across Iowa for prison awareness, television coverage only focussed on our water bottles and our shoes. The underlying issues beyond the footwork and exercise were beyond TV's faith in their audience's ability to think.

The tabloids play the same game as television, in their own medium. Focussing on lurid pictures and sunshine girls, they simply ignore issues too complex to fit within their translation of the 30-second sound bite: the half column sensational story, dwarfed by a lurid picture. So when we accept the widely shared view that truth about the world can only be found by immersing ourselves daily in the corporate media, we invite having our minds stamped with the imprint of a simplistic, corporate coloured, picture dominated torrent. Day by day, we lose touch with reality. We know that our own jobs are insecure, our children lack jobs altogether, our neighbours lost their home, a sick friend was turned away from a scarce hospital bed. We also know that our teachers are telling us of their desperation in serving larger and larger classes with less and less time to teach constructively. But the corporate friendly politicians managing all this community destruction, saturate their media with statements about how they have improved the economy, helped education, health and housing, and voters actually believe these statements in the face of their own experience!

As I reflected on all this, I came to the conclusion that I was allowing my own reality to be defined by the media. I also concluded that I had choices I had not previously considered, and I became positively excited by the freedom and power those choices offered. I realized that we have as many grassroots groups as ever, even if corporate controlled governments have pulled funding from many agencies, and even if the media deny their existence by ignoring their press releases and events. Our community celebrations and demonstrations are significant, whether the corporate media lie about them or ignore them. So how can we become proactive so that we and others will get closer in touch with the reality our biased media obscure? How can we overcome this subversion of democracy by the co-optation of our minds? I have several suggestions:

- Develop consumer ratings of community friendliness in the media and get these published in community media.
- Promote use of the top rated media and boycott the worst ones.
- Rethink our grasp of reality. Discount corporate media in our personal reading, quoting, thinking, advertising, and buying.

One group I worked with began developing a zero to five rating of media for honesty, and for interest in reporting on community building events and perspectives. We worked on identifying the top media, and promoting use of them in every way. Our message was "Read, watch, listen to, quote, advertise in, and use these media."

Similarly, we planned to identify the worst media and promote a boycott of them. Personally, it astonishes me how many socially aware people devote large portions of their time, life and energy to reading, watching, quoting and reacting to these dishonest and destructive media. It is as if we are under a spell. There is a fable about an Ice Queen who puts a splinter of ice in the heart of a little girl, and the child loses her freedom to live as the loving, delightful little girl she was. She is in the thrall of the Ice Queen. When we saturate our minds with corporate dominated media, we allow our souls to be saturated with the power of the Ice Queen.

One day as I was walking down the street thinking about all this, I walked past a pool of dirty, polluted water on the street. I thought, "I would not kneel down and drink from that pool. I would not dream of filling my body with such polluted water! But we pollute our minds with sources of dishonest information, distortion, and omission of all that is most important in community and reality. That is just as destructive. Let's begin avoiding cholera infected media."

Since I have begun to challenge my own thinking about reality, I feel lighter already. When we reject the corporate media perspective, we begin to see a better world already. Life is like one of those connect the dot pictures where the mass of dots thrown at us by corporate advertising and promotion of corporate views obscure the picture, till we begin to draw lines for ourselves, that make the true connections and unveil the real picture beneath it all. Grassroots people *are* helping each other. Many bus drivers *are* helpful. Neighbours want to be caring toward one another. Many agency people and church folk are giving their all in these times to keep community going. Activists are working at an incredible rate, meeting everywhere, organizing demonstrations, disseminating information, and giving beyond belief.

Are we letting our energies be sapped, and missing these wonderful realities because we listen to the deliberately draining messages of corporate media, telling us we don't count? Recently a clerk I was explaining the value of recycling plastic bags to responded, "It's one of those things that when everybody does it, it will help, but until everybody does it, it doesn't do any good." I explained to him that life doesn't work that way: every bit we do contributes to a better or worse world, and the world is the sum total of the choices each of us makes, all day long. But the myth that clerk believed is the one that is disempowering the struggle of individuals to survive over corporate greed. Every time we can unlock for one person faith in their power to act, and the truth that their choices matter, we light a candle of hope.

Fannie Lou Hamer was one who lived this more than most. Considered by many to be second only to Martin Luther King in eloquence and leadership in the civil rights movement in the American south, Fannie Lou Hamer had every reason to feel helpless and defeated in her native, violent, thoroughly racist Mississippi. The twentieth child in a poor sharecropper family, involuntarily sterilized herself, only able to afford a sixth grade education, Fannie Lou was one of life's hopeless victims of racism and classism, it would have seemed. But she chose to act, and when the moment came, Fannie Lou Hamer made choices that transformed electoral politics throughout the USA, especially the south.

In 1962 the courageous youth of the Southern Non-violent Co-ordinating Committee (SNCC) came to Mississippi, a bastion of entrenched and violently held white power, to try to organize Blacks to register to vote. They called a meeting in a church, and they made their case, then pleaded for volunteers to go with them to make the attempt. Fannie Lou Hamer was one of three middle-aged Black women who dared to put up their hands and volunteer for this perilous and terrifying venture (Mills, p. 24).

Courageous young Charles McLaurin organized his faithful few to make the effort. What courage it took for the women and McLaurin to walk up those courthouse steps — and be told the clerk would be gone for a month! Fannie Lou joined a later group of seventeen persons, making the same attempt, and this time facing White people in cowboy hats, with dogs and guns. When the would-be voters had to state their employers, they knew they would be fired before they got back home. They were given hard sections of the state constitution to interpret, told they had failed the test, and sent home. On the way back, their bus was stopped, and the driver was arrested because his bus was too yellow, the police said!

In the midst of the fear and insecurity of the passengers left stranded, one woman penetrated the growing anxiety by leading out in song, with a powerful voice: "Down by the Riverside," "Ain't Gonna Let Nobody Turn Me Around," and above all, "This Little Light of Mine." That voice was Fannie Lou Hamer's. A number of people claimed the credit of discovering this amazing woman, hidden in the poverty and locked-in racism of rural Mississippi, but at heart, Fannie Lou Hamer discovered herself. She went on to challenge the President of the USA, the national Democratic Party, the voting system of the United States, and the continued existence of White rule in Mississippi.

Fannie Lou Hamer lost every election she ever ran for. She was beaten by police, thrown off of the farm her family rented by the White owner, and had her life threatened repeatedly. Her spirit shone through every disappointment and every terror. It was expressed again and again in her theme song: "This little light of mine, I'm gonna let it shine, all over Mississippi, I'm gonna let it shine." She died at 59, partly from injuries from police beatings, still in poverty, but she liberated herself and she created a south where the most powerful bigoted politician of the south, Senator Eastland, could no longer run, because the electorate was beyond his mean smallness.

Fannie Lou Hamer's philosophy of letting each of our little lights shine where we are, is the perfect foil for that clerk's belief that nothing will happen till everyone suddenly decides to move together. Every one of us can choose to wait for social justice to descend on the world with the wave of a magic wand from on high, when several billion persons suddenly change at once, or we can let our lights shine, by discovering ourselves. We won't discover the power in ourselves by reading the corporate press!

Where would my energy level have been if I had spent my time recently reading their accounts of life, with their misleading language, "welfare *reform*" (for destruction of the lives of those who need financial supports), "neo-*liberalism*" (for a philosophy which normal language would call ultraconservative)? Behind their language is misleading reporting, telling only the story of corporate power, sinking into our subconscious that there is no alternative to a world running entirely on corporate greed. Instead, I chose to spend time reading magazines reporting the facts of the damage of corporate rule, facts about the world-wide struggle for democracy and the environment, and the inspiring story of Fannie Lou Hamer!

We do count, and our choices matter. There is hope, energy, and inspiration in challenging corporate media myths and transforming our ways of seeking information. Corporate media are alternatives to reality. The evidence of our eyes and ears, and the truths of community media can put us in touch with the world of our living communities.

5.   Changing our Political Systems to Achieve Democracy

Democracy is being subverted to begin with by the ways corporate media twist truth so that poor and middle class people vote against their true interests, and waste energy fighting among each other, and blaming themselves for the selfishness of the greed agenda. An exercise on world poverty has ten chairs, and invites one person representing the Western wealthy to lie across eight of them, while the other nine try to jam on to the remaining two. When we blame one another instead of noticing who is occupying eight chairs, we are submitting to the absurd myths propagated by the corporate media.

But secondly, democracy is subverted because even when we ferret out the truth in spite of corporate media monopoly, our electoral systems limit our choices to variations in the corporate agenda. In the USA, people can vote for Corporate Party A or B. In Canada, it is broadened to Corporate Party C, and sometimes even D. But even the NDP in power bows largely to the corporate agenda.

Corporations control candidate selection and party platforms by the might of their donation power, their advertising revenue, and their threat to pull out of the economy. When labour unions strike for better safety conditions, benefit packages or a more reasonable wage, it is called "union blackmail by big bad union bosses" (in the corporate press). When corporations threaten to pull out of a community if they are not more heavily subsidized, or if they are asked to pay a modest share of taxes, no such language is used about this blackmail for the sake of widening the gap between rich and poor still further.

Corporate lobbyists get more perks for corporations in tax dodges, immunities, and rights to endanger our lives and health than would be possible if we had true democracy in operation. Their control of our governments is ensured on several levels:

- By keeping in place voting systems that deny forward looking groups a voice in elected governments
- By financial donations to election campaigns, ensuring that those elected are heavily dependent on corporate wealth and favours, and sometimes by direct corruption of elected officials through illegal bribes and threats
- By attacks in the corporate press on those who do stand for human rights, the social safety net, or the rights of workers
- By open threats to pull out of communities that do not follow their dictates

This is a hard set of behaviours to overcome. In my view, it cannot be overcome without regaining control of corporations themselves, which we will discuss in the next section. In this century, the electorate has been widened repeatedly: first women gained the vote, then Native people, and then in some areas, even prisoners, the most scapegoated of all! But for every widening of the electorate, the corporate oligopoly has narrowed our choices, so their measure of control has more than remained constant: it has grown.

One important electoral tool that has helped many countries around the world to regain a greater measure of democracy is proportional representation. There are many variations on proportional representation. Some have been accused of being too unstable, so that splintering occurs to such an extent that continuity in government is too limited. But the better systems have minimum numbers (such as five percent of voters needed to elect a representative), and have much to recommend them:

1. **Proportion Representation Almost Guarantees Minority Government**. In 40 years of adult living in three countries, I have found minority government by any party always superior to majority government by any party. With minority government, legislators have to listen to other opinions, and they have to listen to the people.

2. **Proportional Representation Guarantees Opinions of Minorities, Even Relatively Small Ones, Will Be Heard**. The argument that rightwing extremists will be represented, if they can muster five percent of the vote, is true. That is part of democracy too! But only with some form of proportional representation will the voices of progressive idealists, and of the most informed academics and intellectuals, always a minority, be heard and spoken for in Parliament. We can actually be represented at last! We can vote for someone and know they will feel motivated and obligated to try to follow the platform we voted for, not the latest corporate orders.

3. **The Opposition of Transnational Corporations to Proportional Representation Demonstrates How Much It Threatens Their Power Monopoly**. When proportional representation threatened to win in New Zealand, the transnational corporations dropped all other priorities to put so much money into paid ads and propaganda against it that their dollars against proportional representation exceeded those of all parties in the national election! When the TNCs put that

much money into a campaign, they clearly believe proportional representation will undermine their power monopoly. Although they are sometimes wrong in their estimates, they are fairly sophisticated at power games, and their investment in this case is further evidence that proportional representation has liberating power for the community.

In addition to proportional representation, there is one other reform that is basic to regaining political power for the people, in true democracy. That reform is based on the powerful truth enunciated years ago by Schumacher in his book, *Small Is Beautiful*. The truth of Schumacher's principle has been proven again and again, as the sheer size of corporations has been part of their dysfunctionality. The more layers any organization has, the more impersonal, uncaring, and in many ways inefficient it becomes. I have been amazed at how power seeps into the cracks of each status layer even in comparatively small social agencies of fifteen to twenty-five persons. As the Executive Director of such organizations, I was supposed to be the most powerful person, and in many ways I was. Yet I knew that my power to make choices, for good or for ill, was constrained more than others realized by the many layers I had to juggle and take account of.

We have all heard the plaintive cry; "I didn't have any choice." We always do have a choice, but if our bottom line is to stay within the bounds of a large organization, and play by its rules, then our choices are very limited. Large corporations have been pointing this out about large governments, without acknowledging that large corporations are even more unhealthy, because they have no semblance of democratic accountability. So how does this principle apply to regaining democracy?

While we need governments large and powerful enough at some level to control corporations, we also need very strong local governments, directly accountable to their voters. When a legislator represents 100,000 persons, their personal access to her or him is very limited. When they represent a million, it is almost non-existent. But when legislators have to convince 10,000 voters that they have their personal interests at heart, then real democracy has a chance. Real democracy is flawed, but as Winston Churchill said, it's the worst system in the world, except for all the rest. So to regain it, we need to strengthen local governments, ensuring that the ratio of legislators to voters is small enough to let democracy happen.

6. Regaining Control of Corporations

The movement to regain control over corporations is already happening around the world, and a number of writers and groups point out specific measures to achieve it. Fundamentally, these are rooted in the fact that corporations are legally created entities with no bodies, minds, consciences or spirits of their own. They exist because governments created legislation to allow them to exist, and reversing that legislation can end them.

Moreover, their control over us is rooted in our buying their values. They do hold enormous power over money and consumer goods. As Korten and others have pointed out, they control us through our value for money. When we move to the spiritual basis of life, and let go of our fascination with money, the golden chains by which they hold us largely melt away. There is a spiritual liberation in that awareness, which is a major step in itself. But we also need to be further liberated from their power to oppress those who do not choose materialism, but are bound by their cruel oppression and exploitation of the marginalized. Helpless children, for example, working under excruciating conditions in the world's sweatshops to build profits for billionaires who cannot even count their wealth if they devoted their whole lives to it!

Four basic steps are important ways of regaining control of corporations:

- Abolish their Status as Persons
- Set Standards of Social Responsibility for Them, with Strong Measures, and Revoke Corporate Charters When Necessary
- Deny Them the Right to Move Businesses to the Country of Lowest Standards
- Curb International Speculation

Abolish their Status as Persons

A single American judge established the fiction that corporations are persons with the rights of persons (but not many of the obligations) years ago. The power of corporations no doubt played a part in this strange decision many decades ago, but no one foresaw its huge implications. Corporations use the privilege of personhood along with the power of corporate status to gag opponents in all kinds of ways, but they are not subject to the same obligations as people.

This fiction is back of many corporate abuses, and precedents of other judges in many countries have extended it, and so the naked emperor continues to parade his naked power around the world. To clothe the emperor we need only legislation in each country requiring that he be clothed. The Alliance for Democracy has 49 chapters in the USA, and is pursuing several remedies for corporate power. One of these is an amendment to the US Constitution declaring that corporations are not persons, and do not have the rights of persons. Those who choose to act in every country can join or create their own groups working on this objective. As the Pete Seeger song goes, "If two and two and fifty make a million... we'll see those walls come down, we'll see those walls come down." Taking away the greatly abused special privileges of corporations removes the walls that are dividing and destroying our society.

Set Standards of Social Responsibility for Corporations

A number of groups are working on variations of this simple principle. Michael Lerner, editor of *Tikkun* magazine, has sparked a group called "The Politics of Meaning," in the USA (Korten, p. 204). They have proposed model resolutions for adoption by any level of government, and a Social Responsibility amendment to the US Constitution. Both of these mechanisms would require corporations with annual revenues over twenty million dollars to file reports every five years on their "Ethical Impact" — on the communities they work in, on their employees, on consumers, and on the environment! To ensure greater accuracy, employees would file a separate report from the corporation itself, and the wider community a third. Renewal of the corporate charter, every twenty years, would depend on the content of these reports! This is regaining power indeed.

Corporations basically impact enormously on four groups:

- Consumers
- Employees
- Stockholders
- Wider community, through environmental and social impact

Yet most corporate decisions are made as if all but the stockholders were invisible and of no value or consequence whatever. The Ethical Impact Reports would right the balance of corporate perspective.

Deny Right of Corporate Flight

Some countries have passed legislation that denies corporations the right to pick up and move without very heavy penalties. Given the huge amount of community and government subsidies given to corporations to settle in a community, this seems reasonable. This step would end corporate blackmail on politicians to follow every bidding of corporations, lest the corporation take its jobs and go to some more exploitative country, where workers will be forced to work at even worse wages and under worse health conditions. Children who threaten regularly to take their dollies and go home are usually encouraged by parents to grow up and play more fairly. The same encouragement is needed for corporations.

Another device that supports such moves is the creation and maintenance of strong state corporations, especially for areas of national interest and culture such as key utilities, transportation, information media, and arts groups. Such moves strengthen local cultures and safety nets and environmental standards as well. But they are only effective if controls are created which make it very difficult for any future governments beholden to the corporate sector to sell them off easily and pocket the proceeds, leaving the trusting public again poorer and more defenceless against corporate rule. Legislation, constitutional amendments, or referendums (depending on the particular country's legal structure) could be bulwarks in the struggle to retain control for the people over the privatizing corporate agenda. For example, in a federation like Canada, legislation might require a three-quarters majority of Parliament plus agreement of three-quarters of the provinces for any major change to crown corporations. Or, in a direct democracy approach, a popular referendum with a two-thirds majority voting for the sale of these valuable state holdings might be required.

Curb International Speculation

In addition, there are important measures to control the international speculators whose paper money games create billionaires who do not contribute anything to the world's wellbeing, and contribute much to its undoing. These speculators force countries to the brink of bankruptcy, force on them policies that starve and deprive their people, and then profit on all outcomes of the transaction! Immorality is a weak word for their brutal behaviour, and their activities must be curbed as soon as possible. A key part of gaining control of corporations is regaining control of these games-playing investors, who often force out the few corporate CEOs who try to behave in a more ethical manner. Hostile take-overs and firings are aimed at CEOs who dare to prioritize employees, environment and community over maximum stockholder profits.

The best device for gaining control of and curbing such immoral speculative investing is the Tobin tax (so-named for Nobel Prize economist James Tobin), which would put a very small tax on international financial transactions. Such a tax would not harm genuine international investment, which lasts years, but would penalize those who leap from one investment to another rapidly, and destructively. Each country has the right to legislate its own version of the Tobin tax. Although the amount is tiny, the speculations are large and numerous. The income would be enough, some have pointed out, to stamp out hunger and/or prevent most preventable health problems around the world!

7. Building International Networks for Compassion

Finally, an international disease cannot be fought solely on a national or local basis. Recently there have been conferences in Italy, Mexico, and Barcelona, among other places, bringing together activists, labour unions, and consumer groups from all over the world, to work together in the struggle against corporate rule. Seattle's famous November 1999 struggle between the people of the world and the moneyed interests at the World Trade Organization will go down in world history. We need to read reports on these great events, join proposed international boycotts and support movements, and some of us need to go to them. We need to donate to the cost of such efforts. We need to expose transnational corporate rule, and resist it across the globe.

But the best news is that such networking is possible for most of us from our own homes and workplaces, through the internet. This is one of those tools of technology which is still working more for us than against us, so we had better take full advantage of it before we find a way to damage ourselves with it as we have nearly every other technological "advance."

Through the internet, world-wide resistance stopped the corporations' planned passage of the MAI (Multilateral Agreement on Investment) in the spring of 1998. The internet was also a major vehicle for the miracle of Seattle. Although we still have to resist later versions of the MAI, these were amazing victories of local activists in many countries. They were made possible by a world-wide movement of internet protesters who passed the word, again and again, about this dangerous threat that would have denied the rights of democratic governments to defend their people against labour and environmental devastation by the corporations.

Conclusion

Every one of us can partake in some measure in each of these steps. These actions are hope in living colour, in this wonderful world that we have been entrusted to inhabit. By tuning our lives to sustainable living, by using our consumer power to achieve our dreams, and by disseminating truth with every breath we breathe, we find power, and we become the power of a world revitalized with community caring. By choosing to read this book, instead of watching corporate chosen TV fare, you have added something to your knowledge and power. By supporting and creating truthful media, by rejecting corporate media myths, by creating better political systems, and by supporting international networks, we can build a mighty world movement. Most of all, by joining those who are demanding that our governments hold corporations and speculators responsible for ethical standards, we can take the initiative in this struggle for the future of our world.

The yeast is rising, all over the world. Market capitalism is crumbling, and new community systems that care for people and for the environment are being born. We live in a time when we can assist in their delivery. We feel the labour pains of this delivery, but like all birth periods, it holds the promise of a better future if we do our part. We can help to deliver to this planet and to the rainbow of people and cultures which inhabit it, a beautiful new spirit of community, and healthy economic systems that care first for basic human and environmental needs. The heartbeat of the healthy new infant trying to be born is heard in our community demonstrations. It is a great time to be alive and to have a part in social transformation: let us celebrate it!

Chapter 9

Transformative Justice: Power for the Future

This book has taken us together on an exciting journey. Readers may wonder what the sections of it have in common. We have defined a new and exciting idea: transformative justice. This idea, this vision, has carried us on our journey. We have seen its power in creative listening, and then in my personal adventures with a series of challenging prisoners. Their stories of transformation are mutual, for these men — Pat, Mike, and the others — transformed our lives and understandings at least as much as the other way round.

Then we journeyed to look at circle sentencing and family group conferencing: two of the most popular transformative justice approaches spreading around the world today. I really meant to fill the whole book with these stories, but books have a way of writing themselves, and choosing their own agenda. Valuable as these model stories are, they were only a part of our journey of transformation. In some of them, as in the Alberta story, the community took the initiative in creating transformation, without any formal framework offered by the justice system.

A very important chapter looked at forgiveness: Can we forgive those who seem unforgivable? Why do we forgive? What's in it for us? The stories of forgiveness are so wonderful that it is easy to get carried away with their magic. Forgiveness is liberating, but it does not end grief, nor forestall the pain that comes when a sore place is re-wounded by some new event that rubs the wound. Yet the degree of relief from it is extraordinary. The underlying magic of transformation is making forgiveness more possible. But we can't force it on anyone, nor should we guilt those caught in tragedy struggling through their anger. They need their wrongs recognized fully, and they need to be free to choose forgiveness, of their own free will, in a community that fully supports their sense of outrage at their injustice.

Our journey then took us to look at the evidence that transformative justice is indeed vastly more satisfying for victims, for offenders, for their families, and for communities, than the present failed system. As Trish Montour said so eloquently, "Community is the way. Penal 'justice' and prisons are the failed alternatives."

Our last two chapters tell how you and I, here and now, can move this world closer to transformation of our legal system, and of the vast economic injustices in our world. Justice that never examines the growing chasms between privileged and marginalized is no justice at all. Crime has many causes, and offenders need to take responsibility for their choices in it, but most crime, including the overwhelming damage of corporate crime, is rooted in the catastrophic distributive injustices in our world. So we have looked at how social transformation can change them too.

Let's take a last look at the justice system that we have now versus what we could have.

Does Transformative Justice Satisfy Us?

Is there any academic evidence that transformative justice satisfies victims, offenders, and community? In fact, a European Conference reviewing victim offender mediation approaches around the world concluded that many studies have shown high victim dissatisfaction with the existing system. Generally speaking, less than 40 percent of victims express satisfaction with their experiences of retributive justice (Messmer & Otto, 1992).

Why is that? Victims' needs clash with those of the retributive justice system. The literature on victims shows victims have five core needs: the need for answers, for recognition of their wrong, for safety, for restitution, and to find significance or meaning from their tragedy. The retributive or misery justice system on the other hand is interested in punishment, deterrence, incapacitation, and rehabilitation of the offender. Table One below (Needs of Victims and of Retributive Justice System) compares these purposes, and shows how little they harmonize. The criminal justice system and the victims of crime are like ships in a boundless ocean, whose courses are set for a collision, as they churn through troubled waters, unaware of each other's proximity.

In contrast, the same studies show that victims express more than 90 percent satisfaction with the processes of transformative justice (Messmer & Otto, 1992). There are many reasons for this. There is something ultimately satisfying in facing down your worst fears, as many of our stories have illustrated. Table Two below compares the Needs of Victims, and the Processes of Transformative Justice, demonstrating the much greater harmony. This harmony is no accident: transformative justice methods are in part a response to the crying unmet needs of crime victims suffering under our present system.

TABLE ONE: VICTIM NEEDS AND RETRIBUTIVE JUSTICE NEEDS

<u>VICTIM NEEDS</u>	<u>RETRIBUTIVE JUSTICE NEEDS</u>
1. ANSWERS: Key questions include — WHY ME? HOW COULD GOD LET THIS HAPPEN? HOW COULD I HAVE PREVENTED THIS? WHY DID THE OFFENDER DO ... ?	1. ANSWERS: Key question is: WHO DID IT? CAN WE CONVICT THEM? HOW HARD CAN WE PUNISH THEM? Truth is a casualty in the legal battle between the skills of a set of lawyers, bounded by an archaic set of rules and precedence. Not only can victim needs not be asked, the alienation makes it unlikely they ever will be.
2. RECOGNITION OF WRONG Victim needs to have their wrong recognized by the offender, the significant community of the victim, and the world. Victim needs to be assured that no one blames them, that they did not cause this. Victim needs the chance to reframe their understanding of themselves as a worthy person TO WHOM THIS COULD HAVE HAPPENED.	2. RECOGNITION OF WRONG Wrong is recognized only by LENGTH OF SENTENCE meted to offender, based on precedents which may not match victims' sense of violation at all. Victim may be blamed by lawyers, judge, and police for having laid themselves open to violation, which REVICTIMIZES them.

3. SAFETY

Victim needs to feel their need to feel safe again is a high priority.

Victim wants to be reassured that this will not happen again.

Victim needs to be assured by offender that they will not do this again, or anything like it.

3. SAFETY

Demonizing of the offender adds to victim fear.

Process takes some account of victim protection, but not much.

Whole process emphasizes normality of crime among officials whose business it is to deal with it all the time. Fear exacerbated.

Offender infuriated by adversarial process, any hostility to victim is greater, fears of victim increase.

4. RESTITUTION

Victim wants some kind of restitution, reassuring them they are part of a safe, caring world again.

If reparation is possible or relevant, victim wants that to be a high priority in the resolution.

4. RESTITUTION

Until recently victim restitution wasn't even on the court menu. Even now it is a low priority.

The retributive process incapacitates and aggravates offenders, making restitution less possible by the offender. The energy and funds spent on retribution drain community resources which could better be spent on significant restitution for victims.

5. MEANING OR SIGNIFICANCE

Victim wants to feel that when the whole process is concluded, THE WORLD WILL SOMEHOW BE A BETTER SAFER PLACE FOR WHAT HAPPENED TO THEM.

Victim wants their pain to help make the world a place where others are not as likely to suffer what they have suffered.

5. MEANING OR SIGNIFICANCE

The resources which the impact of crime could galvanize from victim, offender, and their significant community to find a significant outcome are dissipated in the thirsty quest for revenge.

The victim is told the punishment of the offender should satisfy them, and when it doesn't, feels their inner emptiness is yet another proof something is wrong with them.

TABLE TWO: VICTIM NEEDS AND
TRANSFORMATIVE JUSTICE OUTCOMES

VICTIM NEEDS	TRANSFORMATIVE JUSTICE OUTCOMES
1. ANSWERS TO KEY QUESTIONS: Why me? How could I have prevented this? Why did the offender do...?	1. ANSWERS TO KEY QUESTIONS Offender and community participate in answering why this victim suffered, how it could or could not have been prevented, and why the offender did what she or he did. Answers are found which could not be found by any other approach.
2. RECOGNITION OF WRONG Victim needs their wrong recognized by: * Offender * Their own significant community * Community of the offender * The world	2. RECOGNITION OF WRONG Victim's wrong is fully recognized by: * Offender * Victim's own significant community * Significant community of offender * Wider community and world
3. SAFETY Victim needs to feel SAFE again. Victim needs to feel REPETITION UNLIKELY TO THEM. Victim needs to feel THIS OFFENDER WON'T HARM THEM AGAIN.	3. SAFETY Although victim will never feel safe in the old way, the new sense of community support *assures* victim that the community will do all it can to prevent repetition. Seeing the offender as a humble part of the community defuses their power, and seeing the offender humble and apologetic makes them seem more incapable of wanting or achieving further harm.
4. RESTITUTION Victim wants the world to feel safe and caring and secure again. Victim wants offender and community to participate in their healing process.	4. RESTITUTION Transformative justice creates a blending of communities that wraps the victim in a cocoon of caring. Everyone focusses on healing process of victim, as well as prevention of further harm by offender.
5. MEANING OR SIGNIFICANCE Victim wants to feel they have a part in healing and protecting the whole community from what happened to them. Victim wants to feel control over their life space, and power to do good are returned to them.	5. MEANING OR SIGNIFICANCE Victim holds the only key that can unlock the door to resolution for all: the power to choose to forgive. Transformative process empowers whole group to find creative expressions of significance that will honour victims' suffering and the healing work of the whole group.

The literature is less clear about long-term impact on offenders. In the short term, offenders say confronting their victims is harder, but has a lot more meaning for them. Yet one Family Group Conference cannot unmake twenty years of abusive, deprived living, nor open the doors of community to a young offender who has no foothold in it. So a single meeting does not always change patterns, which is why I believe Transformative Justice needs to be a process and at least a series of meetings over time. Nevertheless, offenders report in general a far more relevant and meaningful experience from transformative justice processes than from the vengeful ritualistic disempowering proceedings of our traditional courts, where the offender's only voice is a lawyer they often don't understand.

There are several other parties besides the victim and offender who are vitally involved in the scene, but so often forgotten by our legal system that their very existence is often ignored. These are the family and friends of the victim, the family and friends of the offender, and the wider affected and concerned community. How does transformative justice satisfy each of them?

Those close to a victim feel almost as disempowered and helpless as the primary victim. Our existing criminal justice system ignores them even more completely than it ignores the needs of the primary victim. If the court doesn't need you as a witness to convict, you just don't exist in the scene. I remember a sign I saw on the door of a Crown Attorney's office when I was accompanying a victim to court, "The Crown cannot see any victims before court." If that is the case for victims, it is much more the case for their family and friends!

So the rage, anguish, and fears of these secondary victims are lost in the overweening need to find, punish and convict, and they too are usually revictimized in many ways. What a contrast to transformative justice, which seeks them out, asks them to participate, and includes them as honoured, vital contributors to the whole process.

Similarly, there are few statuses in life lower than being the parent or spouse of an offender, except for being an offender. Because of the tendency to blame parents for their children's deeds, one researcher wrote an article maintaining that the trauma in having a child labelled delinquent or criminal was greater than that of losing a child to death. These forgotten victims, the close families of offenders, suffer revictimization in every way through our legal system. The police are likely to feel contempt for them, and the Crown considers them as hostile witnesses or irrelevant. Judges are often likely to view them with a quiet, indifferent contempt, or even address scathing remarks to them.

A Quaker friend of mine who struggled hard to raise her boys after her marriage broke up, was attending court once for the one son who went through delinquent behaviour. The Judge that day referred to the co-accused as a boy from a good home, and to her own son as one from a bad home, since it was broken. She recalled years later how devastating it was for her to sit in court and hear her heroic efforts at parenting under adversity tossed aside as providing a "bad home."

Even the defence attorney, the one party who is supposed to balance the unequal scene out, often makes clear that he or she is there for the accused only. The family of the offender is excluded from the confidential relationship and from the very limited protection and caring of the defence lawyer. This is more so where there are any differences between the accused and their family; and when a person is accused of a crime, even small differences are likely to be widened. The adversarial system digs deep trenches where there are gaps, and adds to the stress and isolation of each party.

In contrast, transformative justice treats all affected as respected community members. Instead of widening family rifts, it does everything possible to encourage families to work together. Because participation of everyone affected is essential to its success, those who come are welcomed with genuine enthusiasm and joy, such a contrast to the court's impersonal indifference blended with confusing, offensive and hurtful procedures! The close family and friends of the offender play one of the most vital roles in transformative processes, for their pain, instead of being ignored, is one of the key ways to reach the offender. Offenders learn to take responsibility in these processes from two main things:

- Seeing the victims' humanity, suffering and concerns, and identifying with them
- Seeing that their conduct has wounded those who care about the offender themselves, and about whom they care

Therefore, the participation of the offender's family and friends is critical, and valued. They are the building blocks of the process, both in initial awareness of impact, and in later search for solutions and resources. No wonder transformative justice is so satisfying to all the secondary victims of a crime!

Finally, the wider community is affected by every breach in the social fabric. Fear and anger and a sense of helplessness escalate. The existing justice system offers nothing more than a process to lock up and further damage and enrage a person defined as bad, while doing nothing significant for victims or for public safety. Far from protecting the public, it maximizes the chance of recidivism by increasing offender alienation and anger, and decreasing their chance of any healthy integration into the community.

In contrast, transformative processes enable the wider community to participate in denouncing crime, supporting victims, and building true solutions. They also enable the wider community to take responsibility for the underlying causes of crime: poverty, abused children, unemployment, discrimination, and other deep social problems. The community is enabled to take these on in digestible servings. It does not need to solve the whole unemployment or poverty problem at once, but each case dealt with transformatively enables the community to work on a portion of it, contribute to its healing, and understand and address better the larger issues that lie behind it. Transformative justice processes are the building blocks of an informed, concerned, and healthy community, one that cares for and includes all its members.

The Magic Power of Forgiveness

The greatest power in transformative justice is the power of forgiveness. Its power cannot be overstated: first for the person who gives it, and beyond that, for all who are touched by its warmth and light. It is no accident that Murder Victims' Families for Reconciliation have the energy to organize long walks and speaking tours across America most years — one has to find an outlet for all that joyful release! It is no accident that all across New Zealand, people with light shining in their eyes would tell of the forgiveness and healing ceremony between the families of the two boys killed by the reckless young driver, and the family of the driver himself.

It is no accident that my friend from Boston, who had run out of gas after eight years on the revenge path, who had barely energy to get up in the morning, now proceeded through life with a lighter step, and with warmth and peace in her eye, as she planned her life-skills tutoring for the man who killed her son. It is no accident that I have often described the completed act of forgiveness between myself and Stacey, the reporter whose work helped destroy my agency and my career dream, as the nearest thing to heaven on earth I will ever know. It is no accident that I have never known a moment's experience of anything but love and joy when her name recurs in my world, since that day.

This is not to deny that many traumas carry lasting pain. You don't forget the loss of a child, or the betrayal of values you thought you shared with those you trusted. Many compare it to learning to walk with an artificial leg. But forgiveness is like the best physiotherapy, and enables us to walk cheerfully and courageously, even though we continue to miss the lost limb. We give up resenting the loss of that limb, and engage ourselves fully and freely in learning to walk in the new world since its loss.

For forgiveness has in it the most powerful satisfaction of all. It holds the riddle of how we can live together in community in this crowded world, where everyone's life-space intrudes on someone else's. It holds a spiritual alchemy that is indescribable. Satisfaction? It holds something much deeper than satisfaction — it holds a mystical peace that is close to the purpose for which we were born.

Conclusion

For these reasons, transformative justice processes are deeply satisfying and healing. There are two approaches to security in our world. One seeks security in locks and bars and walls of separation and complex electronic security systems. If it does not lock offenders in, it locks inside the privileged, who live in their own self-imposed prisons of security system upon security system, and still live in deeper fear and chosen isolation every day.

The other approach recognizes that no security system in the world can protect us from natural or human disasters. Reasonable precautions make sense to minimize undue risk, but beyond such a minimum, there is a freedom for all in unlocked lives and doors. We cannot guarantee that floods, falls, human violence, or other disasters will avoid our doors, however much structural security we build. But we can provide the best insurance system when we build a caring community for all. When we do all we can to support all those around us in trouble, we are building that kind of insurance. We have helped to build a world where, because we have been there for all those in need, we can be surer that others will be there for us when our time comes. For trouble comes to all, however many locks and walls we immure ourselves behind. The issue is not whether trouble will come, but whether we will be alone in it, or whether a caring community will uphold us in a cradle of love which will surround us with love, comfort and healing.

Retributive justice rests on the security of bars and locks and separations. Transformative justice rests on the security of a caring community that includes all and never deserts those in trouble. Transformative justice uses the power of community to heal wrongs, and to change the world. It challenges unhealthy barriers of race, class, and status. It rebuilds community where community has broken down. It heals the broken-hearted, because it listens to and cares about pain of all kinds. No wonder transformative processes are so much more satisfying to all of us! Transformative justice is the way of the future.

Every problem is an opportunity, but if we miss that opportunity, it is a step toward disaster. Transformative justice dares to risk community. But without taking that risk, we plod robot-like toward a more and more divided world in which the powers of greed breed violence and unrest and anger, while destroying the environmental inheritance essential to the survival of all. Transformative justice is a risk; but continuing on the failed road of retributive justice is like the buffalo herds which plunged blindly forward toward the precipices over which they fell to their deaths. Transformative justice is the choice of life. These stories show how much joy can come from each adventure, even adventures with so much pain. Transformative justice is absorbing pain, and walking forward with the power of love and truth to build a stronger community from that painful experience. Some call that love and truth God. Others call it the caring community. In this book, we have called it transformation. By whatever name, it is our hope.

Bibliography

Barlow, Maude, *The Fight of My Life,* HarperCollins, Toronto, 1998.

Boers, Arthur P., *Justice that Heals,* Faith & Life Press, Newton, KS, 1992.

Canadian Sentencing Commission (Archambault Commission), *Report,* Queen's Printer, Ottawa, 1986.

Coffin, William Sloane, *Once to Every Man and Nation,* Atheneum, New York, 1977.

"Conferences help keep offenders out of court," *Boggabilla Argus,* Boggabilla, New South Wales, May 21, 1994.

Consedine, Jim and Helen Bowen (eds.), *Restorative Justice: Contemporary Themes and Practice.* Ploughshares Publishers, Lyttelton, NZ, 1999.

Craig, Mary, *Blessings,* Hodder & Stoughton, London, 1979.

Crowe, Avis, "Taking the First Step: A Story Retold," *Fellowship* 61: July/August 1995: 8.

Daubney Committee (Daubney Commission on Sentencing, Conditional Release and Related Aspects of Corrections), *Taking Responsibility,* Queen's Printer, Ottawa, 1988.

Evers, Tag, "The Healing Approach to Crime," *The Progressive,* September, 1998: 30-33.

Genesee County Sherriff's Department, New York, *Genesee Justice,* Batavia, NY, n.d.

Genesee County Sherriff's Department, New York, *Genesee Justice Report,* Batavia, NY, Dec. 1990.

Goudzwaard, R. and H. De Lange, *Beyond Poverty and Affluence,* University of Toronto Press, Toronto, 1995.

Gustafson, Dave, "Victim Offender Reconciliation in Serious Crime: Debunking the Myths," *Accord* Vol. 9, no. 2, 1990: 4-5.

Henderson, Michael, *The Forgiveness Factor,* Grosvenor Books, London, 1996.

Horner, Robert, *Crime Prevention in Canada,* Canadian Communication Group, Ottawa, 1993.

Jaeger, Marietta, *The Lost Child,* Zondervan, Grand Rapids, MI, 1985.

Jaeger, Marietta, *Marietta Jaeger on Forgiveness,* Mennonite Central Committee video, 1988.

Karim, Nazim, "Forgiveness in a Violent World," *Fellowship* Vol. 64 no. 1-2, Jan/Feb. 1998: 7,18.

Knudsen-Hoffman, Gene, "Victims and Victimizers — Mutual Sorrow, Mutual Suffering," *Fellowship,* March 1993: 25-27.

Korten, David, *The Post-Corporate World,* Kumarian Press, West Hartford, CT, 1998.

Leach, Pamela, "A Tale of Two Justices," *Accord* Vol. 11 no. 1, April 1992.

Marshall, Catherine, *Something More,* McGraw-Hill, New York, 1974

Mathiesen, Thomas, "Towards the 21st Century: Abolition, an Impossible Dream?" Paper read to the VIII International Conference on Penal Abolition, Auckland, NZ, 1997.

McElrea, Judge Fred, Personal Communication, 1994.

McMurtry, John, *Unequal Freedoms,* Garamond Press, Toronto, 1998.

Mennonite Central Committee, *Murder Close Up: From Fury to Forgiveness,* video, 1995.

Messmer, Heinz and Hans-Uwe Otto (eds.), *Restorative Justice on Trial: Pitfalls and Potentials of Victim-Offender Mediation,* Kluwer Academic Publishers, Dordrecht, 1992.

Mills, Kay, *This Little Light of Mine: The Life of Fannie Lou Hamer,* Penguin Books, New York, 1994.

Morris, Ruth, "Beyond the Barrier of Grief," *Friends' Journal,* Jan. 1988: 14-15.

Morris, Ruth, *Penal Abolition,* Canadian Scholars' Press, Toronto, 1995.

Northey, Wayne, "The Frank Brown Story," *Accord* Vol. 10 no. 1, May 1991: 5-7.

"Story of a Reconciliation," *Accord* Vol. 9 no. 2, July 1990: 6-12.

Stuart, Barry, *Building Community Justice Partnerships: Community Peacemaking Circles,* Dept. of Justice, Ottawa, 1997.

Umbreit, Mark, *Victim Meets Offender,* Criminal Justice Press, Monsey, NJ, 1994.

Yantzi, Mark, *Sexual Offending and Restoration,* Herald Press, Waterloo, Ont., 1998.

Zehr, Howard J., *Changing Lenses: A New Focus for Crime and Justice,* Herald Press, Scottdale, PA, 1990

Organizations

Murder Victims' Families For Reconciliation can be reached at MVFR, 2161 Massachusetts Avenue, Cambridge, Massachusetts, 02140, phone 617-868-0007; fax 617-354-2832. Their book, *Not In Our Name: Murder Victims' Families Speak Out Against the Death Penalty,* is available for $10 U.S.

Index

About Rittenhouse

Founded in 1990, Rittenhouse is an agency dedicated to bringing transformative justice instead of retributive justice to our criminal justice system. Transformative justice simply means making the basic goal of a criminal justice system healing, not revenge. Rittenhouse believes that crime can become an opportunity to bring transformation into the lives of victims, offenders and their families. If you'd like to find out more about Rittenhouse and transformative justice, please contact us:

Rittenhouse
157 Carleton St, Suite 202
Toronto ON
M5A 2K3
Canada

Co-ordinator Giselle Dias

Phone (416) 972-9992
Fax (416) 923-8742
www.interlog.com/~ritten/icopa.html

Also of Interest from Canadian Scholars' Press

Test of Faith: Hope, Courage and the Prison Experience
By Eva Evelyn Hanks

Test of Faith is one in the series of Canadian Scholar's Press Justice books. It offers a unique perspective on prison life seen predominantly from the view of the wife of an inmate — but also from the views of her husband, other inmates and guards, as well as mainstream society. In this startling insider's view Eva Evelyn Hanks walks us through the difficult years between her husband's incarceration for bank robbery to his release from prison. Through her eyes we learn about the arbitrary and cruel nature of the penitentiary system.

$19.95   Paperback   6x9   ISBN 1-55130-176-8   Published May 2000

The Case for Penal Abolition
Edited by W. Gordon West and Ruth Morris

The Case for Penal Abolition marshals convincing arguments from a number of scholars and activists for abolishing not only imprisonment, but overhauling our entire penal injustice system. The movement for penal abolition is as old as prisons themselves, which from their beginning have failed to achieve any of their stated objects — individual and general deterrence, rehabilitation, and restoring a sense of justice. Both street crime and corporate crime are considered, acknowledging that corporate crime causes more damage and death than recognized criminals do.

The Case for Penal Abolition challenges us all to move away from failing penal systems towards a new democratic global humanity in resolving human conflicts and legal issues.

$19.95   Paperback   6x9   ISBN 1-55130-147-4   Published May 2000

Penal Abolition: The Practical Choice
By Ruth Morris

Most people would agree that the criminal justice system does not satisfy our society's growing needs. Despite this dissatisfaction, the criminal justice system continues to grow into what is universally recognized as a failure. Morris believes that if society is to find its way out of this predicament, we must focus on these key questions: What's wrong with the system we have? Why is it still in place? What do we want instead? How do we get there? In a concise style this text answers these questions citing evidence and giving examples. This book is an excellent addition to the criminologist's library.

$14.95   Paperback   6x9   ISBN 1-55130-078-8   Published 1995